PENGUIN BOOKS

Selected Writings

Anna Freud, the daughter of Sigmund Freud, was born in Vienna in 1895. She was educated at the Cottage Lyceum, a Viennese girls' school where she later taught. After taking her final teachers' examination in 1918, she undertook psychoanalytic training, qualifying as a psychoanalyst with the Vienna Psychoanalytical Society in 1922.

In 1927 she published *Four Lectures on Child Analysis* which established her leadership of the Vienna School of Child Analysis. There followed a period of major theoretical development which culminated in her classic *The Ego and the Mechanisms of Defence* (1936), which she presented to her father on the occasion of his 80th birthday. Forced by the Nazis to flee Vienna in 1938, Anna Freud and her parents established themselves in Hampstead, London. Her war work with Dorothy Burlingham, with children who were separated from their parents, led to their highly influential *Infants Without Families* (1944). There followed a series of important papers and growing acclaim, particularly in the United States.

Anna Freud's last years, from 1960 to her death in 1982, were marked by an emphasis upon a psychoanalytic psychology of normal development, and the consolidation of her clinic and training centre in Hampstead as the world's major centre for the psychoanalytic study and treatment of the child.

A lay analyst with no formal academic qualification, Anna Freud died at her London home in possession of a large number of honorary doctorates, and as the foremost developer and undisputed world leader of classical psychoanalysis.

Richard Ekins trained with the Northern Ireland Association for the Study of Psycho-Analysis, of which he was a founder member, and at the Institute of Psycho-Analysis in London. He is a psychoanalyst in private practice and Senior Lecturer in Social Psychology at the University of Ulster, where he is Director of the Trans-Gender Archive. His recent books include *Blending Genders* (1996) and *Male Femaling* (1997).

Ruth Freeman trained with the Northern Ireland Association for the Study of Psycho-Analysis. She is a member of the British Confederation of Psychotherapists, a psychoanalytic psychotherapist in private practice and Senior Lecturer in Dental Public Health at the Queen's University of Belfast. Her publications include *Centres and Peripheries of Psychoanalysis* (1994) co-edited with Richard Ekins.

Selected Writings by Anna Freud

Edited, with introductions, by
Richard Ekins and Ruth Freeman

PENGUIN BOOKS

PENGUIN BOOKS

Published by the Penguin Group
Penguin Books Ltd, 27 Wrights Lane, London w8 5tz, England
Penguin Putnam Inc., 375 Hudson Street, New York, New York 10014, USA
Penguin Books Australia Ltd, Ringwood, Victoria, Australia
Penguin Books Canada Ltd, 10 Alcorn Avenue, Toronto, Ontario, Canada m4v 3b2
Penguin Books (NZ) Ltd, 182–190 Wairau Road, Auckland 10, New Zealand

Penguin Books Ltd, Registered Offices: Harmondsworth, Middlesex, England

This edition first published 1998
10 9 8 7 6 5 4 3 2 1

Set in 10/12pt Monotype Bembo
Typeset by Rowland Phototypesetting Ltd, Bury St Edmunds, Suffolk
Printed in England by Clays Ltd, St Ives plc

Contents

For Thomas Freeman MD,
pupil and colleague of Anna Freud

Acknowledgements

The editors would like to thank Sigmund Freud Copyrights Ltd and the Hogarth Press for giving permission to produce this selection of the works of Anna Freud. The photograph on the front cover, taken in 1925, is reproduced by courtesy of Sigmund Freud Copyrights Ltd.

We wish to thank Thomas Freeman, Arthur Couch and Clifford Yorke for our initiation into the classical tradition of psychoanalysis.

Thanks are due to Cesare Sacerdoti for his advice and assistance; to Wendy Saunderson for her invaluable constructive comment throughout the preparation of this volume; to the Psychology Research Unit of Assessment, University of Ulster, for financial support; and to Matthew Ekins, for additional technical assistance.

Foreword

Clifford Yorke, FRCPsych
Formerly Medical Director, The Anna Freud Centre, London

The Northern Ireland Association for the Study of Psycho-Analysis (NIASP) is a thriving body with considerable achievements to its credit. It has established psychoanalysis and psychoanalytic psychotherapy as an active and thriving discipline in a province often seen from London as remote; and it has already made important contributions to the literature. Readers of *Centres and Peripheries of Psychoanalysis* (1994) will already have been impressed by the scope of these contributions, in a cohesive but far-reaching series of papers collected and edited by Richard Ekins and Ruth Freeman. Those same editors are responsible for this fine selection of writings by Anna Freud, expertly put together with clear introductory notes and linking passages. It is a collection that is sorely needed.

It is far from easy to make a selection of papers from Anna Freud's extensive work. The collected writings run to eight volumes, not counting the three books on family law written in cooperation with Professors Solnit and Goldstein of Yale University, the third of which was completed only after Anna Freud's death with the assistance of Sonia Goldstein. Like her father, Anna Freud was equally dedicated to normality and pathology in all matters psychological, and her contributions to each in the field of child development far surpassed in quality and scope those of any other psychoanalytic writer on child development. A selection has to convey the breadth of her many interests and the importance of her contributions to our knowledge of a child's progress towards healthy adaptation, as well as the delays and setbacks that can so readily occur. To have done so in a way that so clearly displays the richness, variety and originality of Anna Freud's thinking, as well as its importance for a better understanding of a wide variety of disciplines relating to child study, is an achievement of first importance. It is here, I believe, that the introduction, as well as the prefatory remarks to individual papers, will be found particularly valuable. They set Anna Freud's work in its proper context, and will be indispensable not only to those encountering this body of work for the first time, but also to those who wish to renew or refresh their acquaintance with it. The authors are to be congratulated on producing a work that not only underlines the clarity and cogency of Anna Freud's thinking, but makes it accessible to a wide audience that will include not only psychoanalysts, but all those with a serious concern for children and the way they become the adults into which they grow.

July 1997

Introduction

Anna Freud was born at Berggasse 19, Vienna, on 3 December 1895, the youngest of Sigmund and Martha Freud's six children. Her birth coincided with her father's founding of psychoanalysis. On 24 July 1895, Sigmund Freud succeeded in 'completely' interpreting a dream for the first time (Masson, 1985, p. 417). It was in the following year, in his 1896 paper, 'Heredity and the Aetiology of the Neuroses', that Freud first used the term 'psycho-analysis'. Later, in *The Interpretation of Dreams* (1900, p. 130), Freud used the young Anna Freud's dream of 'stwawbewwies, wild stwawbewwies, omblet, pudden!' to illustrate the simple wish-fulfilment dreams of childhood.

Anna Freud was educated at the Cottage Lyceum, a Viennese girls' school, where she later taught for many years, stimulated by the educational ideas of Maria Montessori and John Dewey. After taking her final teachers' examination in 1918, she undertook psychoanalytic training, qualifying as a psychoanalyst with the Vienna Psychoanalytical Society in 1922. In 1927, she published *Four Lectures on Child Analysis* which established her leadership of the Vienna School of Child Analysis. Shortly afterwards, she examined the pedagogical importance of psycho-analysis in her *Four Lectures on Psychoanalysis for Teachers and Parents* (1930). There followed a period of major theoretical development culminating in her classic *The Ego and the Mechanisms of Defence* (1936), which she presented to her father on the occasion of his eightieth birthday. By the late 1920s, Sigmund Freud was viewing his daughter in legendary terms as 'my faithful Antigone–Anna' – after Antigone, the daughter of Oedipus Rex, whose loyalty to her family resulted in great personal sacrifice. Anna Freud had long been her father's constant companion, secretary, nurse, professional collaborator and ambassador. Forced by the Nazis to flee Vienna in 1938, Anna Freud and her parents soon established themselves at 20 Maresfield Gardens, Hampstead, London. Following the death of her father in 1939, her war work with Dorothy Burlingham, with children who had been separated from their parents culminated in *Infants Without Families* (1944) and *Reports on the Hampstead Nurseries, 1939–1945*. There followed a series of important papers and growing acclaim, particularly in the United States of America.

Anna Freud's last years, from 1960 to her death in 1982, were marked by an emphasis upon a psychoanalytic psychology of normal development. Her classic *Normality and Pathology in Childhood* (1965) was followed by increasingly subtle elaboration of her position. These final years also witnessed the consolidation of her clinic and training centre in Hampstead as the world's major centre for the psychoanalytic study and treatment of the child. A lay analyst with no formal academic qualification, she died on 9 October 1982 at her London home in possession of a large number of honorary doctorates, and as the foremost developer and undisputed world leader of classical psychoanalysis.

Beginnings and Foundations (1895–1922)

Anna Freud's Early Years and Psychoanalytic Training

Anna Freud's childhood was marked by her gradual immersion in the personalities and work of the nascent psychoanalytic movement. Freud's 'Psychological Wednesday Evening Society' began meeting in his waiting room at Berggasse 19, in October 1902, to discuss psychoanalysis. By 1908, the group was calling itself the 'Vienna Psychoanalytical Society'. Over the years, the young Anna Freud would sit on a library ladder listening to the proceedings (Young-Bruehl, 1988, p. 53). From 1908 onwards, the major names in the history of psychoanalysis were beating their respective paths to Berggasse 19. Young Anna Freud met them all. Whilst barely into her teens she began to read her father's publications as soon as they became available. In 1914–15 she first attended his 'Introduction to Psychoanalysis' lecture course held at the University of Vienna (Freud, 1916–1917), and in 1918 entered into analysis with him. Her first publication, 'Beating Fantasies and Daydreams' (1922), according to Young-Bruehl (1988), told the story of her own analysis. This paper unpacked the story of a patient who had sublimated troublesome private sexual beating phantasies into romantic stories that others could enjoy, and was a continuation of her father's 1919 paper 'A Child is being Beaten: A Contribution to the Study of the Origin of Sexual Perversions'.

Anna Freud and the Foundations of Psychoanalysis

In the year Anna Freud finished her psychoanalytic training, the first major phase of the theoretical development of psychoanalysis had run its course. She had quite literally grown up with it. Most notably, the theory of the mind had been set forth, and the developmental theory of psycho-sexual development had been steadily and continually refined. These were foundations which Anna Freud was never to neglect. In particular, it had become evident that the clinical phenomena of resist-ance and the emergence of reconstructions of childhood, and in some instances of forgotten memories in the treatment situation, presupposed various points of view: a topographical point of view, which postulated systems 'unconscious', 'pre-conscious' and 'conscious'; the dynamic point of view – the explanatory concept of repression denoting forces that sought to withhold thoughts and memories from consciousness; and the economic point of view – that the strength of the opposing forces varied and their relative strength was a major determinant of outcomes in an individual's internal and external life. Furthermore, the fact that the treatment situation pointed to the impact of origins and changes oc-curring over time presupposed a genetic point of view. Thus it was that Anna Freud imbibed a complex metapsychological position which decreed that every clinical 'fact' and every mental act should be con-sidered from the complementary points of view to maximise under-standing. She remained wedded to this standpoint throughout her life.

From the very outset, moreover, the various metapsychological points of view were seen in terms of an overriding commitment to what may be termed the developmental point of view. A commitment to the developmental point of view seeks to account for how 'the given' gets 'given' – by tracing its vicissitudes, its progressions, fixations, regressions, sublimations and so on. It was thus no accident that the thrust of the narrative in her 'Beating Fantasies and Daydreams' is structured around the developmental vicissitudes seen in terms of major phases: a progression from a beating phantasy culminating in masturbation – as a substitute for an incestuous wish between father and daughter – to its replacement by 'nice stories', interpreted as a developmental advance, to the patient's short stories interpreted as still further progress towards social pleasure in communicating with an audience (Murray, 1994, p. 19).

Applying and Clarifiying (1923–1930)

The Development of Child Analysis

Anna Freud's commitment to a balanced approach to the metapsychology was supplemented by two additional overriding themes which were to remain with her throughout her life. Both themes were gradually and variously developed from what was implicit in the work of her father: firstly, what became known as the widening scope of psychoanalysis; and secondly, the concern with both normal and abnormal development (Young-Bruehl, 1996, pp. 61–5).

Psychoanalysis, originally an outcome of the treatment of neurotic disorders, whether of symptom neurosis – conversion hysteria, phobias and obsessional neurosis – or of character neurosis, was later applied, sometimes controversially, to the psychoses, the sexual perversions and so on. In 1925 Freud wrote: 'None of the applications of psycho-analysis has excited so much interest and aroused so many hopes, and none, consequently, has attracted so many capable workers, as its use in the theory and practice of education. It is easy to understand why; for children have become the main subject of psycho-analytic research and have thus replaced in importance the neurotics on whom its studies began' (Freud, 1925, p. 273). As a former teacher of young children seeking to apply and develop the work of her father, it was, perhaps, inevitable that after qualifying as a psychoanalyst in 1922, Anna Freud would launch herself into the intensive analysis of a series of children. As she did so, she took a step that was very characteristic of her way of working: she surrounded herself with a group of co-workers and pioneers to whom she could present her developing ideas. This pioneering work eventually led to the establishment of the Vienna

School of Child Analysis with Anna Freud as its undisputed head.

Anna Freud was part of the so-called second generation of Viennese analysts who – unlike the more erratic and idiosyncratic first generation – underwent systematic training (Leupold-Löwenthal, 1992). Just as this generation imbibed the balanced complexities of the classical metapsychology, so they came to stand for balance in technique. In their clinical work, they pursued a '*balanced* focus on interpretations of transference, resistance, dreams, memories, past and current relationships, character, defences and developmental reconstructions' (Couch, 1997). But how was this technique to be applied to the analysis of the child? Anna Freud set forth her initial findings based on an intensive treatment of ten latency-age children in 1926 (A. Freud, 1927). On the basis of her findings, she argued the following: that child and adult analysis were similar insofar as both entailed arousing the patient's trust and interest in the analytic work; that the analyst is there to help and support the patient; that the patient's version in all his conflicts with his family be accepted; and that the analyst should make himself interesting and useful to the patient. On the other hand, child and adult analysis were different insofar as child analysis required a preparatory period prior to analysis to make the patient analysable: 'to create a tie strong enough to sustain the later analysis'; and to make symptoms not felt by the child as alien or pathological into symptoms consciously felt to be unwanted and distressing. More specifically, she argued that the transference neurosis proper, could not develop in the transferential relationship between child patient and analyst, principally because the child's relationship with its parents was still developing.

During this, her first period of child analysis, her father had put forward his structural model of the mind in *The Ego and the Id* (1923), his last major theoretical work. Drawing upon this radically new conceptualisation of mind and personality in terms of the three psychic agencies – id, ego and superego – Anna Freud summarised the central point of the distinction between adult and child analysis in her 1928 paper 'The Theory of Child Analysis':

> . . . here we have come upon the main and most important difference between analysis of adults and that of children. In the analysis of adults we are dealing with a situation in which the

superego has achieved full independence and is no longer subject to external influences. Here our sole task is to raise all the strivings which contributed to the neurotic conflict to the same level by bringing them to consciousness. On this new conscious level the conflict can then be dealt with in new ways and brought to a different solution.

In the analysis of children, however, we deal with situations where the superego has not yet achieved full independence; where it operates all too clearly for the sake of those from whom it received its commands, the parents and persons in charge of the child, and is swayed in its demands by every change in the relationship with these people and by all the alterations that may occur in their own outlook. As in the case of adults, we work by purely analytic means with children insofar as we attempt to lift the repressed parts of the id and ego from the unconscious. But our task with the childish superego is a double one. It is analytic and proceeds from within in the historical dissolution of the superego, so far as it is already an independent structure, but it is also educational (in the widest sense of that word) in exercising influences from without, by modifying the relations with those who are bringing up the child, by creating new impressions, and revising the demands made on the child by the environment (pp. 171–2).

Psychoanalysis for Parents and Teachers

Anna Freud frequently remarked how often psychoanalysts find a way of returning to their professional interests pursued before their psychoanalytic training. In her case, it was the teacher in her that remained irrepressible. The first of many didactic presentations of psychoanalysis directed specifically at teachers and parents was published in 1930 as *Four Lectures on Psychoanalysis for Teachers and Parents*.

The book begins with observations of children's behaviour with which teachers and parents could readily identify. Anna Freud explains the observed behaviours in terms of the fundamental terms and concepts of psychoanalysis: the unconscious, repression, reaction formation, sublimation, transference, the Oedipus complex and the castration complex, the libido and the theory of infantile sexuality. Once again, she emphasizes psychoanalysis as a developmental theory set within the structural model of a divided personality. What teachers witness in the classroom 'are really only repetitions and new editions of very old conflicts of which you are the target but not the cause' (p. 88). Teachers should recognize that the child is divided within himself, and therefore assume the role of the superego for each child. 'The teacher inherits more than merely the child's oedipus complex. He assumes for each of the children under his control the role of superego, and in this way acquires the right to their submission' (p. 120). Compulsory obedience will then become voluntary submission. 'Moreover, all the children under his guidance will develop ties to each other and become a united group' (p. 120). In the final lecture on the relation between psychoanalysis and education, Anna Freud identifies the three major contributions of psychoanalysis to education: it provides a perspective from which to criticize existing educational methods; as a theory of the instinctual drives, the unconscious and the libido, it extends the teacher's knowledge and understanding of the complex relations between children and adults; and as a method of treatment, psychoanalysis 'could repair the injuries inflicted upon the child during the process of education' (p. 129).

Developing Theory and Technique (1931–7)

By their nature, theoretical models are both constraining and enabling. Furthermore, new models necessitate reorientations and further work if their implications are to be grasped. Even amongst Freud's Viennese followers there were those that remained wedded to his pre-structural models (Sterba, 1982, pp. 73–8), just as there were many who would later come to believe they had moved beyond the structural model. Anna Freud was an early convert to the structural model at its inception, but was never wholeheartedly influenced by her father's refinements to it which he had introduced in his *Inhibitions, Symptoms and Anxiety* (1926). After reading Freud's *An Outline of Psycho-Analysis* (1940), in which his final statement on his metapsychology set great store by the structural model, Anna Freud may have abandoned the topographical *model* but was unable to dispense with the topographical *point of view*, which she frequently found useful in the understanding of dreams. She was, however, committed to developing and refining the structural model and its implications, and set about this task in earnest from 1925 onwards in a series of innovative presentations which culminated in her 1936 classic *The Ego and the Mechanisms of Defence*.

It is a serious mistake to see *The Ego and the Mechanisms of Defence* as merely adding to our knowledge of the mechanisms of defence. It is an innovatory statement of an ego psychology designed to balance psychoanalysis as analysis of id irruptions; analysis of the complex interplay between id derivatives, ego and superego manifestations; and analysis of the relationship between endopsychic and external worlds. Furthermore, whereas Freud (1926) had emphasized the drive derivatives and representatives that threaten the child with basic danger situations, Anna Freud highlighted the defences against affects that threaten the child with psychic pain. These had largely been neglected by psychoanalysts until that time (Yorke, 1996: 10). This led to the development of classical technique which, in moving from the analysis of defence to content, and from surface to depth, developed the tradition begun in the 1920s by Wilhelm Reich. However, whereas Reich focused almost entirely upon character resistance and character analysis, for Anna Freud the task of analysis was to gain the fullest possible knowledge of all three psychic institutions, with the analyst taking his standpoint at a point equidistant from the id, the ego and the superego. Thus it was that Anna Freud's 1936 text became the groundbreaking work which enabled the development of a specifically classical 'balanced' approach to technique, later developed so effectively by Otto Fenichel (1941) and Ralph Greenson (1967) and recently consolidated by Arthur Couch (1997).

It is instructive to trace the major steps taken by Anna Freud in the preparation of her classic 1936 book, and for this, Kris's (1938) review remains unrivalled. He details how the groundwork for the text was laid down in a series of unpublished papers beginning in 1929, when Anna Freud had first described how components of what might ordinarily become an infantile animal phobia might contribute to the formation of an animal phantasy. Here, in the service of the pleasure principle, the feared animal of the phobia becomes the child's protector. In chapter

6 of her 1936 book, she terms this preliminary defence 'denial in fantasy', a method appropriate to the earliest period of childhood and illustrated by the case of the seven-year-old boy who, in his phantasies, owned a tame lion which terrified everyone else and loved nobody but him. The boy was thereby spared the unpleasure of confronting his hatred and fear of the lion, itself a father-substitute.

In her unpublished 1932 paper Anna Freud had given examples of the interaction between the internal and the external world in the development of infantile neurosis. Children who behave like adults are practising what Anna Freud terms 'denial in word and act'. They thereby produce an agreeable phantasy that they can control the world. Such matters become the topic of chapter 7. As a final 'preliminary stage of defense' Anna Freud turns to 'Restriction of the Ego', the subject of chapter 8, where children suddenly change their direction of interest – again to avoid the unpleasure associated with activities they find anxiety-provoking. Most striking is her couching of her arguments in terms of the pleasure–unpleasure principle, her commitment to the developmental point of view and her unwillingness to overpathologize. Whilst the adaption to reality demanded by the mature ego will make many childhood denials inappropriate at a later developmental stage, when seen in terms of the phase of development within which they occur they may well be healthy adaptations.

Anna Freud's commitment to understanding what is specific to each phase of development leads her to a consideration of adolescence, a previously neglected topic. Chapters 11 and 12 of the 1936 text use the phenomena of puberty to illustrate defence motivated by fear of the strength of the instincts. Moving on from where her father had left off in his *Three Essays on the Theory of Sexuality* (1905), she shows how instinctual anxiety during puberty gives rise to the defences of asceticism and intellectualization that are so often a feature of adolescence. These chapters set the stage for the development of a more systematic psycho-analytic study of preadolescence and adolescence. Indeed, Anna Freud herself returned to the topic in later years. Her papers 'On Certain Difficulties in the Preadolescent's Relation to His Parents' (1949b) and 'Adolescence' (1958b) are included in this selection of her writings.

Arguably, the third part of *The Ego and the Mechanisms of Defence* (1936) is its most original section. Here Anna Freud articulates two new defences: identification with the aggressor and altruistic surrender. Both are particular combinations of projection and identification. In identification with the aggressor, the individual perceives aspects of the external world as threatening; becomes the threatening individual through identification or impersonation; and then projects the threatening and aggressive aspects back into the outside world. Alternatively, identification with the aggressor may be identification with the aggression itself, as in the illustration of the six-year-old boy who, having been hurt by his dentist, did not play the role of the dentist but broke pencils and cut up an India rubber and string.

In altruistic surrender, the individual projects his forbidden drive wishes into others; identifies with those others; and is then able to obtain 'a kind of gratification by proxy' (Holder, 1995: 330). In terms of the structural model:

> This defensive process serves two purposes. On the one hand it enables the subject to take a friendly interest in the gratification of other people's instincts and so, indirectly and in spite of the superego's prohibition, to gratify his own, while, on the other hand, it liberates the inhibited activity and aggression primarily designed to secure the fulfilment of the instinctual wishes in their original relation to himself (p. 129).

In this volume of selected writings, we have prefaced these two chapters ('Identification with the Aggressor' and 'A Form of Altruism') with Anna Freud's own review of 'The Mechanisms of Defense' (chapter 4 of the 1936 text). In this chapter she reviews the meaning of the term 'defense' in her father's writings, tracing shifts in meaning, listing his descriptions of the ego's defensive methods and comparing results achieved by the different defence mechanisms in individual cases. She makes it quite explicit that for her, like her father, introjection and projection presuppose the development of an ego that has been differentiated from the outside world, in contradistinction to the followers of Melanie Klein, and others, who see the structure of the ego being developed in and through these mechanisms.

Observing and Augmenting (1938–1959)

Observational Studies

To Anna Freud, psychoanalysis was above all else an observational science. She was no naive empiricist, however. As her father had put it in Freud (1915):

> The true beginning of scientific activity consists . . . in describing phenomena and then in proceeding to group, classify and correlate them. Even at this stage of description it is not possible to avoid applying certain abstract ideas to the material in hand, ideas from somewhere else or other but certainly not from the new observations alone. Such ideas – which will later become the basic concepts of the science – are still more indispensable as the material is further worked over . . . It is only after more thorough investigation of the field of observation that we are able to formulate its basic scientific concepts with increased precision, and progressively so to modify them that they become serviceable and consistent over a wide area (p. 117).

It was in this spirit that Anna Freud had applied the conceptual framework developed by her father when she turned her attention to the analysis of children. In that instance, she was led to modify child technique and saw no reason to depart from the framework developed by her father. On the other hand, when she had focused upon the ego and its defence mechanisms, she was led to major refinements in the framework applied, as well as to explicating the implications for technique of her balanced approach between id, ego and superego analysis. As she began to focus on observational work with children outside of the analytic setting, however, she did so in the spirit of an investigator seeking to apply the framework, to confirm its existing findings where appropriate and to augment them when necessary. In this phase of 'observing and augmenting' she did not expect her observational work to lead to major revisions of theories developed within the analytic setting or to refutations of major findings.

In one sense, of course, her work as a teacher had enabled her to observe the development of children from a psychoanalytic viewpoint.

1937, however, marked the beginning of a lifelong commitment to systematic observation and care of both infants and children. Edith Jackson, an American psychiatrist, provided funds to establish a nursery for children aged one to three years. And so it was that the Jackson nursery opened in Vienna in February 1937 with a roll of 11 children. Infant observation was noted on small cards, filed thematically at the end of each day, providing the basis for later discussions. Thus began Anna Freud's developmental studies on separation and substitute care-givers, and her focus on the preoedipal years.

Forced to flee Vienna a year later, consequent on the Nazi occupation of Austria, she soon established the Hampstead War Nurseries in her new home city of London. *Young Children in War-time: A Year's Work in a Residential War Nursery* (1942) summarized the first year of work. Central was the survey of psychological reactions to the dissolution of family life whether by separation from, or death of, the father and, in all cases, separation from the mother. Contrary to what might have been expected, children were not disturbed by the violence and destruction of war – for Anna Freud, these characteristics of war largely mirrored the child's endopsychic state. Rather, it was the separation that constituted the major trauma. More particularly, it was the form in which the separation took place that was so important. This led her to making recommendations aimed at easing the abruptness of the separation, which came to be widely followed in other areas, thus giving this work an applicability and salience far beyond the circumstances of war. Her recommendations to make the separation a slow process, by introducing the child to its substitute mother beforehand, and by having the real mother reappear several times to see her child while weaning the infant from one mother figure to another, which may seem common sense now, were strikingly innovative at the time. Such has been the fate, too, of her major findings put forward in her other major wartime publication (with Dorothy Burlingham), *Infants Without Families: The Case For and Against Residential Nurseries* (1944).

In this latter text Anna Freud, with her collaborator Dorothy Bur-lingham, carefully profiles the development of the child in residential care as opposed to those brought up in the conventional family. The personality achievements of the infant's first two years in respect of predominantly maturational advances, such as muscular control and independent motility, are comparatively independent of external circumstances. On the other hand, speech, food intake and bladder and bowel control are more dependent on an intimate mother–child relationship and on the constant interaction of maturational forces with external stimulation. Many of these themes were taken up in later publications. As regards eating, she comments:

> But the experiences of the first year, when love for food and love for mother were identical, leave their imprint on the reaction to food throughout life. The child from his side shows every inclination to treat food given by the mother as he treats the mother, which means that all the possible disturbances of the mother–child relationship turn easily into eating disturbances (p. 566).

This was a theme she returned to in 'The Psychoanalytic Study of Infant Feeding Disturbances' (1946) and again in 'The Establishment of Feeding Habits' (1947). Particularly evident in such writings is Anna Freud's characteristic balance of the practical and the applied with the testing of selected areas of theory with corroboration or modification as necessary. As Murray (1994, p. 39) puts it: 'Because the primary purpose of eating is a biological one based on the body's need for nourishment, one would expect a harmony of id and ego forces united in the self-preservation of the individual. However, "(e)ating may, on the other hand, become invested with sexual and aggressive meaning and thereby, secondarily become the symbolic representative of id forces which are opposed to the ego" (A. Freud, 1946, p. 41). Such occurrences will result in eating disturbances.' Anna Freud adds: 'Considerate handling of the child's feeding, with a reasonable amount of self-determination, to safeguard the child's appetite, makes the function of eating less vulnerable and less favorable ground for neurotic superstructures' (ibid., p. 59).

Augmenting

Wartime circumstances had left little time for Anna Freud to write up the results of her observational studies and the theoretical refinement that accompanied them. The years 1945 to the end of the 1950s saw a profusion of papers which consolidated her position as the doyenne of child analysis and psychoanalytic observer of the developing child. Particularly important were her 'Indications for Child Analysis' (1945), which summarized her position on child analysis, and 'Observations on Child Development' (1951a), which detailed the essence and substance of her observational work. Both papers are included in this volume.

These years also saw the development of her characteristic approach to the incorporation of new ideas being developed by psychoanalytic traditions that differed from her own. Her 'Notes on Aggression' (1949a) is paradigmatic in this respect. Faced with the aggression manifest in wartime and the increasing emphasis placed on aggressive as opposed to sexual drives by alternative traditions in psychoanalysis, she sets herself the task of situating the new emphasis *vis-à-vis* her own position. Once again she reiterates the fundamentals of the classical psychoanalytic position rooted in the work of her father. She restates the sexual theory and the significance of the anal-sadistic phase of development in terms of the preponderance of aggressive tendencies at the anal level. Following her father's 1920 formulation of the division of instinctual drives into the life and death instincts, she sees sex as representative of the life force; aggression of the destructive force. However, in clinical observation, neither sex nor aggression can be studied in a pure form. Always it is a question of differing combinations producing the observed phenomena. Sexuality will become ineffective where there is an overabundance of repression or inhibition of aggression. Aggression, when not fused with sexual urges, manifests itself as destructive and criminal tendencies. Observation suggested to her that both are innate, so aggression cannot be the result merely of environmental influences (*contra* John Bowlby). Furthermore, since clinical observation shows states which represent a successful fusion between destructive and erotic urges, and in young infants derivatives of each instinct can be seen successively and seemingly unaffected by each other, the two forces by themselves cannot create a state of conflict in the mind (*contra* Melanie Klein). Rather, it is the development of a focal point (the ego) 'which results in the gradual integration of all instinctual strivings, and during this process may lead to clashes and realization of incompatibility between them' (p. 70).

Anna Freud was, however, constantly developing the classical tradition. Her father had, of course, placed particular emphasis upon the importance of the father and the triadic constellation of the oedipal years. Her own work with young infants and her observations of the consequences of separation from the mother led to important contributions which focused on the preoedipal years. However, unlike those many who saw the new findings as overturning the old, Anna Freud saw her task as finding the appropriate place for the new observations within the old, and the preservation of the old insofar as contemporary work could be seen as compatible with it. Her plea, once again, was for a balanced approach. Illustrative of this is 'The Concept of the Rejecting Mother' (1955). Here she points to the simplifying tendencies amongst certain writers and practitioners to attribute monocausal determinants to a 'rejecting mother' without discriminating the very different ways a mother might be 'rejecting'. 'Rejecting actions or attitudes' take on many different forms and have many different consequences, which it is the task of psychoanalysis and psychoanalytic observation to unravel. Furthermore, '. . . we, the observers, must not share the infants' delusion. We must guard against the error of confusing the inevitably frustrating aspects of extrauterine life with the rejecting actions or attitudes of the individual mothers' (p. 602).

Also evident in these post-war papers is a commitment to the balanced and comprehensive approach which commitment to her father's metapsychology enables. 'About Losing and Being Lost', written in 1953, although not published in full until 1967, is particularly instructive in this regard. After detailing the significance of the dynamic aspect of losing and mislaying objects (we have the unconscious desire to discard something which consciously we wish to retain), Anna Freud goes on to break new ground when she indicates how the libido—economic aspects of losing and being lost enable a theory concerning the attitude of human beings to their possessions.

> We begin to understand . . . why losing things is the exception rather than the rule . . . Obviously, it is the distribution of libido between the animate and the inanimate world and the resulting positive cathexis of material objects which assures that our possessions remain tied to us, or, rather, we to them . . . We understand, further, why some people become chronic losers. If their

libidinal processes are seriously altered, they cease to have a hold
on their possessions, without the latter having changed for the
worse in any respect (pp. 306–7).

The post-war years were also marked by an increasing involvement
in the international psychoanalytical movement. Anna Freud renewed
her position as the general secretary to the International Psychoanalytical
Association, a position which she held until 1949 – she had previously
been elected to the vice-presidency in 1934. Her Hampstead Child
Therapy Training Course began in 1947 and produced qualified analytical child therapists who would eventually establish 'little Anna Freud
Centres' (Dyer, 1983, p. 189) in both the United States and Europe.
The 1950s saw her being increasingly heralded, particularly in the
United States. Her first visit to America, in 1950, was marked by the
conferment upon her of an honorary LLD by Clark University, which
had likewise honoured her father forty years earlier – when Anna Freud
had been denied her wish to accompany him on the grounds that she
was too young. The late 1950s also saw her initiating a number of
collaborative research projects at the Hampstead Child-Therapy Course
and Clinic (now the Anna Freud Centre), including those on adolescence, borderline cases, motherless children and on blind children. The
Hampstead Index, which classified and summarized the data collected,
and which later would form the basis of numerous studies, was also
begun during this period.

The period was also peppered with excursions beyond the psychoanalytic study of the child. In 1954 she tackled the problem of 'The
Widening Scope of Indications for Psychoanalysis: Discussion'; and
'Problems of Technique in Adult Psychoanalysis'. Both are included
in this volume's selection.

Innovating and Conserving (1960–82)

Innovating

Anna Freud has rightly been referred to as both a staunch conservative
and a radical innovator (Wallerstein, 1984). These two themes are
particularly evident in the long, final and highly productive phase which

began in 1960 and ended with her death in 1982. The innovatory aspects of this final phase were signposted in her paper 'Child Observation and Prediction of Development: A Memorial Lecture in Honor of Ernst Kris' (1958a). Previously, she had taken the view that direct child observation would not break new ground – rather, it would prove or disprove the correctness of reconstructions obtained from the analytic situation. Here she endorses Kris's view that, if used appropriately, observations and analytic reconstructions would be comparable. Quoting Kris (1950), 'while the former would certainly not replace the latter, they would implement, supplement, control, and enlarge the picture in various ways' (p. 105). In particular, Kris had set store on systematic longitudinal studies of life histories, supplemented and checked by analytic investigation. This was the domain that Anna Freud was to make her own for the next two decades.

Her innovations focused on three major contributions: her concept of developmental lines; her diagnostic recommendations based on developmental considerations; and what she referred to as 'the metapsychological profile'. Whilst all these contributions had their roots in previous work, it was only from the 1960s onwards that she set out to systematically develop what had previously been merely embryonic. First came a series of lectures delivered in New York in 1960, entitled 'Four Contributions to the Psychoanalytic Study of the Child'. These were supplemented in 1962 by two lectures given as Visiting Sloan Professor at the Menninger School of Psychiatry and one further C.F. Menninger Memorial Lecture. Then followed her *Normality and Pathology in Childhood* (1965), which contained her more mature reflections on the matters introduced in the previous talks (Dyer, 1983, pp. 227–68). These contributions were then further refined and expanded in a series of papers stemming from the late 1960s. For this volume, we have selected the most significant papers stemming from this final phase of development of the 1960 lectures, namely, 'The Symptomatology of Childhood: A Preliminary Attempt at Classification' (1970); 'A Psychoanalytic View of Developmental Psychopathology' (1974a); and 'Psychopathology Seen Against the Background of Normal Development' (1976).

Anna Freud's concept of developmental lines had its roots in her father's delineation of the psycho-sexual stages of development. She had herself begun to delineate a developmental sequence for the relationship between the mother and child in her *Young Children in War-time: A Year's Work in a Residential War Nursery* (1942), a sequence which accounted for both preoedipal and oedipal object relations. While others were content to base developmental concepts on reconstructed abnormal states, Anna Freud's observations of normal as well as disturbed children over many years had convinced her that psychopathology could only be determined against the background of normal development. This was particularly evident in the context of diagnosis and assessment. Similar symptoms may have very different underlying psychopathologies, whilst different presenting symptomatologies may have similar underlying psychopathologies. Further, similar symptoms in different developmental phases may have quite different meanings. This necessitated putting forward 'lines of development' which functioned as ideal-types against which individuals could be assessed. To those lines of libidinal development, and the development of preobjectal and objectal relations, she added those from suckling to rational eating; from wetting and soiling to bladder and bowel control; and from irresponsibility to responsibility in body management; as well as others, such as from egocentricity to companionship; from the body to the toy; and from play to work.

Anna Freud was well aware that particular trajectories along developmental lines were socially and historically situated. She was also tolerant of different trajectories on each line of development, and their various combinations. Indeed, she conceptualized personality and character difference in terms of the unique developmental pathways of each and every individual. However, when regressive tendencies outweigh the progressive ones, the clinician should be put on his guard that intervention may be appropriate.

In particular, she conceptualized psychopathology in terms of disharmony between the developmental lines. Here, it is evident that the various lines are not merely descriptive. Rather, the lines function as complex regulatory structures embracing the multiplicity of possible interactions between maturation, adaptation and structuralization (Mayes and Cohen, 1996). Specifically, it is the interplay between the lines that is crucial in maintaining progressive or regressive tendencies. She gives the example of the child with exceptionally high verbal intelligence quotients linked with exceptionally low performance levels, and exceptional backwardness on the lines towards emotional maturity, towards companionship and towards body management. 'The resulting distortion of behavior is alarming, particularly in such areas as acting out of sexual and aggressive trends, profusion of organized fantasy life, clever rationalization of delinquent attitudes, and lack of control over anal and urethral tendencies. In the usual way, such cases would be classified as ' "borderline" or "prepsychotic" ' (A. Freud, 1965, p. 127).

Conserving

The essence of Anna Freud's new approach is that developmental considerations take precedence over considerations of symptomatology and manifest abnormal behaviour. Insofar as she viewed childhood disturbances against the background of mental disorders in adult life, the primary focus was on the ways in which childhood disturbances differ from the psychopathology of adults. Therein lies the innovatory aspects of the detailed work carried out in Anna Freud's phase of 'innovating and conserving'. However, while adding to her father's corpus, she always does so in a way that conserves the old. This is particularly evident in the way she constructs the metapsychological profile used for the purposes of diagnosis and assessment. Assessments of development are made in terms of drive development and ego and superego development. These are supplemented with dynamic and structural assessments – all in terms of the complementary viewpoints of classical metapsychology: the dynamic, economic, genetic and structural aspects of psychic functioning. Moreover, as she makes particularly clear in the 'The Symptomatology of Childhood: A Preliminary Attempt at Classification', she is concerned to forge links between symptomatology and metapsychology. She does not feel the need to underplay the importance of diagnostic classification and assessment, as was fashionable in some psychoanalytic quarters.

Conserving is also evident in Anna Freud's approach to the varieties of psychopathology – both as regards classification and treatment. She was led to the construction of the various lines of development when confronted with increasing numbers of children who did not fit into categories of the 'normal' or the neurotic. In terms of her developmental approach, these were best seen in terms of non-neurotic developmental disorders. A neurosis presupposes structuralization to have advanced to the extent where there can be inter-systemic conflict. With the non-neurotic developmental disorders, on the other hand, this need not be so. These latter disorders are based on developmental defects caused by developmental irregularities and failures. The failure to recognize the distinction between neurotic disorders and non-neurotic developmental disorders leads to errors in assessing psychopathology, leading the clinician to erroneously link neurotic symptoms in either children or adults to events in the first year of life. Whereas for Anna Freud: 'Whatever clashes occur at that time proceed externally between the infant and the environment, not internally within a not yet existing structure. Where deprivation and frustration are excessive, this leads not to symptom formation but to developmental setbacks' (A. Freud, 1974a, p. 71).

Early developmental defects may well predispose the individual to neurosis and the clinical picture may well be mixed, but conceptually, the two different types of disorder are quite distinct. The twofold classification enabled her to go 'Beyond the Infantile Neurosis' (A. Freud, 1974b) and show how developmental defects in the personality, a result of irregularities and failures in development, are responsible for psychosomatic symptomatology, backwardness and the atypical and borderline states. The twofold distinction also led her to caution against an over-optimistic therapeutic zeal. While psychoanalysis was still the treatment of choice for neurotic disorders, she remained pessimistic about the possibilities of analysis providing the patient with what was never there in the first place. The best that could be hoped for, in such cases, was for the patient to come to a greater understanding and accommodation of the consequences of developmental defects and disharmonies. She elaborates these points in 'A Psychoanalytic View of Developmental Psychopathology' (1974a).

Anna Freud never found it necessary to abandon her father's theory of mind. She remained particularly wedded to the metapsychology and the structural model. It was no mere loyalty to her father that kept Anna Freud attached to the metapsychology, however. She strongly supported it from the outset, extending it with her own innovations and using its comprehensive framework to re-work findings from alternative approaches, when to do so furthered psychoanalytic understanding and explanation. Such an approach enabled both consistency and range – in both the linking of theory and method, and in substantive conclusions. Most particularly, it enabled her to maintain the 'balanced' approach to psychoanalysis she so favoured throughout her life. In 1962, at the inception of two decades of innovating and conserving, she wrote of the merits of her Developmental Profile:

> In contrast to other diagnostic schemes or categorizations [ours] seems to us to provide a comprehensive guide to the individual and to guard the diagnostician against viewing the child from one aspect only, whether this aspect concerns his object relations . . . his social adaptation . . . or his intellectual achievements (A. Freud, 1962, p. 36).

These arguments, when applied across the range of Anna Freud's contributions, provide her most fitting psychoanalytic legacy.

The organization of this selection of Anna Freud's major writings fell naturally into four parts. It is entirely fitting that we should begin this volume of selected writings with three of the twelve chapters of *The Ego and the Mechanisms of Defence* – a classic in the psychoanalytic literature. Indeed, for many it was the first vital component of the total psychoanalytic edifice created by someone other than Freud (Wallerstein, 1984: 70). Part 1 therefore includes Anna Freud's review of 'The Mechanisms of Defense' together with her two chapters setting forth the two new types of defence she articulated herself.

Very soon after qualifying as a psychoanalyst, Anna Freud made the domain of classical child analysis and psychoanalytic observation of the child her own. Part 2 includes her major papers which stem from this work, while part 3 includes two important papers on preadolescence and adolescence. Finally, in part 4, we have grouped together her most significant contributions on the technique and scope of psychoanalysis. These include both her major review of the indications for child analysis and papers of more general significance for the technique and scope of psychoanalysis.

Editors' Note

The Writings of Anna Freud have been published in eight volumes by International Universities Press, New York and by the Hogarth Press and the Institute of Psycho-Analysis, London. Both editions adopt American spelling in the text. The Hogarth Press and the Institute of Psycho-Analysis edition of *The Ego and the Mechanisms of Defence* adopts the English spelling in the title of the book. We have followed the latter usage.

'Problems of Pathogenesis: Introduction to the Discussion' is not included in *The Writings of Anna Freud*. This paper was first published in *The Psychoanalytic Study of the Child*, volume 38, 1983.

The footnotes throughout the book are Anna Freud's. Supplementary references were included in a number of papers when they were reproduced in *The Writings of Anna Freud*. We have retained these additional references.

The following abbreviations are used:

S.E.   *Standard Edition of the Complete Psychological Works of Sigmund Freud*, Vols 1–24, 1953–74, London: Hogarth Press and the Institute of Psycho-Analysis.

Writings   *The Writings of Anna Freud*, Vols 1–8, 1968–81, New York: International Universities Press.

PART 1

The Ego and the Mechanisms of Defence

The Mechanisms of Defense (1936)

*In this chapter Anna Freud continues with the rehabilitation of the defence
concept which Freud had begun in* Inhibitions, Symptoms and Anxiety
*(1926). The concept of defence, which had such a prominent place in Freud's
early writings ('The Neuro-Psychoses of Defence' (1894) and 'Further Remarks
on the Neuro-Psychoses of Defence' (1896a)), had been displaced in favour of
the concept of repression which was capable of taking different forms. Repression
was envisaged by Freud (1896b) as an involuntary mental process whereby
unacceptable wishes, affects and memories were removed from consciousness.
Repression could take place in different forms:*

- *first, by the individual being unaware of the unacceptable thoughts;*
- *second, by attributing the unacceptable thoughts to someone else (Freud (1911));*
- *third, by turning an unacceptable feeling (love) into its opposite (hate) (Freud
(1911));*
- *fourth, by denying an unacceptable external perception ('turning a blind
eye').*

  *In this chapter Anna Freud describes in detail, with clinical illustrations, how
these mental mechanisms previously subsumed under the concept of repression, can
be conceptualized as separate defence mechanisms of the ego. Now, repression is
only one amongst a series of defence mechanisms – projection, denial, displacement, reversal and so forth. This change in the understanding of repression
took place alongside the introduction of the structural model (ego, id and superego)
of the mind (*The Ego and the Id *(1923)). The defence mechanisms, of which
repression is only one, are now regarded as a function of the ego. Moreover,
whereas Freud (1926) had emphasized the defences against the drives and drive
derivatives, for Anna Freud it is the defences against affects that need highlighting.*

'The Mechanisms of Defense' is the fourth chapter of *The Ego
and the Mechanisms of Defence*. This book was first published in

1936 by the Internationaler Psychoanalytischer Verlag under the title *Das Ich Und Die Abwehrmechanismen*. The English translation by Cecil Baines followed in 1937. The present revised edition, based on the 1937 translation, was first published in 1966.

Psychoanalytic Theory and the Mechanisms of Defense

The term 'defense,' which I have used so freely in the three last chapters [of *The Ego and the Mechanisms of Defence* – eds.], is the earliest representative of the dynamic standpoint in psychoanalytic theory. It occurs for the first time in 1894, in Freud's study 'The Neuro-Psychoses of Defence,' and is employed in this and several of his subsequent works ('The Aetiology of Hysteria,' 'Further Remarks on the Neuro-Psychoses of Defence') to describe the ego's struggle against painful or unendurable ideas or affects. Later, this term was abandoned and, as time went on, was replaced by that of 'repression.' The relation between the two concepts, however, remained undetermined. In an appendix to *Inhibitions, Symptoms and Anxiety* (1926) Freud reverted to the old concept of defense, stating that he thought it would undoubtedly be an advantage to use it again, 'provided we employ it explicitly as a general designation for all the techniques which the ego makes use of in conflicts which may lead to a neurosis, while we retain the word "repression" for the special method of defence which the line of approach taken by our investigations made us better acquainted with in the first instance' (p. 163). Here we have direct refutation of the notion that repression occupies a unique position among the psychic processes, and a place is made in psychoanalytic theory for others which serve the same purpose, namely, 'the protection of the ego against instinctual demands.' The significance of repression is reduced to that of a 'special method of defence.'

This new conception of the role of repression suggests an inquiry into the other specific modes of defense and a comparison of those so far discovered and described by psychoanalytic investigators.

The same appendix to *Inhibitions, Symptoms and Anxiety* contains the conjecture to which I alluded in the last chapter [Chapter 3 of *The Ego and the Mechanisms of Defence* – eds.], namely, that 'further investigations may show that there is an intimate connection between special forms of defence and particular illnesses, as, for instance, between repression and hysteria' (p. 164). Regression and reactive alteration of the ego (reaction formation), isolation and 'undoing' what has been done are all cited as defensive techniques employed in obsessional neurosis.

A lead having thus been given, it is not difficult to complete the enumeration of the ego's defensive methods as described in Freud's other writings. For instance, in 'Jealousy, Paranoia and Homosexuality' (1922), introjection, or identification, and projection are mentioned as important defensive methods employed by the ego in morbid affections of this type and are characterized as 'neurotic mechanisms.' In his work on the theory of instinct (1915) he describes the processes of turning against the self and reversal, and these he designated as 'vicissitudes of instinct.' From the point of view of the ego these two latter mechanisms also must come under the heading of methods of defense, for every vicissitude to which the instincts are liable has its origin in some ego activity. Were it not for the intervention of the ego or of those external forces which the ego represents, every instinct would know only one fate – that of gratification. To these nine methods of defense, which are very familiar in the practice and have been exhaustively described in the theoretical writings of psychoanalysis (regression, repression, reaction formation, isolation, undoing, projection, introjection, turning against the self and reversal), we must add a tenth, which pertains rather to the study of the normal than to that of neurosis: sublimation, or displacement of instinctual aims.

So far as we know at present, the ego has these ten different methods at its disposal in its conflicts with instinctual representatives and affects. It is the task of the practicing analyst to discover how far these methods prove effective in the processes of ego resistance and symptom formation which he has the opportunity of observing in individuals.

A Comparison of the Results Achieved by the Different Mechanisms in Individual Cases

I shall take as an illustration the case of a young woman employed in an institution for children. She was the middle child of several brothers and sisters. Throughout childhood she suffered from passionate penis envy, relating to her elder and her younger brother, and from jealousy, which was repeatedly excited by her mother's successive pregnancies. Finally, envy and jealousy combined in a fierce hostility to her mother. But, since the child's love fixation was no less strong than her hatred, a violent defensive conflict with her negative impulses succeeded an initial period of uninhibited unruliness and naughtiness. She dreaded lest the manifestation of her hate should cause her to lose her mother's love, of which she could not bear to be deprived. She also dreaded that her mother would punish her and she criticized herself most severely for her prohibited longings for revenge. As she entered upon the period of latency, this anxiety situation and conflict of conscience became more and more acute and her ego tried to master her impulses in various ways. In order to solve the problem of ambivalence she displaced outward one side of her ambivalent feeling. Her mother continued to be a love object, but, from that time on, there was always in the girl's life a second important person of the female sex, whom she hated violently. This eased matters: her hatred of the more remote object was not visited with the sense of guilt so mercilessly as was her hatred of her mother. But even the displaced hatred was a source of much suffering. As time went on, it was plain that this first displacement was inadequate as a means of mastering the situation.

The little girl's ego now resorted to a second mechanism. It turned inward the hatred, which hitherto had related exclusively to other people. The child tortured herself with self-accusations and feelings of inferiority and, throughout childhood and adolescence right into adult life, she did everything she could to put herself at a disadvantage and injure her interests, always surrendering her own wishes to the demands made on her by others. To all outward appearance she had become masochistic since adopting this method of defense.

But this measure, too, proved inadequate as a means of mastering the situation. The patient then entered on a process of projection. The hatred which she had felt for female love objects or their substitutes was transformed into the conviction that she herself was hated, slighted or persecuted by them. Her ego thus found relief from the sense of guilt. The naughty child, who cherished wicked feelings against the people around her, underwent a metamorphosis into the victim of cruelty, neglect, and persecution. But the use of this mechanism left upon her character a permanent paranoid imprint, which was a source of very great difficulty to her both in youth and adult years.

The patient was quite grown up when she came to be an analyzed. She was not regarded as ill by those who knew her, but her sufferings were acute. In spite of all the energy which her ego had expended upon its defense she had not succeeded in really mastering her anxiety and sense of guilt. On any occasion when her envy, jealousy, and hatred were in danger of activation, she invariably had recourse to all her defense mechanisms. But her emotional conflicts never came to any issue which could set her ego at rest and, apart from this, the final result of all her struggles was meager in the extreme. She succeeded in maintaining the fiction that she loved her mother, but she felt herself to be full of hatred and on this account she despised and mistrusted herself. She did not succeed in preserving the sense of being loved; it had been destroyed by the mechanism of projection. Nor did she succeed in escaping the punishments which she had feared in childhood; by turning her aggressive impulses inward she inflicted upon herself all the suffering which she had formerly anticipated in the form of punishment by her mother. The three mechanisms of which she had made use could not prevent her ego from being in a perpetual state of uneasy tension and vigilance, nor relieve it of the exaggerated demands made upon it and the sense of acute torment from which it suffered.

Let us compare these processes with the corresponding relations in hysteria or obsessional neurosis. We will assume that the problem is the same in each case: how to master that hatred of the mother which springs from penis envy. Hysteria solves it by means of repression. The hatred of the mother is obliterated from consciousness and any possible derivatives which seek entry into the ego are vigorously warded off. The aggressive impulses associated with hatred and the sexual impulses associated with penis envy may be transformed into bodily symptoms,

7

if the patient possesses the capacity for conversion and somatic conditions are favorable. In other cases the ego protects itself against the reactivation of the original conflict by developing a phobia and avoiding the occasions of trouble. It imposes restrictions upon its activity, thus evading any situation which might lead to a return of the repressed impulses.

In obsessional neurosis, as in hysteria, hatred of the mother and penis envy are in the first instance repressed. Subsequently the ego secures itself against their return by means of reaction formations. A child who had been aggressive toward her mother develops an excessive tenderness toward her and is worried about her safety; envy and jealousy are transformed into unselfishness and thoughtfulness for others. By instituting obsessional ceremonials and various precautionary measures she protects the beloved persons from any outbreak of her aggressive impulses, while by means of a moral code of exaggerated strictness she checks the manifestation of her sexual impulses.

A child who masters her infantile conflicts in the hysterical or obsessional manner here described presents a more pathological picture than the patient whose case we first considered. The repression which has taken place has deprived such children of the control of part of their affective life. The original relation to the mother and brothers and the important relation to their own femininity have been withdrawn from further conscious assimilation and have become obsessively and irrevocably fixed in the reactive alteration undergone by the ego. A great part of their activity is consumed in maintaining the anticathexes which are designed subsequently to secure the repression, and this loss of energy is apparent in the inhibition and curtailment of other vital activities. But the ego of the child who has solved her conflicts by means of repression, with all its pathological sequels, is at peace. It suffers secondarily through the consequences of the neurosis which repression has brought upon it. But it has, at least within the limits of the conversion hysteria or obsessional neurosis, bound its anxiety, disposed of its sense of guilt, and gratified its ideas of punishment. The difference is that, if the ego employs repression, the formation of symptoms relieves it of the task of mastering its conflicts, while, if it employs the other defensive methods, it still has to deal with the problem.

In practice, the use of repression as distinct from other defensive

8

methods is less common than a combination in one and the same individual of the two techniques. This is well illustrated by the history of a patient who also suffered in very early childhood from acute penis envy, in her case in relation to her father. The sexual fantasies of this phase reached their climax in the wish to bite off her father's penis. At this point the ego set up its defense. The shocking idea was repressed. It was replaced by its opposite – a general disinclination to bite, which soon developed into a difficulty in eating, accompanied by hysterical feelings of disgust. One part of the prohibited impulse – that represented by the oral fantasy – had now been mastered. But the aggressive content, i.e., the wish to rob her father or a father substitute, remained in consciousness for a time, until, as the superego developed, the ego's moral sense repudiated this impulse. By means of a mechanism of displacement, which I shall discuss more fully later [Chapter 3, this volume – eds.], the urge to rob was transformed into a peculiar kind of contentedness and unassumingness. We see that the two successive methods of defense produced a substratum of hysteria and, superimposed on this, a specific ego modification, not in itself of a pathological character.

The impression conveyed by these examples is confirmed when we examine in detail the effect of the different defense mechanisms in other cases. Theoretically, repression may be subsumed under the general concept of defense and placed side by side with the other specific methods. Nevertheless, from the point of view of efficacy it occupies a unique position in comparison with the rest. In terms of quantity it accomplishes more than they; that is to say, it is capable of mastering powerful instinctual impulses, in face of which the other defensive measures are quite ineffective. It acts once only, though the anticathexis, effected to secure the repression, is a permanent institution demanding a constant expenditure of energy. The other mechanisms, on the contrary, have to be brought into operation again whenever there is an accession of instinctual energy. But repression is not only the most efficacious, it is also the most dangerous mechanism. The dissociation from the ego entailed by the withdrawal of consciousness from whole tracts of instinctual and affective life may destroy the integrity of the personality for good and all. Thus repression becomes the basis of compromise formation and neurosis. The consequences of the other defensive methods are not less serious but, even when they assume an acute form, they remain more within the limits of the normal. They manifest themselves in innumerable transformations, distortions, and deformities of the ego, which are in part the accompaniment of and in part substitutes for neurosis.

Suggestions for a Chronological Classification

Even when we have accorded to repression its exceptional position among the ego's methods of defense, we still feel with regard to the rest that we are including under a single heading a number of heterogeneous phenomena. Methods such as that of isolation and undoing stand side by side with genuine instinctual processes, such as regression, reversal, and turning against the self. Some of these serve to master large quantities of instinct or affect, others only small quantities. The considerations which determine the ego's choice of mechanism remain uncertain. Perhaps repression is pre-eminently of value in combating sexual wishes, while other methods can more readily be employed against instinctual forces of a different kind, in particular, against aggressive impulses. Or it may be that these other methods have only to complete what repression has left undone or to deal with such prohibited ideas as return to consciousness when repression fails.[1] Or possibly each defense mechanism is first evolved in order to master some specific instinctual urge and so is associated with a particular phase of infantile development.[2]

The appendix to *Inhibitions, Symptoms and Anxiety*, from which I have already quoted more than once, contains a provisional answer to these suggestions. 'It may well be that before its sharp cleavage into an ego and an id, and before the formation of a super-ego, the mental apparatus makes use of different methods of defence from those which it employs after it has reached these stages of organization' (p. 164). This may be expanded as follows. Repression consists in the withholding or expulsion of an idea or affect from the conscious ego. It is meaningless to speak of repression where the ego is still merged with the id. Similarly we might suppose that projection and introjection were methods which depended on the differentiation of the ego from the outside world.

The expulsion of ideas or affects from the ego and their relegation to the outside world would be a relief to the ego only when it had learnt to distinguish itself from that world. Or again, introjection from the outside world into the ego could not be said to have the effect of enriching the latter unless there were already a clear differentiation between that which belonged to the one and that which belonged to the other. But the situation is by no means so simple. In the case of projection and introjection the first beginnings are much more obscure.[3] Sublimation, i.e., the displacement of the instinctual aim in conformity with higher social values, presupposes the acceptance or at least the knowledge of such values, that is to say, presupposes the existence of the superego. Accordingly, the defense mechanisms of repression and sublimation could not be employed until relatively late in the process of development, while the position in time which we shall assign to projection and introjection depends upon the theoretical standpoint which happens to be adopted. Such processes as regression, reversal, or turning round upon the self are probably independent of the stage which the psychic structure has reached and as old as the instincts themselves, or at least as old as the conflict between instinctual impulses and any hindrance which they may encounter on their way to gratification. We should not be surprised to find that these are the very earliest defense mechanisms employed by the ego.

But this suggested chronological classification does not accord with our experience that the earliest manifestations of neurosis which we observe in young children are hysterical symptoms, of whose connection with repression there can be no doubt; on the other hand, the genuine masochistic phenomena, which result from the turning round of the instinct upon the self, are very rarely met with in earliest childhood. According to the theory of the English school of analysis, introjection and projection, which in our view should be assigned to the period after the ego has been differentiated from the outside world, are the very processes by which the structure of the ego is developed and but for which differentiation would never have taken place. These differences of opinion bring home to us the fact that the chronology of psychic processes is still one of the most obscure fields of analytic theory. We have a good illustration of this in the disputed question of when the individual superego is actually formed. So a classification of the defense mechanisms according to position in time inevitably partakes of all the doubt and uncertainty which even today attach to chronological pronouncements in analysis. It will probably be best to abandon the attempt so to classify them and, instead, to study in detail the situations which call for the defensive reactions.

Notes

1. I am following here a suggestion made by Jeanne Lampl-de Groot during a discussion by the Vienna Society.
2. According to a suggestion by Helene Deutsch.
3. Freud, *Totem and Taboo* (1913, p. 64). Compare also the view held by the English school, to which I refer on page 11.

2

Identification with the Aggressor (1936)

'Identification with the Aggressor' constitutes one of Anna Freud's most important contributions to the technique of psychoanalysis. She begins this chapter by describing the way in which children may overcome their real or phantasied fear of an angry or frightening adult. The child becomes as angry or frightening as he fears the adult is/was with him. To illustrate this movement from being the passive object to the active agent Anna Freud uses the example of a child after his visit to the dentist. The principle function of the mechanism of identification with the aggressor is to dispel anxiety.

Anna Freud uses material from the analysis of children to illustrate the way in which identification with the aggressor represents a staging post on the way to the development of conscience in both its conscious and unconscious aspects (superego). At this stage the child has internalized the parental prohibitions and restraints but as yet has been unable to make them her own. The examples used by Anna Freud demonstrate how the child dissociates herself from her own reprehensible thoughts and actions, attributing responsibility to others. This allows her to attack the other rather than herself.

The fact that the offence is externalized shows that projection is involved in the mechanism of identification with the aggressor. 'True morality begins,' Anna Freud writes, 'when the internalized criticism now embodied in the standard exacted by the superego, coincides with the ego perception of its own fault.' Many individuals fail to pass beyond this intermediate stage in the development of the superego, as represented in the mechanism of identification with the aggressor. Thus the individual has difficulty in acknowledging responsibility for her blameworthy thoughts and actions, attributing them to others.

'Identification with the Aggressor' is the ninth chapter of *The Ego and the Mechanisms of Defence*. This book was first published in 1936 by the Internationaler Psychoanalytischer Verlag under

3

the title *Das Ich Und Die Abwehrmechanismen*. The English translation by Cecil Baines followed in 1937. The present revised edition, based on the 1937 translation, was first published in 1966.

It is comparatively easy to discover the defense mechanisms to which the ego habitually resorts, so long as each is employed separately and only in conflict with some specific danger. When we find denial, we know that it is a reaction to external danger; when repression takes place, the ego is struggling with instinctual stimuli. The strong outward resemblance between inhibition and ego restriction makes it less certain whether these processes are part of an external or an internal conflict. The matter is still more intricate when defensive measures are combined or when the same mechanism is employed sometimes against an internal and sometimes against an external force. We have an excellent illustration of both these complications in the process of identification. Since it is one of the factors in the development of the superego, it contributes to the mastery of instinct. But, as I hope to show in what follows, there are occasions when it combines with other mechanisms to form one of the ego's most potent weapons in its dealings with external objects which arouse its anxiety.

August Aichhorn relates that, when he was giving advice on a child guidance committee, he had to deal with the case of a boy at an elementary school, who was brought to him because of a habit of making faces. The master complained that the boy's behavior, when he was blamed or reproved, was quite abnormal. On such occasions he made faces which caused the whole class to burst out laughing. The master's view was that either the boy was consciously making fun of him or else the twitching of his face must be due to some kind of tic. His report was at once corroborated, for the boy began to make faces during the consultation, but, when master, pupil, and psychologist were together, the situation was explained. Observing the two attentively, Aichhorn saw that the boy's grimaces were simply a caricature of the angry expression of the teacher and that, when he had to face a scolding by the latter, he tried to master his anxiety by involuntarily imitating him. The boy identified himself with the teacher's anger and copied his expression as he spoke, though the imitation was not recognized. Through his grimaces he was assimilating himself to or identifying with the dreaded external object.

My readers will remember the case of the little girl who tried by means of magic gestures to get over the mortification associated with her penis envy [A. Freud, 1936, p. 40 – eds]. This child was purposely and consciously making use of a mechanism to which the boy resorted involuntarily. At home she was afraid to cross the hall in the dark, because she had a dread of seeing ghosts. Suddenly, however, she hit on a device which enabled her to do it: she would run across the hall, making all sorts of peculiar gestures as she went. Before long, she triumphantly told her little brother the secret of how she had got over her anxiety. 'There's no need to be afraid in the hall,' she said, 'you just have to pretend that you're the ghost who might meet you.' This shows that her magic gestures represented the movements which she imagined ghosts would make.

We might be inclined to regard this kind of conduct as an idiosyncrasy in the two children whose cases I have quoted, but it is really one of the most natural and widespread modes of behavior on the part of the primitive ego and has long been familiar to those who have made a study of primitive methods of invoking and exorcizing spirits and of primitive religious ceremonies. Moreover, there are many children's games in which through the metamorphosis of the subject into a dreaded object anxiety is converted into pleasurable security. Here is another angle from which to study the games of impersonation which children love to play.

Now the physical imitation of an antagonist represents the assimilation of only one part of a composite anxiety experience. We learn from observation that the other elements also have to be mastered.

The six-year-old patient to whom I have several times alluded had to pay a series of visits to a dentist. At first everything went splendidly; the treatment did not hurt him and he was triumphant and made merry over the idea of anyone's being afraid of the dentist. But there came a time when my little patient arrived at my house in an extremely bad temper. The dentist had just hurt him. He was cross and unfriendly and vented his feelings on the things in my room. His first victim was a piece of India rubber. He wanted me to give it to him and, when I refused, he took a knife and tried to cut it in half. Next, he coveted a large ball of string. He wanted me to give him that too and painted me a vivid picture of what a good leash it would make for his animals. When I refused to give him the whole ball, he took the knife again and secured a large piece of the string. But he did not use it; instead, he began after a few minutes to cut it into tiny pieces. Finally, he threw away the string too, turned his attention to some pencils, and went on indefatigably sharpening them, breaking off the points, and sharpening them again. It would not be correct to say that he was playing at 'dentists.' There was no actual impersonation of the dentist. The child was identifying himself not with the person of the aggressor but with his aggression.

On another occasion this little boy came to me just after he had had a slight accident. He had been joining in an outdoor game at school and had run full tilt against the fist of the games master, which the latter happened to be holding up in front of him. My little patient's lip was bleeding and his face tear-stained, and he tried to conceal both facts by putting up his hand as a screen. I endeavored to comfort and reassure him. He was in a woebegone condition when he left me, but next day he appeared holding himself very erect and dressed in full armor. On his head he wore a military cap and he had a toy sword at his side and a pistol in his hand. When he saw my surprise at this transformation, he simply said, 'I just wanted to have these things on when I was playing with you.' He did not, however, play; instead, he sat down and wrote a letter to his mother: 'Dear Mummy, please, please, please, please send me the pocketknife you promised me and don't wait till Easter!' Here again we cannot say that, in order to master the anxiety experience of the previous day, he was impersonating the teacher with whom he had collided. Nor, in this instance, was he imitating the latter's aggression. The weapons and armor, being manly attributes, evidently symbolized the teacher's strength and, like the attributes of the father in the animal fantasies [A. Freud, 1936, pp. 74–9 – eds], helped the child to identify himself with the masculinity of the adult and so to defend himself against narcissistic mortification or actual mishaps.

The examples which I have so far cited illustrate a process with which we are quite familiar. A child introjects some characteristic of an anxiety object and so assimilates an anxiety experience which he has just undergone. Here, the mechanism of identification or introjection is combined with a second important mechanism. By impersonating the aggressor, assuming his attributes or imitating his aggression, the child transforms himself from the person threatened into the person who makes the threat. In *Beyond the Pleasure Principle* (1920) the significance of this change from the passive to the active role as a means of assimilating unpleasant or traumatic experiences in infancy is discussed in detail: 'If the doctor looks down a child's throat or carries out some small operation, we may be quite sure that these frightening experiences will be the subject of the next game; but we must not in that connection overlook the fact that there is a yield of pleasure from another source. As the child passes over from the passivity of the experience to the activity of the game, he hands on the disagreeable experience to one of his playmates and in this way revenges himself on a substitute' (p. 17).

What is true of play is equally true of other behavior in children. In the cases of the boy who made faces and the little girl who practiced magic, it is not clear what finally became of the threat with which they identified themselves, but in the other little boy's ill temper the aggression taken over from the dentist and the games master was directed against the world at large.

This process of transformation strikes us as more curious when the anxiety relates not to some event in the past but to something expected in the future. I remember a boy who had the habit of furiously pealing the bell of the children's home where he lived. As soon as the door opened, he would scold the housemaid loudly for being so slow and not listening for the bell. In the interval between pulling the bell and flying into a rage he experienced anxiety lest he should be reproved for his lack of consideration in ringing so loudly. He upbraided the servant before she had time to complain of his conduct. The vehemence with which he scolded her – a prophylactic measure – indicated the intensity of his anxiety. The aggressiveness which he assumed was turned against the actual person from whom he expected aggression and not against some substitute. The reversal of the roles of attacker and attacked was in this case carried to its logical conclusion.

Jenny Waelder has given a vivid picture of this process in a five-year-old boy whom she treated.[1] When his analysis was about to touch on the material connected with masturbation and the fantasies associated with it, this little boy, who was usually shy and inhibited, became

17

fiercely aggressive. His habitually passive attitude disappeared and there was no trace left of his feminine characteristics. In the analytic hour he pretended to be a roaring lion and attacked the analyst. He carried a rod about with him and played at 'Krampus,'[2] i.e., he laid about him with it on the stairs, in his own house, and in my room. His grandmother and mother complained that he tried to strike them in the face. His mother's uneasiness reached its climax when he took to brandishing kitchen knives. Analysis showed that the child's aggressiveness could not be construed as indicating that some inhibition on his instinctual impulses had been lifted. The release of his masculine tendencies was still a long way off. He was simply suffering from anxiety. The bringing into consciousness and the necessary confession of his former and recent sexual activities aroused in him the expectation of punishment. According to his experience, grown-up people were angry when they discovered a child indulging in such practices. They shouted at him, checked him sharply with a box on the ears or beat him with a rod; perhaps they would even cut off some part of him with a knife. When my little patient assumed the active role, roaring like a lion and laying about him with the rod and the knife, he was dramatizing and forestalling the punishment which he feared. He had introjected the aggression of the adults in whose eyes he felt guilty and, having exchanged the passive for the active part, he directed his own aggressive acts against those same people. Every time that he found himself on the verge of communicating to me what he regarded as dangerous material, his aggressiveness increased. But directly his forbidden thoughts and feelings broke through and had been discussed and interpreted, he felt no further need of the 'Krampus' rod, which till then he had constantly carried about with him, and he left it at my house. His compulsion to beat other people disappeared simultaneously with his anxious expectation of being beaten himself.

In 'identification with the aggressor' we recognize a by no means uncommon stage in the normal development of the superego. When the two boys whose cases I have just described identified themselves with their elders' threats of punishment, they were taking an important step toward the formation of that institution: they were internalizing other people's criticisms of their behavior. When a child constantly repeats this process of internalization and introjects the qualities of those responsible for his upbringing, making their characteristics and opinions his own, he is all the time providing material from which the superego may take shape. But at this point children are not quite whole-hearted in acknowledging that institution. The internalized criticism is not yet immediately transformed into self-criticism. As we have seen in the examples which I have given, it is dissociated from the child's own reprehensible activity and turned back on the outside world. By means of a new defensive process identification with the aggressor is succeeded by an active assault on the outside world.

Here is a more complicated example, which will perhaps throw light on this new development in the defensive process. A certain boy, when his oedipus complex was at its height, employed this particular mechanism to master his fixation to his mother. His happy relations with her were disturbed by outbursts of resentment. He would upbraid her passionately and on all sorts of grounds, but one mysterious accusation invariably recurred: he persistently complained of her curiosity. It is easy to see the first step in the working over of his prohibited affects. In his fantasy his mother knew of his libidinal feeling for her and indignantly rejected his advances. Her indignation was actively reproduced in his own fits of resentment against her. In contrast to Jenny Waelder's patient, however, he did not reproach her on general grounds but on the specific ground of curiosity. Analysis showed that this curiosity was an element not in his mother's instinctual life but in his own. Of all the component instincts which entered into his relation with her, his scoptophilic impulse was the most difficult to master. The reversal of roles was complete. He assumed his mother's indignation and, in exchange, ascribed to her his own curiosity.

In certain phases of resistance a young patient used bitterly to reproach her analyst with being secretive. She complained that the analyst was too reserved and she would torment her with questions on personal matters and be miserable when she received no answer. Then the reproaches would cease, only to begin again after a short time, always in the same stereotyped and, as it seemed, automatic fashion. In this case again we can detect two phases in the psychic process. From time to time, because of a certain inhibition which prevented her speaking out, the patient herself consciously suppressed some very private material. She knew that she was thereby breaking the fundamental rule of analysis and she expected the analyst to rebuke her. She introjected the fantasied rebuke and, adopting the active role, applied the accusation to the analyst. Her phases of aggression exactly coincided in time with her phases of secretiveness. She criticized the analyst for the very fault of which she herself was guilty. Her own secretive behavior was perceived as reprehensible conduct on the analyst's part.

Another young patient used periodically to have fits of violent aggressiveness. I myself, her parents, and other people in less close relation with her were almost equally the objects of her resentment. There were two things in particular of which she constantly complained. First, during these phases she always had the feeling that people were keeping from her some secret which everyone knew but herself, and she was tormented by the desire to find out what it was. Secondly, she felt deeply disappointed by the shortcomings of all her friends. Just as, in the case which I last quoted, the periods in which the patient kept back material coincided with those in which she complained of secretiveness in the analyst, so this patient's aggressive phases set in automatically whenever her repressed masturbation fantasies, of which she herself was unaware, were about to emerge into consciousness. Her strictures on her love objects corresponded to the blame which she expected from them because of her masturbation in childhood. She identified herself fully with this condemnation and turned it back upon the outside world. The secret which everybody kept from her was the secret of her own masturbation, which she kept not only from others but from herself. Here again, the patient's aggressiveness corresponded to that of other people and their 'secret' was a reflection of her own repression.

These three examples have given us some ideas of the origin of this particular phase in the development of the function of the superego. Even when the external criticism has been introjected, the threat of punishment and the offense committed have not yet been connected up in the patient's mind. The moment the criticism is internalized, the offense is externalized. This means that the mechanism of identification with the aggressor is supplemented by another defensive measure, namely, the projection of guilt.

An ego which with the aid of the defense mechanism of projection develops along this particular line introjects the authorities to whose criticism it is exposed and incorporates them in the superego. It is then able to project the prohibited impulses outward. Its intolerance of other people precedes its severity toward itself. It learns what is regarded as blameworthy but protects itself by means of this defense mechanism from unpleasant self-criticism. Vehement indignation at someone else's wrongdoing is the precursor of and substitute for guilty feelings on its own account. Its indignation increases automatically when the perception of its own guilt is imminent. This stage in the development of the superego is a kind of preliminary phase of morality. True morality begins when the internalized criticism, now embodied in the standard exacted by the superego, coincides with the ego's perception of its own fault. From that moment, the severity of the superego is turned inward instead of outward and the subject becomes less intolerant of other people. But, when once it has reached this stage in its development, the ego has to endure the more acute unpleasure occasioned by self-criticism and the sense of guilt.

It is possible that a number of people remain arrested at the intermediate stage in the development of the superego and never quite complete the internalization of the critical process. Although perceiving their own guilt, they continue to be peculiarly aggressive in their attitude to other people. In such cases the behavior of the superego toward others is as ruthless as that of the superego toward the patient's own ego in melancholia. Perhaps when the evolution of the superego is thus inhibited, it indicates an abortive beginning of the development of melancholic states.

'Identification with the aggressor' represents, on the one hand, a preliminary phase of superego development and, on the other, an intermediate stage in the development of paranoia. It resembles the former in the mechanism of identification and the latter in that of projection. At the same time, identification and projection are normal activities of the ego and their results vary greatly according to the material upon which they are employed.

The particular combination of introjection and projection to which we have applied the term 'identification with the aggressor' can be regarded as normal only so long as the ego employs this mechanism in its conflict with authority, i.e., in its efforts to deal with anxiety objects. It is a defensive process which ceases to be innocuous and becomes pathological when it is carried over into a person's love life. When a husband displaces onto his wife his own impulses to be unfaithful and then reproaches her passionately with unfaithfulness, he is really introjecting her reproaches and projecting part of his own id.[3] His intention, however, is to protect himself not against aggression from without but against the shattering of his positive libidinal fixation to her by disturbing forces from within. Accordingly the result is different. Instead of an aggressive attitude toward some former external assailants the patient develops an obsessional fixation to his wife, which takes the form of projected jealousy.

When the mechanism of projection is employed as a defense against homosexual love impulses, it is combined with yet other mechanisms. Reversal (in this case the reversal of love into hate) completes what introjection and projection have begun, and the result is the development of paranoid delusions. In either case – defense against heterosexual or against homosexual love impulses – the projection is no longer arbitrary. The ego's choice of a billet for its own unconscious impulses is determined by 'the perceptual material which betrays unconscious impulses of the same kind in the partner.'[4]

From the theoretical standpoint, analysis of the process of 'identification with the aggressor' assists us to differentiate the various modes in which the specific defense mechanisms are employed; in practice, it enables us to distinguish in the transference anxiety attacks from outbursts of aggression. When analysis brings into the patient's consciousness genuine, unconscious, aggressive impulses, the dammed-up affect will seek relief through abreaction in the transference. But, if his aggression is due to identifying himself with what he supposed to be our criticism, it will not be in the least affected by his 'giving it practical expression' and 'abreacting' it. As long as the unconscious impulses are prohibited, it increases, and it vanishes, as in the case of the little boy who confessed his masturbation, only when the dread of punishment and of the superego has been dissipated.

Notes

1. Presented at the Vienna Seminar on child analysis (see Hall, 1946).
2. A devil who accompanied St. Nicholas and punished naughty children. –
   Translator's note.
3. Cf. 'Some Neurotic Mechanisms in Jealousy, Paranoia and Homosexuality'
   (Freud, 1922, p. 223).
4. Ibid., p. 224.

3

A Form of Altruism (1936)

Anna Freud conceived of 'altruistic surrender' (a term first coined by Bibring) as a means of illustrating how projection need not always be harmful but can provide a valuable contribution to sound and satisfying interpersonal relationships. She had in mind individuals who are by nature selfless and devoted to the interest of others. When these characteristics are carried to extreme it is possible to discern that unconsciously they are attributing wishes, to which they are unable to give conscious expression, to another individual. She gives the example of Cyrano de Bergerac as illustrative of this process. Here identification and projection are used as defences against anxiety – anxiety arising from unrealizable wishes.

It is important to add that Anna Freud was later to distinguish between projection and externalisation. Following Freud (1911) she came to regard projection as a reflexive process in the sense that an unwanted wish or feeling attributed to another person feels as if it is directed towards the self. Externalization would simply be endowing another person with wished for or unacceptable thoughts and feelings. A simple example of this difference is as follows: Projection is involved when an individual who has difficulties with her own jealousy comes to believe that another person is jealous of her. Externalization is in operation when a jealous individual describes another person of her acquaintance as jealous. In view of this distinction the projection to which Anna Freud refers in this chapter would have been described by her in later writings as externalization (Sandler, 1985, pp. 136–45).

'A Form of Altruism' is the tenth chapter of *The Ego and the Mechanisms of Defence*. The book was first published in 1936 by the Internationaler Psychoanalytischer Verlag under the title *Das Ich Und Die Abwehrmechanismen*. The English translation by Cecil Baines followed in 1937. The present revised edition, based on the 1937 translation, was first published in 1966.

The effect of the mechanism of projection is to break the connection between the ideational representatives of dangerous instinctual impulses and the ego. In this it resembles most closely the process of repression. Other defensive processes, such as displacement, reversal or turning round upon the self, affect the instinctual process itself: repression and projection merely prevent its being perceived. In repression the objectionable idea is thrust back into the id, while in projection it is displaced into the outside world. Another point in which projection resembles repression is that it is not associated with any particular anxiety situation but may be motivated equally by objective anxiety, superego anxiety, and instinctual anxiety. Writers of the English school of psychoanalysis maintain that in the earliest months of life, before any repression has taken place, the infant already projects its first aggressive impulses and that this process is of crucial importance for the picture which the child forms of the world around him and the way in which his personality develops.

At all events the use of the mechanism of projection is quite natural to the ego of little children throughout the earliest period of development. They employ it as a means of repudiating their own activities and wishes when these become dangerous and of laying the responsibility for them at the door of some external agent. A 'strange child,' an animal, even inanimate objects are all equally useful to the infantile ego for the purpose of disposing of its own faults. It is normal for it constantly to get rid of prohibited impulses and wishes in this way, handing them over in full measure to other people. If these wishes entail punishment by the authorities, the ego puts forward as whipping boys the persons upon whom it has projected them; if, on the other hand, the projection was prompted by a sense of guilt, instead of criticizing itself it accuses others. In either case it dissociates itself from its proxies and is excessively intolerant of its judgment of them.

The mechanism of projection disturbs our human relations when we project our own jealousy and attribute to other people our own aggressive acts. But it may work in another way as well, enabling us to form valuable positive attachments and so to consolidate our relations with one another. This normal and less conspicuous form of projection might be described as 'altruistic surrender'[1] of our instinctual impulses in favor of other people.

The following is an example of what I mean.

A young governess reported in her analysis that, as a child, she was possessed by two ideas: she wanted to have beautiful clothes and a number of children. In her fantasies she was almost obsessionally absorbed in picturing the fulfillment of these two wishes. But there were a great many other things that she demanded as well: she wished to have and to do everything that her much older playmates had and did – indeed, she wanted to do everything better than they and to be admired for her cleverness. Her everlasting cry of 'Me too!' was a nuisance to her elders. It was characteristic of her desires that they were at once urgent and insatiable.

What chiefly struck one about her as an adult was her unassuming character and the modesty of the demands which she made on life. When she came to be analyzed, she was unmarried and childless and her dress was rather shabby and inconspicuous. She showed little sign of envy or ambition and would compete with other people only if she were forced to do so by external circumstances. One's first impression was that, as so often happens, she had developed in exactly the opposite direction from what her childhood would have led one to expect and that her wishes had been repressed and replaced in consciousness by reaction formations (unobtrusiveness instead of a craving for admiration and unassumingness instead of ambition). One would have expected to find that the repression was caused by a prohibition of sexuality, extending from her exhibitionistic impulses and the desire for children to the whole of her instinctual life.

But there were features in her behavior at the time when I knew her which contradicted this impression. When her life was examined in more detail, it was clear that her original wishes were affirmed in a manner which seemed scarcely possible if repression had taken place. The repudiation of her own sexuality did not prevent her from taking an affectionate interest in the love life of women friends and colleagues. She was an enthusiastic matchmaker and many love affairs were confided to her. Although she took no trouble about her own dress, she displayed a lively interest in her friends' clothes. Childless herself, she was devoted to other people's children, as was indicated by her choice of a profession. She might be said to display an unusual degree of concern about her friends' having pretty clothes, being admired, and having children.

Similarly, in spite of her own retiring behavior, she was ambitious for the men whom she loved and followed their careers with the utmost interest. It looked as if her own life had been emptied of interests and wishes; up to the time of her analysis it was almost entirely uneventful. Instead of exerting herself to achieve any aims of her own, she expended all her energy in sympathizing with the experiences of people she cared for. She lived in the lives of other people, instead of having any experience of her own.

The analysis of her infantile relations to her mother and father revealed clearly the nature of the inner transformation which had taken place. Her early renunciation of instinct had resulted in the formation of an exceptionally severe superego, which made it impossible for her to gratify her own wishes. Her penis wish, with its offshoots in the shape of ambitious masculine fantasies, was prohibited, so too her feminine wish for children and the desire to display herself, naked or in beautiful clothes, to her father, and to win his admiration. But these impulses were not repressed: she found some proxy in the outside world to serve as a repository for each of them. The vanity of her women friends provided, as it were, a foothold for the projection of her own vanity, while her libidinal wishes and ambitious fantasies were likewise deposited in the outside world. She projected her prohibited instinctual impulses onto other people, just as the patients did whose cases I quoted in the last chapter [chapter 2, this volume – eds]. The only difference lay in the way in which these impulses were subsequently dealt with. The patient did not dissociate herself from her proxies but identified herself with them. She showed her sympathy with their wishes and felt that there was an extraordinarily strong bond between these people and herself. Her superego, which condemned a particular instinctual impulse when it related to her own ego, was surprisingly tolerant of it in other people. She gratified her instincts by sharing in the gratification of others, employing for this purpose the mechanisms of projection and identification.[2] The retiring attitude which the prohibition of her impulses caused her to adopt where she herself was concerned vanished when it was a question of fulfilling the same wishes after they had been projected onto someone else. The surrender of her instinctual impulses in favor of other people had thus an egoistic significance, but in her efforts to gratify the impulses of others her behavior could only be called altruistic.

This passing on of her own wishes to other people was characteristic of her whole life and could be traced very clearly in the analysis of little isolated incidents. For instance, at the age of thirteen she secretly fell in love with a friend of her elder sister who had formerly been the special object of her jealousy. She had an idea that, at times, he preferred her to her sister and she was always hoping that he would give some sign of loving her. On one occasion it happened, as it had often happened before, that she found herself slighted. The young man called unexpectedly one evening to take her sister for a walk. In analysis the patient remembered perfectly distinctly how, from having been at first paralyzed with disappointment, she suddenly began to bustle about, fetching things to make her sister 'pretty' for her outing and eagerly helping her to get ready. While doing this, the patient was blissfully happy and quite forgot that it was not she, but her sister, who was going out to enjoy herself. She had projected her own desire for love and her craving for admiration onto her rival and, having identified herself with the object of her envy, she enjoyed the fulfillment of her desire.

She went through the same process when frustration rather than fulfillment was in question. She loved to give the children of whom she was in charge good things to eat. On one occasion a mother refused to give up a particular tit-bit for her child. Although the patient herself was, in general, indifferent to the pleasures of the table, the mother's refusal made her furiously indignant. She experienced the frustration of the child's wish as if it were her own, just as in the other case she had rejoiced vicariously in the fulfillment of her sister's desires. It is plain that what she had made over to other people was the right to have her wishes fulfilled without hindrance.

The last trait comes out even more clearly in the experiences of another patient of the same type. A young woman, whose relation to her father-in-law was a particularly friendly one, reacted very strangely to the death of her mother-in-law. The patient, with other women of the family, undertook to dispose of the dead woman's clothes. Unlike all the others, my patient refused to take even a single garment for her own use. Instead, she set aside one coat as a present for a cousin who was badly off. The mother-in-law's sister wanted to cut off the fur collar of the coat and keep it herself, whereupon the patient, who so far had been quite indifferent and uninterested, flew into a blind rage. She turned the full fury of her usually inhibited aggression upon her aunt and insisted on her protégée's having what she had intended for her. Analysis of this incident showed that the patient's sense of guilt prevented her from appropriating anything which had belonged to her mother-in-law. To take a garment symbolized to her the gratifying of her wish to fill her mother-in-law's place with her father-in-law. She therefore renounced any claim herself and surrendered in favor of her cousin the desire to be her 'mother's' successor. Having done so, however, she felt the full force of the wish and its disappointment and was able to insist on its fulfillment, a thing which she could never do when she herself was concerned. The superego, which took up so implacable an attitude toward her own instinctual impulse, assented to the desire when it was no longer associated with the patient's own ego. When the fulfillment of another person's wish was in question, the aggressive behavior which was usually inhibited suddenly became ego syntonic.

Any number of cases similar to those which I have quoted can be observed in everyday life, when once our attention has been called to this combination of projection and identification for purposes of defense. For instance, a young girl, who had scruples of conscience about marrying herself, did all she could to encourage her sister's engagement. A patient, who suffered from obsessional inhibitions in spending any money on herself, had no hesitation in spending lavishly on presents. Another patient, who was prevented by anxiety from carrying out her plans for travel, was quite unexpectedly pressing in her advice to her friends to do so. In all these cases the patient's identification of herself with a sister, a friend, or the recipient of a gift betrayed itself by a sudden warm sense of a bond between them, which lasted as long as her own wish was being vicariously fulfilled. Jokes about 'matchmaking old maids' and 'meddlesome onlookers, for whom no stakes are too high'[3] are perennial. The surrender of one's own wishes to another person and the attempt to secure their fulfillment thus vicariously are, indeed, comparable to the interest and pleasure with which one watches a game in which one has no stake oneself.

This defensive process serves two purposes. On the one hand it enables the subject to take a friendly interest in the gratification of other people's instincts and so, indirectly and in spite of the superego's prohibition, to gratify his own, while, on the other, it liberates the inhibited activity and aggression primarily designed to secure the fulfillment of the instinctual wishes in their original relation to himself. The patient who could not lift a finger to gratify her own oral impulses could feel indignant at the mother's refusal to indulge her child, i.e., at oral renunciation imposed on someone else. The daughter-in-law who was prohibited from claiming the rights of the dead wife felt it permissible to defend the symbolic right of another with the full force of her aggression. An employee who would never venture to ask for a raise in salary for herself suddenly besieged the manageress with demands that one of her fellow workers should have her rights. Analysis of such situations shows that this defensive process has its origin in the infantile conflict with parental authority about some form of instinctual gratification. Aggressive impulses against the mother, prohibited so long as it is a question of fulfilling the subject's own wishes, are given rein when the wishes are ostensibly those of someone else. The most familiar representative of this type of person is the public benefactor, who with the utmost aggressiveness and energy demands money from one set of people in order to give it to another. Perhaps the most extreme instance is that of the assassin who, in the name of the oppressed, murders the oppressor. The object against which the liberated aggression is directed is invariably the representative of the authority which imposed renunciation of instinct on the subject in infancy.

Various factors determine the selection of the object in favor of whom instinctual impulses are surrendered. Possibly the perception of the prohibited impulse in another person is sufficient to suggest to the ego that here is an opportunity for projection. In the case of the patient who assisted in the disposal of her mother-in-law's property, the fact that the vicarious figure was not a near relation was a guarantee of the harmlessness of the wish which, when cherished by the patient herself, represented her incestuous impulses. In most cases the substitute has once been the object of envy. The altruistic governess in my first example displaced her ambitious fantasies onto her men friends and her libidinal wishes onto her women friends. The former succeeded to her affection for her father and her big brother, both of whom had been the object of her penis envy, while the latter represented the sister upon whom, at a rather later period of childhood, that envy was displaced in the form of envy of her beauty. The patient felt that the fact that she was a girl prevented her from achieving her ambitions and, at the same time, that she was not even a pretty enough girl really to be attractive to men. In her disappointment with herself she displaced her wishes onto objects who she felt were better qualified to fulfill them. Her men friends were vicariously to achieve for her in professional life that which she herself could never achieve, and the girls who were better-looking than herself were to do the same in the sphere of love. Her altruistic surrender was a method of overcoming her narcissistic mortification.

The surrender of instinctual wishes to an object better qualified to fulfill them often determines the relation of a girl to some man whom she chooses to represent her – to the detriment of any true object relation. On the grounds of this 'altruistic' attachment she expects him to carry out the projects in which she believes herself to be handicapped by her sex: for instance, she wants him to lead the life of a student or to adopt a particular profession or to become famous or rich in her place. In such cases egoism and altruism may be blended in very various proportions. We know that parents sometimes delegate to their children their projects for their own lives, in a manner at once altruistic and egoistic. It is as if they hoped through the child, whom they regard as better qualified for the purpose than themselves, to wrest from life the fulfillment of the ambitions which they themselves have failed to realize. Perhaps even the purely altruistic relation of a mother to her son is largely determined by such a surrender of her own wishes to the object whose sex makes him 'better qualified' to carry them out. A man's success in life does, indeed, go far to compensate the women of his family for the renunciation of their own ambitions.

The finest and most detailed study of this altruistic surrender is to be found in Edmond Rostand's play *Cyrano de Bergerac*. The hero of the play is a historical figure, a French nobleman of the seventeenth century, a poet and officer of the Guards, famous for his intellect and valor but handicapped in his wooing of women by a peculiarly ugly nose. He falls in love with his beautiful cousin, Roxane, but, conscious of his ugliness, he at once resigns every hope of winning her. Instead of using his formidable skill as a fencer to keep all rivals at a distance, he surrenders his own aspirations to her love in favor of a man better looking than himself. Having made this renunciation, he devotes his strength, his courage, and his brains to the service of this more fortunate lover and does all he can to help him to attain his desire. The climax of the play is a scene at night, under the balcony of the woman who both men love. Cyrano whispers to his rival the words with which to win her. Then he takes the other's place in the dark and speaks for him, forgetting in the ardor of his wooing that he himself is not the wooer and only at the last moment falling back into his attitude of surrender when the suit of Christian, the handsome lover, is accepted and he goes up to the balcony to embrace his love. Cyrano becomes more and more devoted to his rival and in battle tries to save Christian's life rather than his own. When this vicarious figure is taken from him by death, he feels that it is not permissible for him to woo Roxane. That the poet is depicting in Cyrano's 'altruism' something more than a strange love adventure is clear from the parallel which he draws between Cyrano's love life and his fate as a poet. Just as Christian woos Roxane with the help of Cyrano's poems and letters, writers like Corneille, Molière and Swift borrow whole scenes from unknown works, thus enhancing their own fame. In the play Cyrano accepts this fate. He is as ready to lend his words to Christian, who is handsomer than himself, as to Molière, who is a greater genius. The personal defect which he thinks renders him contemptible makes him feel that the others who are preferred to himself are better qualified than he to realize his wish fantasies.

In conclusion, we may for a moment study the notion of altruistic surrender from another angle, namely, in its relation to the fear of death. Anyone who has very largely projected his instinctual impulses onto other people knows nothing of this fear. In the moment of danger his ego is not really concerned for his own life. He experiences instead excessive concern and anxiety for the lives of his love objects. Observation shows that these objects, whose safety is so vital to him, are the vicarious figures upon whom he has displaced his instinctual wishes. For instance, the young governess, whose case I have described, suffered from quite excessive anxiety about the safety of her friends in pregnancy and childbirth. Again, as is shown in the sketch which I have given, Cyrano sets Christian's safety in battle far above his own. It would be a mistake to suppose that this is a question of suppressed rivalry breaking through in death wishes, which are then warded off. Analysis shows that both the anxiety and the absence of anxiety are due rather to the subject's feeling that his own life is worth living and preserving only insofar as there is opportunity in it for gratification of his instincts. When his impulses have been surrendered in favor of other people, their lives become precious rather than his own. The death of the vicarious figure means – as Christian's death meant for Cyrano – the destruction of all hope of fulfillment.

It was only after analysis, when she happened to fall ill, that the young governess discovered that the thought of dying was painful to her. To her own surprise she found that she ardently desired to live long to furnish her new home and to pass an examination which would secure her promotion in her profession. Her home and the examination signified, though in a sublimated form, the fulfillment of instinctual wishes which analysis had enabled her to relate once more to her own life.[4]

Notes

1. '*Altruistische Abtretung.*' This term was coined by Edward Bibring.
2. Compare in this connection Paul Federn's notion (1936) of 'sympathetic' identification and his remarks on this subject.
3. '*Kiebitze, denen kein Spiel zu hoch ist.*'
4. There is an obvious similarity between the situation in altruistic surrender and the conditions which determine male homosexuality. The homosexual makes over his claim on his mother's love to a younger brother whom he has previously envied. It is true that he proceeds to satisfy this demand himself by adopting a maternal attitude, i.e., by enjoying both the active and the passive side of the relation between mother and son. It is difficult to determine how far this process contributed to the various forms of altruistic surrender which I have described. Cyrano and the altruistic young governess must have both derived pleasure from this mechanism even before they could rejoice vicariously in the successes of their substitutes. Their rapture of giving and helping shows that the surrender is in itself a gratification of instinct. As in the process of identification with the aggressor, passivity is transformed into activity, narcissistic mortification is compensated for by the sense of power associated with the role of benefactor, while the passive experience of frustration finds compensation in the active conferring of happiness on others.

It remains an open question whether there is such a thing as a genuinely altruistic relation to one's fellowmen, in which the gratification of one's own instinct plays no part at all, even in some displaced and sublimated form. In any case it is certain that projection and identification are not the only means of acquiring an attitude which has every appearance of altruism; for instance, another and easy route to the same goal is by way of the various forms of masochism.

34

PART 2

Child Development – Normal and Pathological

4

Notes on Aggression (1949 [1948])

In this paper, Anna Freud describes the development of Freud's theory of aggression. In his early work, Freud (1905, 1916–1917) related aggressive and destructive attitudes and behaviours to the child's developing sexuality (oral, anal, etc.). At the same time, aggression was at the disposal of the self-preservative instincts. This was all to change with his theory of the life and death instincts. Aggression now became a derivative of the death instinct turned away from the self and on to others. For optimal development, the aggressive and sexual instincts fused so that each expression of the sexual instincts was accompanied by an appropriate manifestation of aggression. Thus the successful achievement of genitality in the male is dependent upon a necessary quota of aggression. In this final formulation on aggression, sadism, which was previously an inherent element of sexuality, is now a derivative of the death instinct.

With the theory of the life and death instincts, aggression is regarded as innate and not a response to frustrations and disappointments (cf. Bowlby, 1951). In the course of development, 'the naked aggression' of the young child is transformed through displacement, reaction formations and turning in on the self (see 'The Mechanisms of Defense'). These transformations of aggression are dependent on a loving relationship between mother and child.

'Notes on Aggression' was first published in *Proceedings of the International Conference on Child Psychiatry* [International Congress on Mental Health, London, 1948, Vol. II], J.C. Flugel, ed. London: H.K. Lewis; New York: Columbia University Press, 1949, pp. 16–23. The paper was also published in the *Bulletin of the Menninger Clinic*, 13: 143–51, 1949; and *The Yearbook of Psychoanalysis*, 6: 143–154. New York: International Universities Press, 1950. Excerpts were included in *The Family and the Law*, by Joseph Goldstein and Jay Katz. New York: Free Press, 1965, pp. 983–4.

Recent Trends in Child Psychology

In recent years, aggression, destruction, their expressions and their development have assumed central interest for workers in the field of education, child psychology, and child therapy. There seems to be an increasing recognition of the fact that normal or abnormal emotional development cannot be understood without adequate explanation of the role played by aggressive tendencies and attitudes. In normal children, the problem of aggression is studied with special regard to their social responses. In abnormal children (children with retarded development, with states of regression in development, dissocial or criminal tendencies), aggression is known to play an important pathogenic part.

It is in accordance with this trend in modern child psychology that the role of aggression in normal and abnormal child development has been chosen as the topic for discussion by an overwhelming majority of Congress members from many nations and countries. Some contributions made by previous speakers may have created the impression that this choice is not unconnected with experience and clinical observations made during the recent war years. Psychologists, all over the world, have been impressed by the quantity and crude quality of aggression released in individuals and nations during the war, and by the impact of this aggression on those children and adults who were exposed to it as victims. Practical experience of this kind might naturally lead to the wish for better theoretical understanding of the phenomena that have been under observation.

On the other hand, this explanation, obvious though it seems at first glance, proves misleading when examined more closely. The recent war has, in fact, taught us nothing about aggression which might not have been learned before. There has been no period in history when ample opportunities were not available for observations of the same nature. The role played by aggression in human relations was open to view throughout historical times in the wars between nations, the civil wars, the race wars, the oppression or extermination of minorities, religious persecutions, or the crimes of violence committed by individuals. Further material for the observation of aggressive behavior has, at all times, been provided by children.

Young children, throughout the ages, have shown traits of violence, aggression, and destruction. If anything, the parents and educators of past times seem to have been more impressed by this aspect of the child's nature than those in charge of children are today. The grim severity of many educational measures of the past was, after all, designed to check the 'badness' of the children, i.e., their violence, their search for pleasure, their tendencies to harm, to hurt, and to destroy. What has changed in the field of aggression is, thus, not the range of observable phenomena but the attitude of those who are observing and describing them. The former inclination of psychologists to look away from the crude and more displeasing manifestations of human nature, especially where children are concerned, to deny their occurrence or, at best, to belittle their importance, has given way to the opposite tendency – to a determination to scrutinize these forms of behavior, to study and describe them in detail, to trace them back to their origins, and to assess the part played by them in the normal and abnormal development of the individual child.

Psychoanalytic Reorientation

It is a legitimate claim that this reversal of attitude in child psychology has taken place as a result of the work and findings of psychoanalysis dating back as far as the beginning of this century or the years preceding it. Psychoanalytic psychology has effected a complete reorientation with regard to the role of the instinctual urges in the development of the individual. In preanalytic psychology, childhood was regarded as a more or less peaceful period of progressive growth in which the instinctual urges, where they appeared, merely played the part of disturbing elements. Psychoanalytic psychology, on the other hand, ascribes to these same innate urges the main role in shaping the mind and forming the character.

Instinctual wishes, whether they express the need for food, warmth, and comfort, or the strivings of sex and aggression, arise from the body and make themselves felt in the mind as an urgent claim for satisfaction. They produce painful tension when they remain ungratified and pleasurable relief when their aim is reached and the need fulfilled. Owing to the stimulation arising from them, the infant, from birth onward, gradually develops a whole range of functions which enable him to avoid such pain, to gain such pleasure, and thereby to maintain himself in a state of tolerable comfort. He gradually learns to distinguish between an inner and an outer world, to become aware of his surroundings, to store up and use experience, to control his motor responses; that is, the infant develops the so-called ego functions which serve the purpose of wish fulfillment. Since the infant's environment often withholds or opposes wish fulfillment, conflicts of a new kind arise and require to be solved. All this serves as a stimulus toward increasingly higher development of mental functioning. Far from disturbing this process of growth, the instinctual urges, through the constant pressure they exert, serve as mind builders.

Sexual Theory

For more than thirty years the psychoanalytic study of instinctual life was almost exclusively directed toward the manifestations of sexuality. The result of these investigations is, by now, well known. According to the psychoanalytic theory of sexuality, diffuse sources of sexual excitation exist in various parts of the body from birth onward and give rise to the pregenital sexual urges of infantile life. The origin of these component urges (the skin, the mucous membranes of the mouth and anus, the penis and clitoris) determines a sequence of sex organizations ranging from birth to approximately the fifth or sixth year of life: the oral, anal, and phallic sexual phases. Residues of these phases continue to exist in adult life, either as normal preparatory acts to genital intercourse (kissing, looking, touching) or, in the form of sexual perversions, as abnormal nongenital substitutes for genital intercourse. The psychoanalytic theory of sex thus widens the concept of sexuality so as to include the pregenital and extragenital activities, and antedates its onset from puberty to the beginning of life.

It took considerable time and a persistent struggle before these findings were accepted as valid for child psychology. In fact, the battle for a new, 'dynamic' type of child psychology was fought out over this question of infantile sexuality. Owing to an overwhelming mass of evidence contributed by the clinical observations of psychoanalysts, a number of child psychologists gradually accepted the new views. This paved the way for the acceptance of further findings about the child's instinctual life. After the investigators of infantile sexuality had borne the brunt of the attacks by a public unwilling to abandon the notion of childhood as a period of innocence, the investigators of infantile aggression have comparatively easy play. Indeed, at times, their researches into aggressive behavior of the child are received with an eagerness which suggests that the change of subject is welcome to the wider public, which has never overcome all its resistance against dealing with the sexual problems of the child.

The Psychoanalytic Theories of Aggression

Aggression as a Quality of the Pregenital Sex Manifestations

In Freudian psychoanalysis, the aggressive behavior of children was observed first where it appeared in conjunction with their sex behavior. Young children, while pursuing their pregenital sexual aims, were found to possess a substantial amount of inconsiderateness for the feelings of others, hostility toward the environment, sadism, aggression, and destructiveness. In analytic work, these qualities became evident first in the phallic phase of sexual development, in connection with the manifestations of the so-called oedipus complex, i.e., the violent love of the child for the parent of the opposite sex, accompanied by hostility and death wishes against the rival parent of the same sex. The occurrence of sadistic and aggressive attitudes in the latter part of the oral phase (after teething) was also described. Above all, the peak period of aggressiveness was found to coincide with the anal stage of sexuality. On this level of instinctual development the wishes to harm or to destroy things or people, and to make sadistic attacks on loved persons were shown to assume equal importance with the anal interests themselves. This preponderance of aggressive tendencies on the anal level led to the description of this stage as the *anal-sadistic* phase, a term which is still in use.

Aggression as a Function of the Ego: the 'Frustration Theory'

Further inquiry into the functions of the ego and their role in the process of wish fulfillment led to the tentative classification of aggression as an 'ego instinct.' This implied that the aggressive impulses were at the disposal of the ego for its purposes of preserving life and safeguarding the gaining of instinctual satisfaction. The child was found to react with aggression whenever an instinctual wish failed to be gratified or was deliberately thwarted through intervention by the environment. Such occasions arise continually and inevitably during the pregenital phases of development since pregenital sexual wishes, owing to their primitive, fantastic, and unrealistic character, are to a large extent doomed to remain unsatisfied. This so-called 'frustration theory' of aggression is still maintained by many psychoanalytic workers.

Aggression as the Expression of the Destructive Instinct: the Theory of Life and Death Instincts

In the further development of his theory of instincts Freud (1920) abandoned the conception of 'ego instincts,' decided to ascribe instinctual nature and origin to the aggressive manifestations, and thereby gave them in his evaluation equal status with the manifestations of sex. In this assumption, which is known as the 'theory of the life and death instincts,' the whole range of instinctual urges is grouped under these two main forces, the life force serving the purposes of preservation, propagation, and unification of life, the death instinct or destructive force serving the opposite aim of undoing connections and destroying life.

Sex is the representative of the life force, aggression of the destructive force. In clinical observation neither sex nor aggression can be studied in a pure form. The two fundamental instincts combine forces with each other or act against each other, and through these combinations produce the phenomena of life. The development of aggression is inseparably bound up with the developmental phases of infantile sexuality. On each level of sex development (oral, anal, phallic) the aggressive urges manifest themselves in different ways, and by their manifestations lend force to the expressions of the child's love life. Without this admixture of aggression, the sexual impulses remain unable to reach any of their aims.

The fusion of sexual instincts with aggression makes it possible for the child to assert his rights to the possession of his love objects, to compete with his rivals, to satisfy his curiosities, to display his body or his abilities – even to obtain possession of his food and destroy it by eating it. Equally, in normal adult sex life, the carrying out of the sexual act presupposes on the part of the male sufficient aggression to obtain mastery over the sexual partner. Where in abnormal cases, through repression or inhibition of aggression, this admixture from the side of the destructive forces is lacking, sexuality becomes ineffective. In adult genital life this results in impotence. In the pregenital stages of childhood the clinical pictures produced are those feeding disturbances, weakness of emotional attachments, especially of the oedipus manifestations, inhibition of curiosity and intellectual achievements, loss of pleasure in play, etc. The aggressive urges, on the other hand, when they are for some reason not fused with the sexual urges, manifest themselves as purely destructive, criminal, and – in this form – uncontrollable and unmanageable tendencies.

Implications of the Theory of the Life and Death Instincts for Psychology

This, essentially biological, theory contains several far-reaching implications for psychology and child psychology. First, it offers an explanation why the love relations of human individuals are so commonly disturbed and interfered with by emotions of a hostile and aggressive nature. According to the theoretical assertions outlined above, the love and hate reactions of human beings are intermixed by nature, and from the beginning of object relationships in the life of the individual both opposing tendencies are directed toward the same persons. This implies that the infant develops hostile as well as loving feelings toward the mother, over and above the hostility which is aroused whenever the mother frustrates the child's wishes. The same tendency, to turn negative and aggressive feelings toward loved people, then remains throughout

43

life and inevitably carries distress and bewilderment into otherwise happy and positive adult love relationships. This inability to establish purely positive relationships in real life creates the well-known longing of human beings for 'pure love,' which has found expression in countless fantasies, daydreams, utopias, and other poetic productions.

Controversies and Problems

Several controversial points, at present under debate among psychoanalysts, arise from the foregoing theoretical assumptions.

As mentioned above, there is divergence of opinion as to the role of frustration in the development of aggressive tendencies. Those analysts who have adopted Freud's theories of the life and death instincts consider aggression an inborn instinctual urge which develops spontaneously, in response to the environment, but is not produced by environmental influences. Those analysts who maintain his earlier 'frustration theory' regard aggression as the product of environmental influences, that is, as the individual's answer to the thwarting of his instinctual wishes. (See the contributions made, in England, by John Bowlby.)

Further controversial questions are whether the interplay between two biological forces of opposite nature is in itself sufficient to create a state of conflict in the mind; and, if so, how far this conflict, i.e., a basic ambivalence of feeling, is by its very nature of vital and pathogenic significance.

A group of psychoanalysts in England, represented by Melanie Klein and her followers, answers the last two questions in the affirmative. According to their views, a vital stage in the emotional development of every infant is marked by the recognition that a loved object is in danger of being attacked and destroyed by virtue of being loved. When the loved object is no longer merely a part of the other person from which satisfaction is gained (such as the mother's breast) but a whole human being (the mother as a person), the infant feels guilt with regard to his destructive fantasies. This produces feelings of depression which are lessened only when reparative and restitutive ideas appear and bring relief. Melanie Klein considers this phase, which she calls 'the depressive position,' an essential feature in emotional development.

Other analysts, in America and Europe, the author among them, hold the view that the coexistence of the two opposing instinctual forces in themselves is not sufficient to produce mental conflict. Clinical observation shows numerous states which represent a successful fusion between the destructive and erotic urges. (Eating, for instance, destroys the food for the purpose of incorporating it; in sexual intercourse the partner is aggressively mastered for the purpose of intimate union, etc.) Further, in young infants, love and hate, affection and anger, tenderness and aggression, the wish to destroy loved people or toys and the wish to preserve and have them, can be seen to appear in quick succession, seemingly unaffected by each other, each controversial striving attempting with full force to reach its own aim. The mental representatives of the two organic forces remain unrelated to each other so long as no central point of awareness is established in the personality. It is only the growth of this focal point (the ego) which results in the gradual integration of all instinctual strivings, and during this process may lead to clashes and realization of incompatibility between them. According to these views, therefore, the presence of mental conflicts and of the guilt feelings consequent on them presupposes that a specific, comparatively advanced stage in ego development has been reached.

Transformation of Aggression

All psychoanalytic writers agree that, at some moment or other in the development of the young child, the aggressive urges become incompatible with other strivings or with the higher agencies in the individual's mind. Aggression is then felt to be intolerable; the ideas, the fantasies, and wishes representing it are feared as dangerous, provoke outbursts of anxiety, and are, for this reason, rejected by the mind.

The methods used for their attempted elimination are the mechanisms of defense used by the ego to ward off and transform dangerous pregenital sexual strivings. These mechanisms have been listed and described in detail in the course of the psychoanalytic study of the sexual urges.

45

Repression of Aggression, Reaction Formation, and Inhibitions

Repression of aggressive and destructive strivings removes hostile intentions and death wishes against the loved parents from the child's consciousness without otherwise affecting their existence in the unconscious. To lessen the danger of their re-emergence from repression, the contrasting positive, loving tendencies are overemphasized in the conscious mind. The child then develops reactive trends of excessive gentleness, horror of violence, oversolicitude, and anxiety concerning the loved person's safety, health, etc. The crippling effect of such an inhibition of vital aggression for the child's love life and his essential constructive activities has been described above.

Projection and Displacement of Aggression

Before a strict division between the unconscious and the conscious mind has been established, aggression is warded off by other methods. Aggressive and destructive impulses are projected outward; that is, they cease to be felt as part of the child's inner world and are instead ascribed to persons in the external world, usually the same persons against whom the original hostility had been directed. The child then becomes intensely afraid of these formerly loved people who assume the role of aggressors and persecutors.

Aggressive urges, again, may become redirected from the child's main love objects (the parents) to people of lesser importance in the child's life. This relieves the intimate family relationships of their negative admixture. But the gain is offset by the emergence of an excessively negative and hostile attitude toward people outside the family circle (such as complete strangers, casual acquaintances, servants, foreigners).

Attitudes such as these are not reversible by experience, since they are not rooted in a real assessment of the hated persons, but arise from the necessity to prevent the hate reactions from reverting to the original, ambivalently loved objects.

Projection and displacement of aggression are responsible for much of the strain, suspiciousness, and intolerance in the relationships between individuals and nations.

Turning Inward of Aggression

Certain quantities of destructive strivings are invariably directed against the individual's own self; normally their effects are counterbalanced by similar quantities of erotic urges which remain within the self. If, on the other hand, the destructive urges are too consistently directed away from employment against the object world, too much aggression becomes internalized. The harmful consequences of such a distribution of aggressive energy become manifest, in the bodily sphere, as a heightened inclination to develop organic illness; in the mental sphere, as a lack of self-possession, harsh self-criticism, excessive severity of the superego, depressive states, self-destructive and suicidal tendencies.

Sublimation of Aggression

When fused with the erotic impulses, the aggressive urges are relieved of their destructive qualities and make a decisive contribution to the purposes of life.

Practical Implications

Parents, educators, and workers in the allied field of child therapy are, above all, concerned with two questions: how far the fate of the aggressive urges is determined by internal factors (such as hereditary disposition, inborn relative strength of the destructive and erotic urges, constitutionally heightened inability to tolerate the offsprings of aggression in the mind); and how far influence is exerted by external factors (such as parental attitudes, increase or decrease of deprivations and frustrations, strict or lenient methods of upbringing).

The answers to these all-important questions lie beyond the limits of this paper, which can at best provide a short survey of the subject of aggression. Here I can only express the opinion that they will have to be based on the following clinical facts which have become available from the observation of individual children and of groups of children:

1. Increased frustrations of essential libidinal wishes (arising, for instance, from unloving, forbidding, rejecting attitudes of the parents)

abnormally increase the child's aggressive reaction to the normal and inevitable deprivations to which every infant is subjected from birth.

2. The lack of steady love relationships in early childhood caused either by internal or external factors (such as loss of parents or their substitutes, traumatic weaning from the breast, etc.) gives rise to states of emotional starvation with consequent retardation or complete stunting of the child's erotic development. In such cases the normal fusion between the erotic and destructive urges cannot take place, and aggression manifests itself as pure, independent destructiveness. Instances of this kind are observed occasionally in family life but are mostly studied in orphaned or otherwise deprived children, under war conditions, in residential institutions, in camps, etc.

3. Destructiveness, delinquency, and criminality in children, caused by the stunting of their libidinal development as described above, are not open to direct educational influences such as severe control, punishments, admonitions, etc. An appropriate therapy has to be directed to the neglected, defective side of the emotional development so that normal fusion between the erotic and the destructive impulses can follow and aggression be brought under the beneficial, mitigating influence of the child's love life.

4. The child's spontaneous inner conflict with the aggressive urges directed against the loved parents is strongly influenced by the tolerance or intolerance which the parents themselves show in this respect.

5

Observations on Child Development (1951 [1950])

This paper is included in this selection of Anna Freud's work because it illustrates the importance she attached to the direct observation of healthy children under both normal and abnormal conditions of life. A theory of mental development cannot be based only on the information obtained from psychoanalytic work with mentally disturbed adults and children.

The observations she describes in the first part of the paper are drawn from the work carried out at the Hampstead Nurseries between 1940 and 1945. She describes how many analytic concepts were confirmed by observations of children's behaviour. At the same time she draws particular attention to observations which ran counter to analytic assumptions. She highlights the phenomenon of total regression and reconstruction versus observation. The former (total regression) was characteristic of children who had been subjected to loss of parents by death or separation, etc. Not only was there regression of the instincts, but also a loss of important ego achievements (ego regression). This total regression is in contrast to the partial regressions characteristic of symptom and character neuroses in adults. As to the latter (reconstruction versus observation) the reaction of children to traumatic experiences demonstrated that an adult's single memory of a traumatic event in childhood is a condensation of innumerable unpleasant experiences rather than one alone (telescoping).

'Observations on Child Development' was presented as a contribution to the Symposium on Problems of Child Development, held at Stockbridge, Mass., April 1950. Among the other contributors were E. Kris (1951), D. Burlingham (1951b), J. Putnam *et al.* (1951). It was first published in *The Psychoanalytic Study of the Child*, 6: 18–30, 1951. Excerpts appeared in *The Family and the Law* by Joseph Goldstein and Jay Katz. New York: Free Press, 1965, p. 1060.

In a stimulating introduction to this symposium, Ernst Kris (1951) has set up the framework within which an interchange of ideas about current problems in psychoanalytic child psychology may prove fruitful. Since my own contribution to the discussion refers to a piece of direct observation of young children carried out in the Hampstead Nurseries during the war (A. Freud and Burlingham, 1942, 1944), I am particularly grateful to him for his remarks concerning work of this nature. For the psychoanalyst who deals habitually with latent, repressed, and uncon-scious material, which has to be drawn into consciousness by the laborious means of the analytic technique, a shift of interest to the observation of manifest, overt behavior marks a step which is not undertaken without misgivings. As psychoanalysts we are not interested in behavioristic data for their own sake. We ask ourselves whether observational work outside of the analytic setting can ever lead to new discoveries about underlying trends and processes, and can thereby supplement the data gathered through the analyses of adults and children. It is therefore helpful to be reminded that the origin of our analytic knowledge of children is not as exclusively centered in the analytic situation between analyst and patient as we are sometimes inclined to believe. It is true that the basic data concerning the phases of libido development and the oedipus and castration complexes were extracted during the psychoanalytic exploration of normal, neurotic or psychotic adults and children, i.e., with the help of the analytic technique of free association, and the interpretation of dreams and transference manifestations. But in later stages many data were added to this body of knowledge which came from sources less purely analytic. When the knowledge concerning infantile sexuality and its transformations had spread in the circle of psychoanalytic workers, direct observation of children began. Such observations were carried out first by parents, either under analysis or analysts themselves, on their own children, and were recorded regularly in special columns of the psychoanalytic journals of the time. When psychoanalysis began to be applied to the upbringing of children, the analysis of teachers and nursery school workers became a frequent occurrence. The observational work of these, professionally trained, people had the advantage of being undertaken with greater objectivity and more emotional detachment than parents can muster when confronted with the behavior of their own children. It had the further advantage of dealing not only with individuals but with groups. An additional source of information was opened up when psychoanalysis began to be applied, not only to normal educational work, but to work with delinquent and criminal children, and when, again, workers in this field were analyzed, trained, supervised, and encouraged to observe. It was the common characteristic of all these classes of investigators that their observation work was done on the basis of their personal analyses and their analytic training and that it was linked with practical activities with children (upbringing, teaching, therapy). The results helped to swell the body of existing analytic knowledge, even though, as Ernst Kris maintains, they did not break new ground.

This, then, is the category to which the observations carried out in the Hampstead Nurseries (1940–1945) belong. Far from being any form of planned research, they were no more than the by-product of intensive, charitable war work, and financed as such.[1] Since all efforts failed to obtain additional funds for the purposes of observation, recording and classifying of material, etc., all such activities had to be relegated to the spare off-time of the workers and was undertaken as their voluntary effort. Apart from this drawback, the setup of the institution was ideal for the purposes of observation. The choice of the case material was completely in the hands of the organizers; so were the practical arrangements for the children's lives. Contact with the children was of the twenty-four-hour kind. Circumstances made it possible to admit children from the age of ten days upward, and to keep many of them for the whole term of the war. Approximately one fifth of the children were admitted together with their mothers, who remained in the Nurseries for periods ranging from several days to several years. This variation in the case material made it possible to see children, almost from birth, in contact with their mothers or deprived of mother care, breast fed or bottle fed, in the throws of separation or reunited with their lost objects, in contact with their mother substitutes and teachers, and developing relations with their contemporaries. The stages of libidinal and aggressive development, the process and the effects of weaning and toilet training, the acquisition of speech and of the various ego functions with their individual variations could be followed closely. The abnormal circumstances of the children's lives served to stress the importance of certain factors through the distorting influence exerted by their absence (lack of fathers, of a family situation, of normal sexual observation of the parents, imitation of and identification with them, etc.).

It was a further favorable factor that, apart from a small group of highly qualified people (five or six for a resident population of eighty infants and children), the staff was built up of young people, eager for an adventure in education and observation, untrained for this type of work but also untrained in methods hostile to it. While being taught how to handle the children, they were taught as much psychoanalytic child psychology as the material demonstrated, i.e., the essentials of it. They were not analyzed at the time, although for many of them work in the Hampstead Nurseries became a prelude to a later personal analysis and to training in the field of analytic child therapy.[2]

The observational work itself was not governed by a pre-arranged plan. In emulation of the analyst's attitude when observing his patient during the analytic hour, attention was kept free-floating, and the material was followed up wherever it led. The fact that the effects of early separation from the mother, feeding habits, toilet training, sleep, anxiety, etc., were in the center of attention at different times was determined by the happenings among the children, not predetermined by fixed interests of the observers. Although this is a true description of the attitude of the organizers and their qualified colleagues, the position was different where the student workers were concerned. The subjects on the observation cards which arrived in a continuous stream from the staff — the material on which this contribution is based — fluctuated according to the subjects under discussion in the lectures, seminars, and general meeting of the staff. When the eyes of the workers had been opened to see the action of one or another specific factor in the child's life, attention was concentrated for a while on this particular aspect. Some authors may be of the opinion that such an attitude betrays the subjective nature of the observations and detracts from their value. I do not hold this view. Observations such as those described here are not 'objective' in the true sense of the word, in any case. The material which presents itself is seen and assessed neither by an instrument, nor by a blank and therefore unprejudiced mind, but on the basis of pre-existent knowledge, preformed ideas and personal attitudes (although these should be conscious in the case of the analyzed observer).

With the existence of this bias in mind, the participants in the experiment knew that they were not so much recording data as checking the children's behavior against the analytic assumptions about the hidden trends in the child's mind. For the analyst who derives his conviction of the validity of the analytic findings from applying the microscope of the psychoanalytic technique, it is an exciting experience to work for once with the naked eye and to discover how far the happenings in the deeper layers are actually reflected in behavior – if one looks for them. On the other hand, when assessing the value of such work which can be called neither analytic nor purely observational, it will be necessary to keep its limitations in both directions fully in mind.

For the purpose of this particular symposium, I present in what follows, some types of data collected in the Hampstead Nurseries, grouped according to their suitability to illustrate, to confirm, to amend, or to widen existent analytic knowledge.

Illustrations and Confirmations

The Phases of Libido Development Reflected in the Child's Behavior

Ernst Kris has repeatedly drawn attention to the fact that the correct reconstruction of the phases of pregenital development from the analysis of adult neurotics is one of the most impressive achievements of early psychoanalytic work. Although every analyst has had ample opportunity to repeat this discovery in his daily work with patients, we still welcome confirmation of it in direct observation. In adult analysis, infantile sexuality is seen dimly, in retrospect, reconstructed from the conscious and unconscious residues which act as disturbers of adult genitality. In the analysis of neurotic children, on the other hand, the analyst is presented with pictures of fixation and regression to one particular libidinal phase which, through its pathogenic overemphasis, blots out the importance of all others. None of these experiences during analytic work compares therefore in vividness, colorfulness, and convincing strength with the impressions we receive when following the gradual growth and development of a group of normal infants, and seeing the pregenital urges build up a sexual life in its own right undisturbed by later overlays. While observing the coming and going of the manifestations of pregenitality in their inexorable sequence, the observer cannot help feeling that every student of psychoanalysis should be given the opportunity to watch these phenomena at the time when they occur so as to acquire a picture against which he can check his later analytic reconstructions.

In the analytic literature on the subject of libido development, it is stressed repeatedly that the oral, anal, and phallic phases merge into each other at the points of transition and that they should be thought of as distinct from each other only in the sense that in each phase one of the component urges is highly cathected with libido and therefore prominent, whereas the others, earlier as well as later trends, although they may exist, have a low cathexis and therefore play an minor part. Such warnings are useful to the analyst to whom the libidinal phases often appear as closed-off entities when seen in retrospect. Observations, as we were able to make them, on the other hand, bear out the theory fully. What impressed us particularly was the wide overlapping between the oral and the anal stage. Much of this may have been due in our case to the oral deprivations which many of our children had had to undergo when separated from their mothers. But even those who had been breast fed by their own mothers in the Nursery, and remained in close contact with them, showed a survival of oral wishes, oral greed, and oral activities which seemed protracted when compared with our expectations. They kept up thumb sucking as a major autoerotic gratification, and biting as their main aggressive expression, far into the anal phase, and indulged in these activities, alongside with their anal interests. The line of demarcation between anal and phallic interests seemed in comparison to be much sharper.

On the other hand, despite this overlapping of pregenital gratifications, it was possible to distinguish clearly between the libidinal phases on the basis of the child's behavior toward the mother or her substitute. A greedy dependence (oral); a tormenting, harassing possessiveness (anal); a continual bid for attention and admiration, linked with an indulgent protectiveness toward the love object (phallic) – these attitudes were expressed by the children daily, hourly, and from minute to minute in their behavior. As overt expressions of the underlying sexual fantasies, these forms of loving (or hating) the mother seemed firmly tied up with the phases to which they belonged, and exclusive to them. We found that progress from one libidinal phase to the next was usually preceded by a change from one type of manifest behavior to the other. In adult analysis, even though free association, dreams, and transference manifestations revive the early forms of object relationship, they have by then lost much of their distinctiveness, and invariably return from the unconscious intermingled with later reactions, and distorted by them. A patient's oral dependence on the analyst, for example, is never free from anal, phallic, and genital admixtures, i.e., elements from later positions from which regression has taken place. So far as this particular correlation between developmental stage and behavior pattern is concerned, the direct observer of children is therefore more favorably placed than the analyst.

Evidences of the Primary Process in the Second Year of Life

One of the basic principles of metapsychology is the distinction between the primary and secondary process, i.e., the modes of mental functioning which are relevant for the id and the ego. This difficult piece of theory is demonstrated in our institutes to the analyst-in-training on the study of dreams, where the main characteristics of the primary process (lack of synthesis and negation, condensation, displacement of cathexis, exclusive concern with wish fulfillment) become apparent in the dream work. Watching groups of infants between twelve and eighteen months of age, one is impressed by the fact that their behavior is dominated by the principles which we know from dream interpretation and that observation of it may well serve as an additional source of information and illustration for the student. At this stage of ego development, the child is on the point of acquiring speech and, with it, the elaborate modes of logical thought and reasoning which form the indispensable basis for the secondary process. But these new abilities, although they are already in evidence, are not yet strong enough to keep control of motility and to govern actions for any length of time. At one moment, therefore, the infant acts impulsively, unrelated to reality dangers and a moment later, uninfluenced by them, he attacks a loved person or destroys a toy and, a moment later, expects to find them unharmed, as objects of his positive feelings; his anger moves easily from one person or cause to another; his only motive for action is a search for pleasure. On the other hand, an understanding and regard for the consequences of actions, a piece of reasoning, some integration of ambivalent feelings toward the love object, may appear intermittently as representatives of higher ego activity, and interfere with the infant's free, instinctual expressions. His behavior alternates therefore between manifestations of the primary processes with the pleasure principle and those of the secondary process with the beginning of the reality principle, making the contrast between the two forms of functioning extremely instructive.

Behavior at this stage is called 'unpredictable' since we never know whether, in a given situation, the child will react completely in accordance with the primary process or will make use of secondary functioning. Between eighteen and twenty-four months it is possible to demonstrate the growth and strengthening of the secondary elaborations and to see the instinctual, primary reactions and the pleasure principle recede into the background. Observation at this level will impress the student in particular with the importance of the quantitative aspect, since it is easy to demonstrate that relapses into the earlier mode of functioning occur whenever tension from an unsatisfied drive is especially high.

Fusion of Drives, Viewed from the Point of View of Behavior

Another set of observations, more important if confirmed by future work, deals with a point concerning the theory of the life and death instincts, namely, the fusion between libidinal and aggressive energies.

In our Nurseries, as in other homes for homeless and motherless infants, some children were displaying an amount of aggression and destructiveness which was not only greater than anything previously known at this age but also inaccessible to the usual educational measures such as guidance, praise, punishments, etc. Senseless destruction of toys and furniture, open or surreptitious attacks on other children, biting, and frequently soiling, were beyond outside control and not gradually brought under the control of the ego, as is normally the case. Since it can be proved that in the lives of these children the usual stimulant for normal libido development, namely, a mother relationship, had been missing, it seems permissible to assume that the cause of the trouble was not that the aggressive drives of these individual children were stronger than normal, but that, owing to the stunting of their emotional development, their libido was weaker, so that fusion between the drives could not take place in the normal manner. What the children displayed, therefore, was 'aggression in pure culture,' unsuited for the positive purposes of life.

To test our diagnosis, we ceased any attempts to combat the children's aggression directly, and concentrated our efforts instead on stimulating the emotional side which had lagged behind. The results confirmed that, with the development of good object relationships, aggression became bound and its manifestations reduced to normal quantities. It proved possible, as it were, to effect therapeutic results by bringing about the necessary fusion of the two drives.

Some Discrepancies Between Analytic Assumptions and Observation of Behavior

The following are points where the behavior displayed by the children under observation suggested revisions and amendments of existing explanations.

Phenomena of Total Regression

One of the indispensable elements of the psychoanalytic theory of the neuroses is the concept of regression. The individual, in the course of his instinctual development, acquires so-called fixation points to which part of his instinctual energies remains attached, while other quantities of it progress further and reach later stages of development. When on these later stages the individual experiences frustration due to external and internal danger, deprivation, and anxiety, the new libidinal or aggressive position is given up again and the individual reverts to former, more primitive wishes, i.e., he regresses to the fixation points. But since these regressive forms of gratification are not compatible with his comparatively more mature ego and superego attitudes, conflicts arise which have to be solved by compromise formations, i.e., neurotic symptoms. In the analytic exploration of character disorders, psycho-pathic states, etc., it was further shown that regression may occur not only on the instinctual side but also on the side of the ego, the phenomenon showing in varying degrees on each side of the personality. But the analysis neither of the neuroses nor of the character disorders gives us the opportunity to see what one might call 'total regression,' a process with which we became familiar in the Nurseries.

With our children regression under the impact of their traumatic experiences (loss of parents by death or separation) was the order of the day; yet we have hardly ever seen a regressive process which did not concern ego attitudes as well as drives. When left by his mother in the strange environment of the Nursery, a child in the anal phase would regress to the oral, a child in the phallic phase to the anal stage. These regressions were always accompanied by the loss of important ego achievements. It hardly needs mentioning that the children lost bowel and bladder control under such conditions; it is worth noting that many of those who had already learned to speak at home lost their ability to speak. They lost forms of locomotion which had been acquired recently and became clumsier and less coordinated in their movements. They also became more primitive in their modes of play. Especially in those instances where libidinal attitudes returned to the oral position, a full return to functioning under the pleasure principle was effected simultaneously. This phenomenon of total regression explains why the children did not develop neurotic symptoms when regressing to earlier libidinal phases and merely became more primitive beings, undoing development which had taken place. There was no occasion for a pathogenic conflict to arise between their regressive forms of gratifica-tions and their equally regressive ego attitudes.

When watching these phenomena, the observers were led to certain conclusions concerning the degree of vulnerability shown by the ego. It seemed that recent ego achievements were less likely to bear up under the influence of regression in the instinctual sphere than ego achievements of longer standing. A child, for instance, who had acquired speech a year ago or more would not lose it when he regressed from one phase of libido development to another; where speech had not existed for more than three to six months, it would be lost under these conditions. The same was true of locomotion, of moral achievements, etc.

In the light of these observations it might be worthwhile to inquire closely into the happenings which are revealed in the analysis of the adult neurotic and to look for evidence of similar ego losses occurring regularly before the outbreak of a neurosis. Such losses would concern late ego achievements, such as sublimations, idealizations, social adaptations, while older and more basic ego attitudes would remain unaffected.

Reconstruction versus Observation: Telescoping of Events

Early Traumatic Experiences

Early traumatic experiences, when they survive in a person's consciousness, do so in the form of cover memories. In analytic reconstruction it is the analyst's task to undo the distortions, condensations, displacements, and reversals which have constructed the particular cover memory out of the traumatic material and to revive the memory of the original event. The impression arrived at is usually that not one but two or more pathogenic happenings have contributed and been condensed to form the cover memory.

Actual observation of the same processes at the time of their occurrence suggests a correction of this view so far as the multiplicity of the pathogenic happenings is concerned. An action which we see the infant repeat a hundred times may in later life be represented as one traumatic happening. We see the infant play with his excrement, smear with it, try to taste it, over a period of weeks, or even months; the adult patient may remember this period in analysis as a single event of high emotional value. The memory of a traumatic fall, a traumatic injury may cover the whole series of smaller and bigger accidents which happen almost daily in a child's life. One traumatic prohibition or punishment, remembered or reconstructed, becomes the representative of hundreds of frustrations which had been imposed on the child; one longer separation from the mother takes over the combined effect of innumerable times when the infant was left alone in his cot, his room, at bedtime, etc. Although as analysts we realize that past experience is telescoped in this manner, we are in danger of underestimating the extent of the phenomenon, when not reminded of it by the result of direct observation.[3]

Autoerotic Experiences

A similar process of telescoping, though in the qualitative rather than in the quantitative sense, concerns the autoerotic activities. The data collected from our children during their first five years show a fairly equal distribution between rocking, thumb sucking, rhythmical rubbing of various portions of their skin, and masturbating, with the emphasis on the earlier rather than on the later practices. During the reconstruction of infantile sexuality in adult analysis, the emphasis is usually the opposite: although the incidents of early autoerotic practices are revived, they seldom compare in vividness and pathogenic importance with the memories of masturbation around which the oedipal and castration fantasies, and the guilt feelings concerning them, are centered. Allowing for the difference that rocking, part of thumb sucking, and some of the child's skin eroticism express narcissistic and not object-libidinal trends, and may therefore have played an excessive part in our 'homeless' and comparatively unattached children, the possibility remains that phallic masturbation, as the latest of them, becomes invested with and 'covers' the high emotional value of all the other activities which were its equivalents in the early phases.

Differences in Chronology

Some other points where our observers found themselves at variance with established analytic findings concerned chronology. Penis envy, which we expected to see in girls in the phallic phase, appeared with extreme violence according to some of our recordings in girls between eighteen and twenty-four months. In these cases the responsible factor may have been the bodily intimacy between boys and girls as it exists in a residential nursery where the opportunities for watching other children being bathed, dressed, potted, etc., are countless. It is less easily explained why in some cases infants showed definite reactions of disgust *before* toilet training had started, as well as reactions of shame long before exhibitionism had been interfered with.[4]

New Problems, Suggestions, Impressions

A Manifestation of 'Autoaggression'

As reported in *Infants Without Families*, we had ample opportunities to observe a practice which occurs in infants in their second year, namely, 'head knocking.' Children who are afflicted with it beat their heads against hard objects (the bars of their cots, the floor, etc.) when they are in a state of frustration and impotent anger. Although mild in some cases, this habit reaches a considerable and sometimes dangerous intensity in others. Although head knocking is well known to mothers and pediatricians, and is found in children who live under the most normal family conditions, it happens with greater frequency in institutional settings where severe deprivations are inevitable and where the practice may spread by contagion from one head knocker to a whole dormitory.

The factor which this practice and the autoerotic practices (such as rocking) have in common is a rhythm which may lead up to a point of climax, although in the case of head knocking the climax is one of self-destruction. Since, so far, no analytic explanation of this distressing habit has been put forward, it occurred to the observers that it might be an early manifestation in behavior of aggression and destruction turned against the self, i.e., the aggressive equivalent of autoerotism. If this interpretation should be confirmed by future analytic work, head knocking might gain a place of importance in analytic theory as one of the rare representatives of pure destructive expression where fusion of the drives is incomplete, or which occurs after defusion has taken place.

Coitus Play Without Observation of the Primal Scene; Oedipus Reactions Without Oedipal Experiences; The Problem of Innate Attitudes

The most intriguing data of the Nurseries series were those recording play among the young children which every analyst would have assessed at first glance as the result and imitation of coitus observations in the parental bedroom. This happened in spite of the fact that these infants had come to the Nursery directly from the maternity hospitals at the age of ten days and had lived there ever since without returning to their families; that they had never seen their parents alone together, and had never known a private bedroom; and that there was no possibility whatever of their having seen adults in sexual intimacy. With stimulation from outside thus excluded, play of this nature appears to be the expression of innate, preformed, instinctual attitudes, a suggestion which – if found to be true – would throw doubt on some of our analytic reconstructions of early witnessing of a primal scene.

As we reported in *Infants Without Families*, we were similarly puzzled when we observed our boys during the transition from the anal to the phallic phase. In the complete change which took place in their behavior toward their mother substitutes at that time, they developed masculine qualities and a protective, often overbearing, sometimes indulgently affectionate attitude toward the woman – an attitude which under normal conditions would invariably have been classified as a close imitation of the father and an identification with him. These children lived without fathers and, in the cases referred to here, had had no opportunity to watch their father's attitude toward the mother. It is therefore suggested as an explanation that the phenomenon in question was the behavioral manifestation of the phallic trends, with or without identification with the father. In this case, of course, outside stimulation through the occasional observation of other men, or other fathers, cannot be excluded completely.

The assumption that there exist in the child innate, preformed attitudes which are not originated, merely stimulated and developed, by life experience was further suggested by a series of observations revealing the child's readiness to adapt himself to the emotional conditions of family life. We found that it is a very different matter for a young child whether he is taken from the family setting to which he is used and placed in a community of children, or whether the upheaval in his life occurs in the opposite direction: whether he is taken from the community in which he has spent his first years and placed in a family. In the first case, adaptation to the group takes a long time, weeks or months, the social responses having to be acquired step by step by painful experience. In the latter case, when a young child (always, of course, before the latency period) is placed for adoption, or sent on a trial visit to a family, he may develop family attitudes in the course of a few days, without any experiences having led up to them. Our most instructive case in this respect was a boy who had entered the Nursery as a small baby, had never known his (or any other) family, and was visiting for adoption at the age of four and a half. His prospective parents were an affectionate couple, very eager to adopt a child. On the second or third morning, at breakfast, when the man kissed his wife before going to work, the boy had a fit of 'oedipal' jealousy and tried to 'separate the parents.' Under equivalent conditions, a child would take at least a year to develop group reactions of similar emotional strength and adequacy.

Ego and Superego Development under Group Conditions

The observation of a group of toddlers between one and two years of age directed our attention to the differences of ego and superego development where this happens under the influence of the love for the parents and in identification with them, or in a community of children of the same age, on the basis of the necessity of maintaining one's own status and existence in the group. From the abundant material, partly published elsewhere, there seems to be no doubt that social reactions, restraint of immediate gratification of instinct, and an adaptation to the reality principle can be acquired under both conditions. It remains an open question, to be answered by further work, whether the social reactions learned in a group remain mere ego attitudes or whether they are incorporated into the structure of the personality to form part of the superego which, according to our present knowledge, is built up on the basis of the emotional ties to the parents and the identifications which result from them.[5]

Notes

1. By the Foster Parents' Plan for War Children, Inc., New York, an American charitable organization.
2. It would be unfair to ascribe responsibility for any shortcomings of the work to the very severe war conditions which reigned in England at the time. On the contrary, the experience of common danger, common anxiety and strain, created in the staff an atmosphere of enthusiasm and exclusive devotion

to the common interests which it would be difficult to duplicate under peacetime conditions.

3. See Hanna Engl Kennedy, 'Cover Memories in Formation' (1950), a study carried out in connection with the follow-up of the material discussed in this paper.

4. Heinz Hartmann (1950) has recently suggested an explanation for these puzzling manifestations.

5. The same question is followed up further in a later piece of observational work and its theoretical evaluation. See 'An Experiment in Group Upbringing.' (A. Freud, 1951b).

6

The Role of Bodily Illness in the Mental Life of Children (1952)

In this detailed account of the role of bodily illness in the mental life of children, Anna Freud continues with her twin approach (observational and analytic) to an understanding of normal and abnormal mental development. The first part of the paper is taken up with a description of the actual effects of nursing, medical and surgical procedures on the child. The child cannot distinguish between the pain caused by the disease and the suffering caused by the nursing and medical interventions. The experience of being nursed and the restriction of movement carry with them the danger of regression. Surgical procedures in particular evoke phantasies of different kinds, for example, the operation may be experienced as a punishment for unacceptable wishes. The child's capacity to tolerate a painful process may be caused by the presence of such phantasies – 'The "tough" child "does not mind pain," not because he feels less or is more courageous in the real sense of the word, but because in his case latent unconscious fantasies are less dominant and therefore less apt to be connected with the pain' (A. Freud, 1952b).

A child's reaction to illness can be decisively influenced by the mother's attitude to illness in general. The child becomes easily infected with the mother's anxiety. Where there is identification with the mother's anxiety, a vulnerability is established for hypochondria in later life.

'The Role of Bodily Illness in the Mental Life of Children' was first published in *The Psychoanalytic Study of the Child,* 7: 69–81, 1952, and in French translation in 1957: 'Le rôle de la maladie somatique dans la vie psychologique des enfants', in *Revue Française Psychanalyse,* 21: 631–46, 1957. A German translation followed in 1968: 'Die Rolle der körper-lichen Krankheit im Seelenleben des Kindes' in *Erziehung in früher Kindheit,* G. Bittner and E. Schmid-Cords, eds. Munich: Piper, 1968, pp. 235–47.

When trying to evaluate the role of bodily illness in the mental life of children, we find ourselves hampered by the lack of integration in the material at our disposal. With the present-day division between professional teaching, nursing, child guidance work, child analysis, and pediatrics, there is little or no opportunity for the trained worker in one of these fields to function, even in the role of observer, in one of the other services for children.[1] Nursery workers, schoolteachers, and child analysts see nothing of the children under their care when they are ill, while pediatricians and sick-nurses lose contact with their young patients when they are healthy. It is only the mothers who have the opportunity to see their children in health, illness, convalescence, deviating from the norm bodily and mentally and returning to it. On the other hand, during severe bodily illness the mother's own emotional upset and her inevitable concentration on bodily matters act as distorting factors and leave little room for objective observation of the child's psychological reactions.

In recent years a number of analytic authors have made attempts to deal with the effects of hospitalization on young children. One series of studies culminated in a documentary film.[2] But in the case of these studies the interest of the investigators was directed toward the misery and anxiety that invariably arise when young children are removed from their parents, placed in unfamiliar surroundings, and handled and cared for by strangers; hospitalization merely serving as the prototype of a first, short-term separation from home. Instructive as these investigations are as a demonstration of separation anxiety and its consequences, they did not produce – nor were meant to do so – additional knowledge concerning reactions to illness and pain in infantile life.

Data are less scarce where the aftereffects of illness are concerned. In describing the neurotic disorders of their children, parents frequently date back the onset of the trouble to some bodily illness, after which the child appeared to be 'different.' Mood swings, changes in the relationship to parents and siblings, loss of self-confidence, temper tantrums often appear for the first time during convalescence from a severe illness. Symptoms, such as bed wetting, soiling, feeding and sleeping troubles, school phobias, which had existed and been overcome earlier in life, may reappear. Some children who had been considered brilliant in their intellectual performance before illness reappear afterward in school comparatively dull and apathetic; others surprise their parents and teachers by emerging from the same experience curiously ripened and matured. It is true that changes of this kind may happen after a period of hospitalization, but it is equally true that they also happen where hospitalization has not taken place, i.e., in children who have remained at home under the care of their mothers during illness and have been nursed at home. In considering the effects of bodily illness on the life of the child, it is important to note that hospitalization is no more than one factor among several other potentially harmful and upsetting experiences.

The Effects of Nursing, Medical, and Surgical Procedures

Before we can arrive at a correct assessment of this potentially traumatic experience of illness we have to work our way through the action of a large number of factors which, though they are mere by-products of the situation, are in the child's mind inextricably intermixed with it. The child is unable to distinguish between feelings of suffering caused by the disease inside the body and suffering imposed on him from outside for the sake of curing the disease. He has to submit uncomprehendingly, helplessly, and passively to both sets of experiences. In certain instances factors of the latter kind, with their high emotional significance, may even be the decisive ones in causing a child's psychological breakdown during illness, or in determining the aftereffects.

Change of Emotional Climate during Illness

There are few parents who do not, imperceptibly or grossly, change their own attitude to the ill child. There are some parents, with ascetic leanings, who are afraid of overindulging and thereby 'spoiling' the child at such times, and consequently leave him very much alone, to 'sleep out' his indisposition with the minimum of fussing. The majority of parents adopt an opposite attitude. The ill child may find himself more loved and fondled than at any other time of his life; for a child of a large family an infectious disease, with consequent isolation from siblings, may be the one occasion when he is in sole possession of his mother's time and care. The mother, owing to her anxiety for the child's health, may suspend all considerations of discipline and good behavior and indulge the child's wishes to the extreme. Or, on the contrary, in her preoccupation with the child's body, she may forget the most elementary principles of psychological handling which she had applied in times of health; shocks, forcible feeding or evacuation of the bowels, sudden separations (for hospitalization), deceptions (before operations) count for nothing with her so long as they ensure that her child recovers. The child, on the other hand, reacts to such unexpected handling as to traumatic experiences, feels bewildered by the upsetting of formerly rigid emotional and moral standards, or finds himself unable to renounce the incidental emotional gains after recovery.

The Experience of Being Nursed

The child's reaction to the experience of being nursed is understood best in terms of comparison with better known and frequently described reactions of adults to the corresponding situation.[3] A normal adult who is nursed through a severe illness cannot help feeling at the same time that he is exposed to a series of indignities. He has to renounce ownership of his own body and permit it to be handled passively. He is dressed and undressed, fed, cleaned, washed, helped with urination and defecation, turned from one side to the other, his nakedness exposed to nurse and doctor, regardless of sex, decencies, and conventional restrictions. He is, as it were, under orders, subjected to a hygienic routine, which implies a major disregard for his personal attitudes and preferences. Characteristically enough, many adults sum up this experience as being 'treated like a baby' or as a 'complete return to the conditions of their childhood.'

On the other hand, it would be a mistake to conclude from such statements that the situation of being nursed, by virtue of its similarity to infantile experiences, is less upsetting to the child than to the adult. Observation as well as theoretical considerations show that the opposite may well be the case. The gradual mastering of various bodily functions, such as independent eating, independent bowel and bladder evacuation, the ability to wash, dress, undress, etc., mark for the child highly significant stages in ego development as well as advances in detaching his own body from that of the mother and possessing it at least in part. A loss of these abilities, when occasioned by the nursing procedures (or by the weakened bodily condition itself), means an equivalent loss in ego control, a pull back toward the earlier and more passive levels of infantile development. Some children who have built up strong defenses against passive leanings oppose this enforced regression to the utmost, thereby becoming difficult, intractable patients; others lapse back without much opposition into the state of helpless infancy from which they had so recently emerged. Newly acquired and, for that reason, precariously anchored ego achievements are most frequently lost under these conditions. Many mothers report that after a period of illness their young infants have to be retrained so far as their toilet habits are concerned, weaned once more from spoon feeding, from clinging to the constant company of the mother, etc.

Restrictions of Movement, Diet, etc.

In contrast to the comparative ease with which ego skills and abilities are renounced under the impact of being 'nursed,' children defend their freedom of movement in the same situation to the utmost whenever they are not defeated by the type or intensity of the illness itself. It is well known that, at least under the conditions of home nursing, children with minor indispositions cannot be kept in bed consistently, or at least not lying down in bed. Young toddlers, who have only recently learned to walk, are known to stand up stubbornly in their beds for the whole course even of severe illnesses (for instance, measles) until exhaustion forces them to adopt the lying position.[4] Recently some enlightened pediatricians have accepted this state of affairs and treated some of their child patients, whenever possible, without enforcing bed rest.[5]

The psychological significance of the children's negative attitude in this respect becomes apparent in those extreme instances when child patients have to be immobilized after surgery or in the course of orthopedic treatment. Several analytic authors have observed and discussed the consequences of such extreme restraint of movement of limbs and have pointed out the possible connection with the emergence of stereotyped, ticlike movements elsewhere in the body (David Levy,

1928, 1944), the difference between this mechanically enforced restraint and the psychologically enforced restraint (Mahler, Luke, Daltroff, 1945), their bearing on the blocking of aggression discharge as well as on the discharge of stimulation in general with consequent overerotization of the whole body (Greenacre, 1944). Thesi Bergmann (1945), in an observational study carried out during three years' work on an orthopedic ward, gives a vivid description of the defense mechanisms which enable the immobilized children to bear the restraint and even to increase their docility when the restraining measures have to be increased. On the other hand, she describes the rages and temper tantrums which appear when the restraint is partially, but not wholly, lifted or when chance deprivations, outside the expected medical procedure, are added to it unexpectedly. She emphasizes, further, a twofold relationship between the immobilized limbs and other parts of the body. According to her experience, on the one hand, the restraint of one limb may spread in the form of inhibitions to other, nonaffected parts; on the other hand, certain ego skills, speech, etc., may undergo an accelerated development to compensate for motor restriction of one limb. The same processes that occur in children with pulmonary tuberculosis are described in a highly interesting study by Sara Dubo (1950).[6]

These authors' observations are confirmed by much non-recorded experience of parents and teachers. The heightening of aggression during and after motor restraint (in plaster casts, etc.) is especially well known to the general public. The most usual ways in which this dammed-up aggression appears are restlessness, heightened irritability, use of bad language, etc.[7]

In comparison with this massive blocking of a whole system of discharge, the food restrictions imposed on children during illness are of minor importance. Normally, in acute illnesses, the physiological lessening of the child's appetite prepares the way for the acceptance of a reduced diet; it is only the children with strong oral fixations, for whom food and deprivation of food have heightened libidinal significance, who react to this situation with fantasies of being badly treated, unloved, rejected. In chronic illnesses (such as diabetes, kidney trouble, colitis, allergies) where dietary restrictions have to be maintained for long periods of time, children are known to feel 'different,' singled out, discriminated against, or, in defense against being passively deprived, to develop ascetic self-denying tendencies.

On the whole, considerably less harm is done by the necessity of withholding desired foods than by an anxious mother urging or even forcing unwelcome food on an ill child. It is these latter situations that turn even minor, short illnesses into starting points for serious and prolonged eating difficulties, usually by reviving feeding battles which have raged between mother and child in the nursing period.

For some children the taking of medicines presents a major difficulty. Although the bad taste or smell of the drug is in the foreground so far as the child's conscious reasons are concerned, analytic investigation invariably discloses behind these rationalizations the existence of repressed ideas of being attacked by the mother through the symbol of the drug (Melanie Klein), of being poisoned, impregnated by her. Laxatives which force the bowels to move, though the child intends otherwise, may form the connecting link between reality and these unconscious fantasies.

In this connection it is interesting to remember that the punitive character of these restrictive measures has always been known to parents and has been exploited by them. To send a child to bed, confine him to his room, deprive him of favorite dishes have been used as punishments over the ages. In certain societies even the forcible administration of laxatives is used for the same purpose.

Operations

Ever since the discovery of the castration complex analysts have had ample opportunity in their therapeutic work to study the impact of surgical operations on normal and abnormal development. By now it is common knowledge among analysts that any surgical interference with the child's body may serve as a focal point for the activation, reactivation, grouping, and rationalization of ideas of being attacked, overwhelmed, and castrated. The surgeon's action, whether he performs minor surgery or major operations, is interpreted by the child in terms of his level of instinct development, or in regressive terms. What the experience means in his life, therefore, does not depend on the type or seriousness of the operation that has actually been performed, but on the type and depth of the fantasies aroused by it. If, for example, the child's fantasies are concerned with his aggression against the mother projected onto her person, the operation is experienced as a retaliatory attack made by the mother on the inside of the child's body (Melanie Klein); or the operation may be used to represent the child's sadistic conception of what takes place between the parents in intercourse, with the child in the role of the passive sexual partner; or the operation is experienced as mutilation, i.e., as punishment for exhibitionistic desires, for aggressive penis envy, above all for masturbatory practices and oedipal jealousies. If the operation is actually performed on the penis (circumcision, if not carried out shortly after birth), castration fears are aroused whatever the level of libidinal development. In the phallic phase, on the other hand, whatever part of the body is operated on will take over by displacement the role of an injured genital part.[8] The actual experience of the operation lends a feeling of reality to the repressed fantasies, thereby multiplying the anxieties connected with them. Apart from the threatening situation in the outer world, this increase of anxiety presents an internal danger which the child's ego has to face. When the defense mechanisms available at the time are strong enough to master these anxieties, all is well; when they have to be overstrained to integrate the experience, the child reacts to the operation with neurotic manifestations; when the ego is unable to cope with the anxiety released, the operation becomes a trauma for the child.

In a recent Symposium (1949) on Observations on the Emotional Reactions of Children to Tonsillectomy and Adenoidectomy, a representative group of analysts, psychiatrists, pediatricians, and psychologists discussed the subject in the light of these ideas with a view to lessening the traumatic potentialities of the three main factors involved in the situation: reaction to anesthesia, to hospitalization, and to the operative procedure itself. Finding the optimal time for carrying out an operation (Hendrick, Escalona, Sylvester); careful preparation before the event (Fries, 1946); avoidance of separation anxiety (Jackson, 1942; Putnam, Butler); psychiatric support (Rank), facilities for expression of feeling (Spock) were brought forward as the most important precautionary measures (Levy, 1945; Pearson, 1941). (See also Jessner and Kaplan, 1949; Jessner, Blom, Waldfogel, 1952.)

When studying the aftereffects of childhood operations in the analysis of adult patients we find that it is not the castration fear but the feminine castration wish in a male child that is most frequently responsible for serious postoperative breakdowns or permanent postoperative character changes. In these instances, the surgical attack on the patient's body acts like a seduction to passivity to which the child either submits with disastrous results for his masculinity, or against which he has to build up permanent pathologically strong defenses.[9]

Pain and Anxiety

The Mental Interpretation of Pain

The manner in which the child invests bodily events with libidinal and aggressive cathexis and significance creates a phenomenon that has baffled many observers. Parents and others who deal with young children frequently comment on the remarkable individual differences in children's sensitiveness to bodily pain; what is agonizing to one child may be negligible to another. The analytic study of such behavior reveals as different not the actual bodily experience of pain but the degree to which the pain is charged with psychic meaning. Children are apt to ascribe to outside or internalized agencies whatever painful process occurs inside the body or whatever hurt happens to the body (accidental hurts, falls, knocks, cuts, abrasions, surgical interference as discussed above, etc.). Thus, so far as his own interpretation is concerned, the child in pain is a child maltreated, harmed, punished, persecuted, threatened by annihilation. The 'tough' child 'does not mind pain,' not because he feels less or is more courageous in the real sense of the word, but because in his case latent unconscious fantasies are less dominant and therefore less apt to be connected with the pain. Where anxiety derived from fantasy plays a minor or no part, even severe pain is borne well and forgotten quickly. Pain augmented by anxiety, on the other hand, even if slight in itself, represents a major event in the child's life and is remembered a long time afterward, the memory being frequently accompanied by phobic defenses against its possible return.

According to the child's interpretation of the event, young children react to pain not only with anxiety but with other affects appropriate to the content of the unconscious fantasies, i.e., on the one hand, with anger, rage, and revenge feelings; on the other hand, with masochistic submission, guilt, or depression.

The correctness of these assumptions is borne out by the fact that after analytic therapy formerly oversensitive children become more impervious to the effect of pain.

Pain and Anxiety in Infants

Where the direct observation of infants in the first year of life is concerned, the relative proportion of physiological and psychological elements in the experience of pain is an open question. At this stage, any tension, need or frustration is probably felt as 'pain,' no real distinction being made yet between the diffuse experience of discomfort and the sharper and more circumscribed one of real pain arising from specific sources. In the first months of life, the threshold of resistance against stimulation is low and painful sensations quickly assume the dignity of traumatic events. The actual response of the infant, whether it occurs instantaneously, or after a time lag of varying length, or remains invisible altogether, is no reliable guide to an assessment of the shock caused by the pain.

From what age onward the bodily event is presumed to carry psychic meaning for the infant will depend altogether on the analytic observer's theoretical assumptions concerning the date when unconscious fantasies begin to exist.

For the observer of children under medical treatment it is interesting to note that older children (two to three years) may react with almost identical distress to the experience of injections or inoculations and to the experience of sunlight treatment, although the former involves pain (plus anxiety) whereas the latter is merely anxiety-raising without any pain involved.

Passive Devotion to the Doctor

It is the psychological meaning of pain that explains why doctors, and other inflictors of pain, are not merely feared but in many cases highly regarded and loved by the child. The infliction of pain calls forth passive masochistic responses which hold an important place in the child's love life. Frequently the devotion of the child to doctor or nurse becomes very marked on the days after the distress caused by a painful medical procedure has been experienced.

Reaction to Pain as a Diagnostic Factor

With young boys in the oedipal stage, their reaction to body pain provides a useful key to the differential diagnosis between genuine phallic masculinity and the misleading manifestations of reactive over-stressed phallic behavior designed to ward off passive feminine castration ideas. The masculine boy is contemptuous of bodily pain, which means little to him. The boy who has to defend himself against passive leanings cannot tolerate even slight amounts of pain without major distress.

The Effects of Illness

Changes in Libido Distribution

The casual observer, while following with his attention the loud, manifest reactions to anxiety and pain, nursing procedures, and restrictions, is in danger of disregarding another process which, silent and under the surface, is responsible for most important alterations during illness: i.e., the heightened demand of the ill body for libidinal cathexis. Some observant mothers know the mental signs heralding this state and are able to diagnose from them the onset of a disease even before any significant bodily symptoms have appeared.

There are two ways for the patient to react to this demand from the side of the body. Many who, when healthy, are in good contact with their surroundings, full of interest in their toys and occupations, and in the happenings of everyday life, begin their sicknesses by withdrawing from the environment, lying down on the floor or curling up in a corner, listless and bored.[10] At the height of the illness they lie in bed without moving, their faces turned to the wall, refusing toys, food as well as any affectionate advances made to them. Although these reactions regularly occur in certain children, even with harmless sore throats, stomach upsets, raised temperatures, and the most common infectious children's diseases, the impression given by such a child in a state of withdrawal is that of a seriously ill person. Anxious mothers are terrified by this complete reversal of their child's behavior and feel that he is in grave danger. In reality the manifestation is not a physiological but a psychological one and not commensurate with the severity of the illness. It is a change in libido distribution during which cathexis is withdrawn from the object world and concentrated on the body and its needs. Despite its frightening suggestion of malignancy this process is a beneficial one, serving the purpose of recovery.

There are other children who, for some unknown reason rooted in their individual libido economy, use a different manner to achieve the same result. Unable to give their own ill body the additional narcissistic cathexis which it demands from them, they claim this surplus of love and attention from the mothers who nurse them through the illness, i.e., they become demanding, exacting, clinging far beyond their years. In doing so they make use of a natural process dating back to the first year of life, when the mother's libidinal cathexis of the infant's body is the main influence in protecting it from harm, destruction, and self-injury (Hoffer, 1950). To the surface observer, children of this type seem extremely 'fussy' when ill, those of the former type seem undemanding.

In both cases, the gradual return to health is accompanied by a gradual regularization of these movements of libido, though not without difficulties and reversals during which the child appears 'cranky.' Occasionally the abnormal distribution of libido proves irreversible for a certain length of time and produces some of the puzzling personality changes that have been pointed out above.

The Child's Body as the Mother's Property. Hypochondria

Some mothers find it difficult to resign themselves to the fact that their children, even after the toddler stage, cannot really be trusted to take care of their own bodies and to observe the rules serving health and hygiene. Whenever a mother reports with pride that her child washes his hands before eating without being told to do so, analytic exploration will reveal that the child in question is a severe obsessional and his apparently sensible cleanliness a compulsive and magical defense against imaginary, dangerous contact. Children who protect themselves against colds and drafts ward off fears of death; those who choose their foods carefully do so on the basis of fears of being poisoned; those who refrain from eating too much or too many nourishing foods are obsessed by anxieties concerning pregnancy. The average, normal child will observe none of these precautionary measures; he will eat with dirty hands, stuff himself, brave wet and cold weather, eat green apples and other unripe fruits unless forced, urged, or prevented by his mother. In illness he will at best cooperate with her; at worst he will fight the care taken of him and proceed to use his own body as he pleases. So far as health, hygiene, and nursing care are concerned, the mother's ownership of the child's body extends from earliest infancy, when the mother–child unity is an important factor in the libido economy of both, through all the phases of childhood into adolescence. At this last stage, before independence is finally reached, recklessness in matters of health provides one of the familiar battle grounds for bitter struggles between the adolescent and his mother.

It is interesting to observe that the state of affairs is reversed more or less completely where motherless, orphaned, and institutionalized children are concerned, even in those cases where competent professional nursing care is provided. Far from enjoying the freedom from anxious supervision (as the observer might expect from the mothered child's revolt against her care), motherless children proceed to care for their own bodies in an unexpected manner. In an institution known to me it was sometimes difficult to prevail upon a child to shed his sweater or overcoat in hot weather; his answer was that he 'might catch cold.' Rubber boots and galoshes were asked for and conscientiously worn by others so as 'not to get their feet wet.' Some children watched the length of their sleep anxiously, others the adequacy of their food. The impression gained was that all the bogeys concerning the child's health which had troubled their mothers' minds in the past had been taken over by the young children themselves after separation or bereavement, and activated their behavior. In identification with the temporarily or permanently lost mother, they substituted themselves for her by perpetuating the bodily care received from her.[11]

Observing the behavior of such children toward their bodies we are struck with the similarity of their attitudes to that of an adult hypochondriac, to which perhaps it provides a clue. The child actually deprived of a mother's care adopts the mother's role in health matters, thus playing 'mother and child' with his own body. The adult hypochondriac who withdraws cathexis from the object world and places it on his body is in a similar position. It is the overcharging of certain body areas with libido (loving care) that makes the ego of the individual hypersensitive to any changes which occur in them. With children, analytic study seems to make it clear that in the staging of the mother—child relationship, they themselves identify with the lost mother, while the body represents the child (more exactly: the infant in the mother's care). It would be worth investigating whether the hypochondriacal phase which precedes many psychotic disorders corresponds similarly to a regression to and re-establishment of this earliest stage of the mother—child relationship.

Summary

In carrying further my own and other writers' studies of separation anxiety (hospitalization) this paper surveys the other factors which play a part in the child's reaction to bodily illness. The effects of the various nursing, medical, and surgical procedures which are open to modification are distinguished from those elements which are inherent in the process of illness itself, such as the effect of pain and the inevitable changes of libido distribution. Lastly, a comparison is drawn between the state of deprived children who care for their bodies in identification with their lost mothers and the adult hypochondriac who overcathects his body with libido after it has been withdrawn from the object world.

In summarizing these factors which play an important role in every normal development, I wish once more to stress how serious a measure hospitalization is, separating the child from the rightful owner of his body at the very moment when this body is threatened by dangers from inside as well as from the environment.[12]

Notes

1. A notable pioneer exception to this practice has been established by Dr. Milton J. E. Senn, Departments of Pediatrics and Psychiatry, Yale University School of Medicine, New Haven, Conn.
2. See James Robertson (1952), Bowlby, Robertson, and Rosenbluth (1952), and Anna Freud's film review (A. Freud, 1953).
3. Compare in this connection *The Middle of the Journey* (1947), by Lionel Trilling, with its striking description of an adult intellectual returning to responsibility for his own health after having been looked after and nursed during a severe illness.
4. See in contrast to this the remarks on pp. 75–6.
5. In England, Dr. Elsie Wright, formerly physician at the Babies Hospital, Newcastle on Tyne, impressed on the members of the Cassel Hospital Summer School for Ward Sisters (1949) that in children's wards there should be 'no rigidity about the child being kept in bed'; Dr. Josefine Stross, pediatrician, when teaching students of the Hampstead Nurseries (1940–1945) and the Hampstead Child-Therapy Course, emphasized repeatedly that even where children have to be kept off the floor, movement inside the crib should not be restricted.
6. See also Thesi Bergmann and Anna Freud (1965).
7. I have analytic knowledge of a girl who was immobilized during her latency period for orthopedic reasons. She used to pay her friends out of her pocket money for every new swearword which they brought home from school. The use of 'bad language' was the only outlet left for her otherwise paralyzed aggression.
8. In deciding on the length of preparation time before an operation, two factors have to be taken into account. A preparation period which is too lengthy leaves too much room for the spreading out of id fantasies; when the interval between knowledge and performance of the operation is too short, the ego has insufficient time for preparing its defenses.

    [For a detailed description of a mother's effort to prepare her daughter for a tonsillectomy, see Joyce Robertson (1956) and Anna Freud's Comments on this paper (A. Freud, 1956). See also T. Bergmann and A. Freud (1965) – Chapter 7: 'Preparation for Surgery'.]
9. [See Lipton's (1962) discussion of tonsillectomy performed in childhood as a complex experience that may prematurely organize a person's adaptation to reality in not readily predictable ways.]
10. This refers to cases where such listlessness cannot be accounted for on physiological grounds.
11. A most instructive example of this behavior is the instance of a motherless boy of six years who in a long-drawn-out nightly attack of vomiting and

diarrhea was heard to say to himself: 'I, my darling.' When asked what he meant, he answered: 'That I love myself. It is good to love oneself, isn't it?'

12. [Some of the points discussed here have been taken further in subsequent papers (Anna Freud, 1961, 1966a, 1966b).]

7

The Concept of the Rejecting Mother (1955 [1954])

This paper was written at a time when mental illnesses of varying degrees of severity were thought to be attributable to faulty and bad mothering. This was the time of the concept of the schizophrenogenic mother. That children suffered rejection by the mother or suffered as a result of adverse environmental circumstances was not in dispute. It was a matter of what was meant by the concept of rejection.

Rejection of the child can take place by an unwillingness on the part of the mother to care for the child; the child might be rejected as a result of physical or mental illness on the mother's part; rejection might occur as a result of separation; and rejection might occur as a result of the mother's inconstancy of feeling. Most importantly Anna Freud underlines the fact that the mother's relationship to her child fluctuates with his/her phases of development. For example, a mother who is devoted to her helpless baby may withdraw her devotion when the child strives for independence.

This paper details the complexity of the concept of rejection. It corrects the one-sided view that severe mental illnesses are necessarily attributable to a disturbed mother–child relationship.

'The Concept of the Rejecting Mother' was first given as a speech at the Annual Dinner Meeting of the Child Welfare League of America, Atlantic City, N.J., 13 May 1954. It was first published as 'Safeguarding the Emotional Health of Our Children' in *National Conference of Social Work, Casework Papers* in 1954 and in New York: Family Service Association of America, pp. 5–17 as well as in *Child Welfare*, 34 (3): 1–4, in 1955; and in *Parenthood: Its Psychology and Psychopathology*, E. James Anthony and Therese Benedek, eds. Boston: Little, Brown and Company, 1968. Excerpts appeared in *The Family and the Law*, by Joseph Goldstein and Jay Katz. New York: Free Press, 1965, pp. 1059, 1133.

When I received from your President an invitation to speak at the Annual Meeting of the Child Welfare League of America, I took this as a sign of recognition of the close interrelation which exists today between your field of work and mine, the social and the psychoanalytic one. By now, it has been accepted as a fact by many people that child welfare work, to be effective, has to draw heavily on the findings of analytic psychology. I believe that, in reverse, child psychology, for the best results, cannot afford to neglect the inexhaustible fund of material which, in the form of impressions, observations, practical experience, is at the disposal of the welfare worker. Generous American support has enabled me, as an analyst, to undertake repeated ventures into the realm of welfare work.[1] These have impressed me with the value of gaining intimate insight into both sides of a twofold task: that of building up a body of knowledge concerning the child's emotional development, as well as that of applying this hard-won knowledge to the aim of 'protecting the emotional health of our children.'

The Relations Between Psychoanalysis and Child Welfare Work

Historically, the significant cooperation between the two fields began with the analytic discovery that nothing that happens in the later life of an individual is of the same importance for his mental health as the events of his first five years. It was this shift of emphasis from adult to childhood experience that demonstrated the importance of child welfare work for the prevention of mental disturbances, thereby giving it a very special status among the social services. There followed on the analytic side the discovery of the oedipus complex, i.e., the exploration of the child's love and hate relations within the family, which lay the foundation for his love life and his moral adaptation to society. Reacting to this, family agencies became concerned with 'broken homes' and directed their efforts toward maintaining – for normality's sake – complete and, if possible, united families. Analysis discovered that there exists no neurosis in adult life which has not been preceded by an infantile neurosis. This led to the setting up of treatment centers and child guidance clinics. Analysis dug deeper into the beginnings of the child's problems and demonstrated the adverse consequences of parental attitudes, such as withholding sex knowledge, overstrict toilet training or wrong feeding methods; this led on the social side to a campaign for the enlightening of parents. When it emerged that the wrong handling of infants is due not to lack of knowledge but to internal difficulties on the mothers' part, casework with mothers set in to try to remedy their troubles, etc.

In short, during its development toward a new and effective form of mental hygiene, child welfare work seems gradually to have become as dependent on analytic child psychology as physical hygiene is on medicine and medical research. The analogy even includes the mistakes made on both sides. Scientists, whether they work on the secrets of the body or the mind, sometimes release their discoveries while they are still in the experimental stage. Workers in hygiene, whether physical or mental, in their eagerness to relieve or prevent suffering, are not always discriminating and careful enough in their applications. This danger is increased on the psychological side by the less objective nature of the findings, by the less precise language in which the analyst expresses them, and – last but not least – by their emotional appeal.

Rejection as a Pathogenic Factor

The fact of infantile sexuality, the oedipus and castration complexes, the problems of ego and superego development, and the role of aggression having been established, psychoanalytic study then turned to the child's first year of life, i.e., to the beginning of mental functioning and the first emotional contact of the infant with his environment. This brought into special focus how all-important the person of the mother and her attitude are to her child. It was demonstrated that all advantage of a later family life may be wasted on a child who has lacked a warm and satisfying mother relationship in the first instance. The conditions necessary for establishing this first contact to the best advantage have been described by many authors.[2] In this earliest partnership in an individual's life, that of infant and mother, the demands are all on one side (the infant's), while the obligations are all on the other side (the mother's). It is the mother's task to be attentive to the child's needs (for food, sleep, warmth, movement, comfort, company), not to mis-understand them, or to confuse them with each other, and to fulfill them, not according to her own speed and rhythm, but by adapting her actions to the child's. The infant is dependent on the mother for his satisfactions. If she proves a gratifying and accommodating provider for his pressing needs, he begins to love, not only his experiences of wish fulfillment, but her person. Thereby the infant's original state of self-centeredness is changed into an attitude of emotional interest in his environment and he becomes capable of loving, first the mother and — after her — the father and other important figures in his external world.

It is maintained by many analytic authors that it lies wholly with the mother of an infant whether this beneficial development occurs. When the mother welcomes the child's first outflow of feeling toward her and responds to it, she favors his progress from self-centeredness to object love. When she fails in her task at some point and thereby rejects his advances, she may destroy an all-important potentiality in her infant, with disastrous consequences for his future healthy development.

This latest development of analytic theory did not fail to impress welfare workers in the usual manner. Realizing the advantage of directing their effects to the earliest ages, and thus, perhaps, to beginning of all troubles, they began to take serious notice of the vital bond which exists between mother and infant, to protect it against forcible interruptions, to foster its existence where they found it, and to urge mothers to be more forthcoming with their feelings where they seemed reluctant.

These were the legitimate applications of a new insight. But, whether owing to the fault of the analysts who were too emphatic in their statements, or owing to the fault of the caseworkers who were too bent on exchanging a multitude of causes of mental trouble for one single, simple, causal factor — the idea of being 'rejected by the mother' suddenly began to overrun the fields of clinical work and casework. On the clinical side, more and more of the gravest disturbances were attributed to the presence of 'rejection' (such as autism, atypical and psychotic development, mental backwardness, retardation of speech, etc.). On the caseworkers' side, more and more mothers were pronounced to be cold, not outgoing, unresponsive, unloving, hating, in short, 'rejecting' their children. This caused much heart-searching and also much self-accusation, especially among the mothers of abnormal children.

Inquiry into the Concept of the Rejecting Mother

There is, of course, no lack of evidence for the occurrence of rejection of infants. Many infants, instead of being kept as near to the mother as possible, spend many hours of the day in isolation; many are subjected to traumatic separations from their mothers; many, at the end of infancy, have good reason to feel deserted when another child is born; many are, indeed, unwanted. Nevertheless, there is behind these happenings a variety of determinants which decides their outcome. There is not one type of rejecting mother, there are many. There are those who are responsible for their rejecting attitude, who can be exhorted, advised, and helped toward a better adjustment to their child; there are also those with whom rejecting is beyond their control.

Children are deprived of the company and care of their mothers for external, physical reasons, and for internal, mental ones; or both factors are inextricably intermixed in other cases. Also, no child is wholly loved. The idea of 'rejection' in its present form is unprecise, vague, and through overuse has become almost meaningless. Nothing short of definition and classification of the degrees and types of withdrawal of mother love from the infant can restore it to its initial usefulness. Hence the present inquiry into the concept of the rejecting mother.

Rejection by Unwillingness of the Mother

No one who has ever had even a short acquaintance with child welfare work will deny that there are 'bad mothers,' in the same sense in which there are bad partners in every type of human relationship, whether they are mothers or fathers, wives or husbands. As described above, the relationship of a mother to her infant is an exacting one. It is too much to expect that she will fulfill her task if she has not taken on the role of motherhood voluntarily, if it has been forced upon her. That leaves on one side, classed as 'unwilling,' all those mothers who never meant to have a baby, or did not mean to have one at the particular time when pregnancy occurred.

The reasons for their unwillingness may be external ones: financial difficulties, lack of their own home, or of space, the burden of too many other children, illegitimacy of the relations with the child's father. There are emotional reasons such as lack of affection for the husband, which is extended to his child. Or reasons, rationalized merely on the surface by external conditions, may lie much deeper in the mother's nature. There are many women who are incapacitated for motherhood by virtue of their masculinity. They may wish for children for reasons of pride and possessiveness, but their humiliation at finding themselves female, their longing for a career, their competition with the husband preclude any real enjoyment of or with the infant.

There are, further, the mothers who waver between rejection and acceptance of the mother role. During her pregnancy a woman may be wholly unwilling and then be seduced and tempted by the infant himself until she enters into an affectionate relationship; in such cases the living presence of the child arouses in her what one used to call the 'mother instinct.'

Or there may be conflict between internal and external pressure. This is well known from casework with unmarried mothers who reject their infants for social considerations while they accept them emotionally.

It is also interesting to note that wholly external influences are capable of interfering with the mother's tie to the child. When mother and infant are separated for long periods and the mother is relieved of all responsibility for the child – as happened in wartime England for safety's sake or as happens in hospitals when either mother or child has to be isolated – under such conditions mothers have been seen to lose their attachment to the child, and to become unwilling to resume it. Such experiences make one feel that the mother's attachment is bound up with the appeal made by an infant's helplessness and urgent need for care rather than being a mere 'instinct.' This might explain too why mothers who entrust the care of their infants to paid nurses are so often described as 'rejecting.'

On the whole, it is not the truly unwilling mother who exerts the most disastrous influences on her child's future. When she refuses altogether to play her part, the door is left wide open for an accepting mother substitute, as found in adoption and in foster families. It is the mother who wavers between rejection and possessiveness who does the more irreparable harm by forcing her child into an unproductive partnership in which he fails to develop his capacities for object love.

Rejection Through Abnormality of the Mother

Unwillingness, for conscious or unconscious reasons, to assume the special task of motherhood should not be confused with the general failure to establish normal human relationships, as it exists in women whose personalities are distorted by psychotic elements or who suffer from a circumscribed psychosis. The effect of a psychotic mother on the development of her child has been discussed frequently and by many authors in recent years. There is no doubt that infants may react to the lack of outgoing warmth in such a mother as if she 'rejected' them. On the other hand, harmful consequences of an opposite nature can also be observed. The psychotic mother may include a child in her own world of self-centered (narcissistic) feelings and reactions, regarding him as a part of her own self. The normal symbiosis of a mother and infant (see Mahler, 1952) may then become prolonged in an abnormal manner, and mother and child together become an isolated couple in an apparently hostile external world. Such a state of affairs delays, or prevents, the growing child's normal adaptation to the social environment (see Bonnard, 1949).

Rejection by Separation

In contrast to these first two groups, there are the mother–child relationships where a good beginning is made in every respect. The mother may be devoted, happy with her baby, accepting and responsive. The child may respond to her care and make the first steps toward emotional attachment. Then there follows rejection brought about by sudden separation of the couple. Such separations may be the mother's fault (when she leaves the child in the care of strangers for trivial reasons such as trips, visits), but they need not be. The mother may be ill, have to go to the hospital, undergo an operation, need convalescence. The illness of an older child or the needs of the father may remove her from the infant. External conditions may interfere, as they did in wartime. The mother may die and leave her child an orphan.

Such separations act on the child irrespective of their causes. Since the infant cannot grasp the reason for the mother's disappearance, every separation equals for him desertion on her part. Before his sense of time develops, the pressure of his needs makes every period of waiting seem agonizingly long; therefore he does not distinguish between separations of short and long duration. Everybody's sympathy and understanding are automatically extended to the infant whose mother dies; if the mother is absent merely for a few weeks, we are less concerned. Wrongly so; *we* know that the mother will return, the *child* does not. Separations between mother and infant are *rejections*, whether they are brought about for good or bad reasons, whether they are long or short. The infant who is torn from the partnership with his mother is emotionally orphaned, even though he may be an 'artificial' orphan with a living mother (see Burlingham and A. Freud, 1942). It is revealing, for example, to learn in the analyses of adults who lost their mothers through death in infancy that, unconsciously, they have never ceased to blame them for desertion.

Dorothy Burlingham's and my wartime study of *Infants Without Families* (1944), John Bowlby's work on separation anxiety (1951), James Robertson's film of *A Two-Year-Old Goes to Hospital* (1952), René Spitz's film studies (1947) etc., have revealed some of the consequences of 'rejection by separation.' Here I can only summarize results. The shock of separation is often expressed by disturbance of the body functions such as upsets of sleep, feeding, of the digestive apparatus; there is also at such times an increased susceptibility to infection. Further, many infants make backward moves in development: those who have just learned to talk, give up speech; those who have just begun to move independently, give up walking; those who have already undergone toilet training, wet and soil again. It is almost invariably the most recent achievement in development which is lost first.

On the emotional side, all variations have been described, from incessant crying to silent despair. For the infant, to withdraw his feelings from the loved person seems to be as painful as it is for an adult in mourning. The main difference between the two emotional states seems to be that the adult is capable of withdrawing his feelings into himself and attaching them to an inner image of the lost object. The infant needs a living person in the external world who is capable of fulfilling his material needs besides serving as a love object: he cannot live without a mother substitute. Therefore, the interval between withdrawal of affection from the mother and search for another object is a short one. But this ability, or rather need, of the young child to form new ties should not deceive us as to the seriousness of what has happened. The first attempt at object love has been destroyed; the next one will not be of quite the same quality, will be more demanding, more intent on immediate wish fulfillments, i.e., further removed from the more mature forms of 'love.' Repeated 'rejection by separation' intensifies this process of deterioration and produces individuals who are dissatisfied, shallow, and, worst of all, promiscuous in their relationships.

In London we are now carrying out studies of such disturbances in children from institutions who, as infants, were passed from hand to hand.

Rejection by Inconstancy of Feeling

There are many young children who show the effect of rejection, although they have never been subjected to a physical separation from their mothers. The fact is that infants demand more than the bodily presence of the mother, they demand too that the mother's regard for them should not undergo any fluctuations in degree. The younger the infant, the greater is his sensitivity for any lessening in the mother's love, even if this is a very temporary phenomenon. Even when the mother is quite oblivious of such a change in intensity of feeling, the child is not.

In a more specialized paper on the subject, 'About Losing and Being Lost' [see chapter 8 in this volume], I was able to show how young children react if they feel less loved. The mother's loving interest in the child ties him to her and he feels securely held in an atmosphere which is charged with her affection. When the charge (the libido cathexis, to use the technical term) diminishes, insecurity sets in, and the child feels 'lost.' When the infant is old enough to be capable of independent movement, he may even get lost physically; i.e., he may venture away from the mother into what is normally for him 'out of bounds' and not find his way back to her. There is an interesting analogy here between our own hold on our material possessions and a mother's hold on her young child. We are apt to lose possessions if we withdraw interest from them, if 'our mind is elsewhere.' Mothers, under the same conditions, may lose their emotional hold on their young children; this, in its turn, may induce the child to stray, to lose himself, to run away.

Seen from the mother's side, it is an unreasonable demand that there should be no fluctuations in the intensity of her feelings for the child. There are many other claims on her emotions. The most devoted mother of an infant may have older children who have older claims; there are the husband's claims to satisfy and needs vary. Mothers may suffer the loss of another child or of their own parents. If this happens, their feelings become withdrawn from the infant and are engaged in mourning. Infants react to such happenings as to rejections and desertions, with illness, with standstills or regressions in development, with increased naughtiness and aggression toward the mother. The same happens if the mother falls into a morbid depression of some kind, or if there is an upheaval in her love life, or if there are troubles in the marital relations which absorb her interest.

Rejection by desertion also seems to be the most potent factor in the young child's emotional upheaval when a next child is born. So far as the mother is concerned, nothing is more natural, healthy and even biologically necessary than that she should turn her attention to the newborn. But all the psychological advice to mothers on how to handle the older child at that juncture, all the devices of giving him a doll to bathe, of letting him help with the new baby, of telling him what a big child he already is — all this will not for a moment blind him to the all-important fact that his mother has withdrawn libido from him. The child's own explanation of such 'rejection' is invariably that he is no good, or that the mother is no good, both versions leading to anxiety, feelings of guilt, and regressions in behavior.

When the withdrawal of love is occasioned by the birth of a new baby or by some happening in the mother's love life, the child will react with normal jealousy. When mourning or depressions are the cause, children usually react with withdrawal and (immediate or later) pathological depressions of their own.

Alternation of Rejection and Acceptance

It is only natural that a mother's relationship to her child fluctuates with his phases of development. Some mothers during their pregnancy feel a pride, possessiveness, and love for the unborn, attitudes which they can never recapture later on. Others are wholly devoted to the helpless baby and withdraw devotion when the child begins to move and help himself. To most mothers, the appeal of the hungry child is quite different from the appeal (or lack of it) of the dirty or obstreperous one. Some mothers find it difficult to tolerate the awakening masculinity of the three-year-old, and withdraw from him at a period when others turn toward the child with increased and proud affection. A mother may be 'rejecting' toward her baby in his first stages and become accepting at the stage when the child is teachable (see Coleman, Kris, and Provence, 1953), etc.

Such alterations of rejection and acceptance (not of the child as a whole but of his changing aspects) are anchored in the depth of the mother's mind. She cannot help reacting to (i.e., 'rejecting') the child if his behavior arouses old conflicts of her own. His oral demands on her arouse once more her own struggles with her own mother in her own babyhood. His dirtiness and the need for her to be concerned with his body products arouse fantasies and battles in the anal phase. Her reaction to the child's phallic development will be determined by her castration complex and her penis envy. In short, the relationship to the developing infant shakes her personality to its foundation. Her behavior toward the child is understood best when viewed in terms of her own conflicts. She acts rejecting when she defends her own repressions, and accepting when the child's behavior meets with secret wishes and fantasies of her own which she can tolerate.

It is a frequent occurrence that a mother is so fixed to a certain libidinal phase of her own development that her obvious predilection for it acts on the child as a seduction. Thus, mother and child as a couple may meet on the basis of an exaggerated sadomasochistic relationship, provoking each other to endless quarrels. Or their relationship may remain predominately within the sphere of oral fantasies; in the later event, partnership becomes the breeding ground for pathological reactions, such as battles over food, eating and stomach troubles, and attitudes of craving and addiction.

Rejection in Spite of Devotion

Although, as said before, no human being is wholly loved, there are some women who come very near to fulfilling this achievement for their child. They are, emotionally, mothers rather than wives, with few other ties and interests, to whom the possession of a child means the fulfillment of their deepest wishes. They give themselves unreservedly to the infant; they do not separate from him and they do not allow other claims to diminish their attention. Their infant frequently remains their only child. But, surprisingly enough, they too do not escape the blame of being 'rejecting' in the eyes of their children. It throws a new light on the factor of 'rejection' when we realize that no degree of devotion on the part of the mother can successfully cope with the boundless demands made on her by the child.

There is another, more intricate, factor which should not be under-rated. Every good mother of an infant shares his experiences. Not only does she provide satisfactions, she also is at hand when the infant is uncomfortable, in pain, and suffering. It is not reasonable to expect that the child will connect her person only with his pleasures. As the first representative of the external world in which the infant has to learn to orient himself, she becomes the symbol of both frustration and satisfaction, pain and pleasure.[3] The nearer she is to the child, the more convincingly will both roles be thrust on her. Paradoxically enough, the most devoted mother may in this way become the most rejecting one for the child.

Actually, we should have been prepared for this result through earlier observations concerning the role given to the father in the oedipus complex of the boy. There, too, the gentlest and most well-meaning fathers find themselves distorted in the boy's conscious and unconscious fantasies, until they take on the aspect of monsters and ogres; i.e., frightening, terrifying, castrating figures. Analysis has shown that the father assumes this aspect for the child as the representative of the culture in which incest with the mother is forbidden. He is no more, and no less, than a symbol of the moral code. I believe we can say that any infant's mother, for all her reality aspects, is a symbol too. In appraising the circumstances, we, the observers, must not share the infants' delusion. We must guard against the error of confusing the inevitably frustrating aspects of extrauterine life with the rejecting actions or attitudes of the individual mothers.

This inquiry into the concept of the rejecting mother has not been undertaken with the aim of discouraging the welfare worker. On the contrary, discrimination between fantasy and reality factors, between attitudes of willful neglect and inescapable fateful situations seems to me of the first importance in clearing the way for increasingly successful action in the puzzling, delicate, and difficult situations which are met in the fields of therapy and casework.

Notes

1. The Jackson Nursery, Vienna, 1938–1939, maintained by Dr. Edith Jackson, New Haven. The Hampstead Nurseries, London, 1940–1945, maintained by the Foster Parents' Plan for War Children, Inc., New York. The Hampstead Child-Therapy Clinic, London, maintained by the Field Foundation, Inc., New York, since 1952.
2. By none better than by D. W. Winnicott in his popular pamphlet on *The Ordinary Devoted Mother and Her Baby* (1949).
3. See in this connection Melanie Klein's concept (1932) of the 'good' and 'bad' mother.

8

About Losing and Being Lost (1967 [1953])

This is an important paper because it illustrates in the clearest possible fashion the emphasis laid on object relationships in classical (Freud's) psychoanalysis. Losing and forgetting are part of the psychopathology of everyday life. Freud explained these phenomena as the effects of repressed (unwelcome) ideas. While the conflict theory of forgetting and losing is often valid, these phenomena may be the outcome of disturbed object relationships. Anna Freud illustrates the latter with many examples of how the lost item or possession represents the self or part of it. She draws attention to children described by teachers as 'chronic losers'. These children invariably feel unloved at home or are, in fact, unloved. They forget, just as they believe themselves to be forgotten: 'they live out a double identification, passively with the lost objects which symbolize themselves, actively with the parents whom they experience to be as neglectful, indifferent, and unconcerned toward them as they themselves are toward their possessions.'

The paper concludes with a section on the lost object in dreams and in folklore.

'About Losing and Being Lost' is based on a paper read at the 18th Congress of the International Psycho-Analytical Association. The present version was written in 1966 and first published in *The Psychoanalytic Study of the Child*, 22: 9–19, 1967. It was simultaneously published in German: 'Über Verlieren und Ver-lorengehen', in *Hoofdstukken uit de Hedendaagse Psychoanalyse*, P.J. van der Leeuw, E.C.M. Fryling-Schreuder and P.C. Kuiper, eds. Arnhem: Van Loghum Slaterus, 1967, pp. 91–100.

Interpretations of Losing: Dynamic and Libido-Economic

Losing and mislaying objects came under analytic scrutiny at an early date. In 1901, in *The Psychopathology of Everyday Life*, we find it mentioned for the first time, and, further, more explicitly in the chapters on 'Parapraxes' of the *Introductory Lectures* (1916–1917). In both publications, Freud explained losing, as he did the other common errors such as forgetting, slips of the tongue, etc., on the basis of a conscious intention being interfered with by a wish which arises from the unconscious. In the case of losing this means that we have the unconscious desire to discard something which consciously we wish to retain. The unconscious tendency makes use of some favorable moment (when our attention is turned elsewhere, when we are tired, preoccupied, etc.) to have its own way. We then lose the object in question; i.e., we throw it away, or put it away, without realizing that we are doing so.

A number of examples of such happenings were collected in *The Psychopathology of Everyday Life,* aiming, above all, 'at paving the way for the necessary assumption of *unconscious yet operative* mental processes' (p. 272, n.).

For our metapsychological thinking, on the other hand, it is significant that Freud's interest in the phenomenon of losing went, as early as 1916, beyond the explanation of two forces interfering with each other as well as beyond the need to prove the existence of an operative unconscious. In the *Introductory Lectures* he wrote: '*Losing and mislaying* are of particular interest to us owing to the many meanings they may have – owing, that is, to the multiplicity of purposes which can be served by these parapraxes. All cases have in common the fact that there was a wish to lose something; they differ in the basis and aim of that wish. We lose a thing when it is worn out, when we intend to replace it by a better one, when we no longer like it, when it originates from someone with whom we are no longer on good terms or when we acquired it in circumstances we no longer want to recall ... The preserving of *things* may be subject to the same influences as that of children' (p. 77).

Insight into 'the basis and aim' of losing led here from the dynamics of mental life to the libido-economic aspects of it, with which we are all equally familiar. As Freud did then, we now take it for granted that our material possessions are cathected with libido (and aggression) and that retaining, mislaying, losing and rediscovering them are caused by either quantitative or qualitative alterations in this cathexis.

Our material possessions may represent for us parts of our own body, in which case we cathect them narcissistically; or they may represent human love objects, in which case they are cathected with object libido. We increase or decrease cathexis, or change it from positive to negative, from libido to aggression, according to the vicissitudes of our attitude to our own body on the one hand and to the objects in the external world on the other hand.

So far as the symbolic links between body parts and material possessions are concerned, these have been studied most closely with regard to the anal product. Here psychoanalysis has established a direct line leading from the high value attributed to excrements in infantile life to the value attributed to money in adulthood. Many attitudes of the adult which would otherwise remain puzzling are open to explanation on this basis, such as the urge to collect, miserliness, avariciousness, or their opposites.

A new chapter in the understanding of losing and retaining was opened when analysts began to concentrate their attentions on the events of the first year of life and the earliest interactions between infants and their mothers. There is general agreement that the infant directs value cathexis to any object from which satisfaction can be obtained, irrespective of the object being animate or inanimate, part of the internal or of the external world: as observation confirms, the mother's breast, the bottle, the child's own fingers, etc., are periodically searched for, found, lost, recaptured, etc.

On the other hand, it depends on the individual author's theoretical orientation whether the dawning differentiation between the self and the object world is conceived of as happening very early or comparatively late in infancy; and whether inanimate objects (such as the bottle) and body parts (such as fingers) are seen as objects in their own right or merely as derivatives of and substitutes for the mother. It seems to me that any decision in this respect (or the continuing indecision) needs to be based on the fact that we deal here with undifferentiated and unstructured human beings; that this is a period of life when there are no whole objects, only part objects; when there are only anaclitic, i.e., need-satisfying, object relationships; and when even external objects are included in the child's internal, narcissistic milieu.[1]

We are greatly helped in our dilemma by the concept of the 'transitional object' as it was introduced by D. W. Winnicott (1953). Winnicott traced the line which connects the mother's breast as a source of pleasure with the thumb which is sucked and the blanket, pillow, or soft, cuddly toy which is played with. He showed convincingly that all these early objects are cathected doubly, narcissistically and with object love, and that this enables the child to transfer his attachments gradually from the cathected figure of the mother to the external world in general.

Thus, human beings are flexible where their attachments are concerned. Narcissistically colored ties alternate with object ties proper; libidinal with aggressive cathexis; animate with inanimate objects. This creates multiple possibilities for discharge, which remain important far beyond childhood. Children who are frustrated, dissatisfied, jealous, etc., but unable for internal or external reasons to react aggressively to their parents, may turn this same aggression toward material things and become destructive of their toys, their clothing, the furniture, etc. In a temper or rage individuals of all ages may choose as their point of attack either their own bodies, or other people, or any objects within their reach. Children in separation distress may cling to any of their possessions which they invest, for the time being, with cathexis displaced from their human objects. When we analyze adolescents who pass through a phase of withdrawal from the object world, or who suffer from the aftereffects of an unhappy love affair, we often find that they are obsessed with holding on to what is left, in the form of compiling lists either of their remaining friends or of their valuables. People with obsessional characters are well known to displace the reaction formations against their hostile impulses and death wishes from human beings to material things, thereby becoming unable to discard anything, down to the most valueless, useless, and superfluous matters.

There is no doubt in our mind that the libido-economic aspects of the interpretation of losing add considerably to its dynamic explanation and that, on this basis, we advance from the mere understanding of phenomena such as losing, mislaying, discarding, destroying, recapturing, etc., to some theory concerning the attitude of human beings to their possessions. We begin to understand, further, why losing things is the exception rather than the rule, in spite of the multitude of items which we own. Obviously, it is the distribution of our libido between the animate and the inanimate world and the resulting positive cathexis of material objects which assures that our possessions remain tied to us, or, rather, we to them.

We understand further, why some people become chronic losers. If their libidinal processes are seriously altered, they cease to have a hold on their possessions, without the latter having changed for the worse in any respect. We see this happen, for example, in individuals whose whole interest is concentrated on one particular subject (such as a scientific inquiry) and who become 'abstracted' as a result; or in states of high emotional involvement such as mourning, or being in love, when cathexis is similarly sent out in one particular direction only and withdrawn from other uses.

Certain other phenomena may be mentioned in the same connection. We are familiar with the *fear of impoverishment* which appears as a symptom in a number of pre-psychotic states, and we understand it, on the basis of the foregoing, as the result of the individual's libidinal withdrawal from his material possessions and the ensuing fear of losing hold of them; obviously, this is not unlike the graver psychotic delusion of the destruction of the world, which we interpret as a reflection in consciousness of the withdrawal of libido from the object world in general. We know severe states of *negativism* in which the individual withdraws cathexis not only from material possessions but also from his body, which as a consequence is utterly neglected (dirty, unkempt, starved, etc.). We are familiar, further, with the concept of *voluntary poverty*, an attitude which is practiced by many religious, political, and social bodies where it is meant to assure that their members will cathect only ideas and not waste cathexis on material matters. Also, we expect poets, writers, members of the medical profession, and others to be '*high-minded*,' i.e., at least to be partially uninterested in material reward.

Some Reactions to Losing: Identification with the Lost Object

We take it for granted that we feel unhappy and miserable after losing one of our possessions, even if these moods are hardly justified by the circumstances themselves.

We feel *deprived*, in the first instance, not necessarily because of the objective value of the lost item but more frequently because of its subjective value, as representative of an important body part (penis symbol) or an important love object (the giver of it). On this basis we go through a period of detaching ourselves from it, almost as we do when *mourning* a dead person. Also we feel *guilty*, as if we had not lost the thing unintentionally but discarded it in full consciousness.

Nevertheless, this accumulation of castration distress, mourning, and guilt still does not suffice to explain all of the loser's distress. There are further elements involved which originate in deeper layers of the mind and become visible only where losing occurs either during an analysis, or at least in full view of an analyst. When this happens, we notice, first, that the loser seems to ascribe some independent action to the lost object. He can be heard to say not only, 'I have lost something, mislaid it, forgotten where I put it,' etc., but equally often: 'It got lost,' or 'It is gone,' or 'It has come back.' Obviously this signifies a displacement: the libidinal withdrawal responsible for the loss is shifted from the inner world of the loser to the item which has been lost, personifying the latter in the process. We notice, secondly, that the loser's emotions do not confine themselves to his own regrets about the loss, but extend to feelings which allegedly belong to the lost object. Here, projection has led to personification, which in its turn is followed by identification.[2]

I remember in this connection an early observation of my own which left me with a lasting impression of the processes concerned. The central figure of the incident was a young girl, an ardent mountaineer, whose walking trip had taken her high into the Alps. Resting near a waterfall, she had forgotten her cap in the camping area. The loss was insignificant in itself and did not seem to concern her much in the beginning. But this changed during the night which followed the excursion. Lying sleepless in her bed, she was suddenly compelled to imagine the lost cap, exposed and deserted in the dark solitude of the mountain scenery. The misery created by this picture became extreme and intolerable until she sobbed herself to sleep.

Identification of the loser with the lost object, as demonstrated by the above example, can be confirmed by us on the basis of numerous other observations. In child analysis we are struck by the fact that certain children – especially those with increased ambivalence and strong defenses against aggression – cling to their possessions, not only to collect and amass them, but because they fear to hurt the imagined feelings of the toys if they consent to their being given or thrown away. There are many dolls and teddy bears which are preserved in this manner until adolescence or even adulthood, not because their owners have remained 'childish' in this respect, but because they have remained too identified with these former transitional objects to withdraw feeling from them altogether.

Such displacements of affect from the loser to the lost become still more obvious when the lost object is a human one. In our work with separated children during wartime, we had many occasions to observe those who experienced not their own, very real separation distress but the imagined distress, loneliness, and longing of the mother whom they had left behind. 'I have to telephone my Mummy, she will feel so lonely,' was a frequent wish, expressed especially in the evening. Children who went home on short holidays from the residential institution used to try and diminish the imagined distress of their nurses by promising to 'send them parcels,' as their mothers did to comfort them when they left home. Nursery schoolchildren often ask their teacher after a weekend or holiday what she has done 'all alone,' whether she has 'missed' them. Patients in analysis confirm this attitude in the transference when they experience the imagined distress of the analyst in place of their own during a break in treatment.

It is not difficult in analysis to understand and interpret such displacements of feeling. When traced back to their source, they reveal themselves as based on early childhood events when the loser was himself 'lost,' that is, felt deserted, rejected, alone, and experienced in full force as his own all the painful emotions which he later ascribes to the objects lost by him.

The Child as Lost Object and as Loser of Objects

We remember the hint given by Freud in the *Introductory Lectures* with regard to children, and we understand that their protection from danger, or exposure to danger, proceeds on lines similar to the preservation or losing of material things. The parents, as owners of the children, cathect them with libido or aggression. We assume that the younger the child, the greater is the part played by narcissistic libido in this respect; as the child grows older, he becomes increasingly part of his parents' object world, cathected with object libido proper. There is a gap in our theoretical understanding when we try to imagine the ways and means by which this cathexis, of whichever kind, reaches its object. We fall back here on the practical experience that children feel secure, happy, and content while they are loved by their parents, and that they become insecure, unhappy, and hurt in their narcissism if this love is withdrawn, or diminished, or changed into aggression.

As in the case of material objects, for a child to get lost is the exception rather than the rule, which is surprising in view of the lack of reality orientation in our toddlers and under-fives, and of the boisterousness and adventurous spirit of those who are slightly older. Here the children's urge to cling seems to unite with the parents' high valuation of their offspring and, combined, to set limits to the area in which the latter roam freely.

It is only when parental feelings are ineffective or too ambivalent, or when their aggression is more effective than their love, or when the mother's emotions are temporarily engaged elsewhere, that children not only feel lost but, in fact, get lost. This usually happens under conditions which make rationalization easy, but which, on the other hand, are much too common to explain the specific event: such as crowds, a full departmental store, etc. It is interesting that children usually do not blame themselves for getting lost but instead blame the mother who lost them. An example of this was a little boy, lost in a store, who, after being reunited with his mother, accused her tearfully, 'You losted me!' (not 'I lost you!').

Matters are different when the looseness and breaking of the emotional tie originate with the child, not with the parents. We know children of all ages whose capacity for object love is underdeveloped for either internal or external, innate or acquired reasons. This defect may become manifest in the symptoms of early wandering, frequently getting lost, truanting, etc. In these instances, the children do not accuse other people, nor do they feel guilty themselves.

It is a fact, well known especially to schoolteachers, that children become chronic losers if they feel unloved at home or are unloved in fact. They do not turn to possessions to compensate themselves for what they miss in their lives. On the contrary, they are singularly unable to establish or to retain ownership. They come to school without the necessary implements, and they forget in the classroom the items which should be taken home. They forget and mislay their money, their caps and articles of clothing wherever they are. We feel tempted to say that not only are their possessions strewn around, but they actually run away from the children. What we discover in their analyses first is an inability to cathect the inanimate, owing to the general damage done to their capacity for involvement with objects; next, that they direct to their possessions the whole hostility aroused by the frustrations and disappointments imposed on them by their parents. It is only behind these fairly obvious causes that a further, even more far-reaching motive comes into view: by being chronic losers, they live out a double identification, passively with the lost objects which symbolise themselves, actively with the parents whom they experience to be as neglectful, indifferent, and unconcerned toward them as they themselves are toward their possessions.

The Lost Object in Dreams and Folklore

The significance of losing some items which may be of some value in itself differs greatly from that of losing through death a person who plays an important role in our lives such as a parent, a marital partner, a child. Such differences in the magnitude of an event may altogether change the quality of the accompanying emotions, and therefore should not be taken lightly. Nevertheless, certain similarities or even identities between the two types of happenings are open to view in the specific case of losing.

We assume that the process of mourning for a loved person will last while the emotions of the mourner are concentrated on the loss, as well as on the necessity of withdrawing feeling from the inner image of the dead. So far as this means withdrawing from the external world, the task of mourning interferes with life itself. So far as it signifies a reunion with the dead by means of reviving and reliving the memories concerning him, mourning is known to be as absorbing and fulfilling as it is painful.

In analysis, we have occasion to notice that in some persons the later stages of mourning are characterized by a series of typical dreams, the latent content of which is fairly easy to interpret. In these dreams the dead person appears, either manifestly or slightly disguised, and makes every effort to bring himself to the notice of the survivor. He searches for him, or pleads with him, or beseeches him to come and stay; he expresses longing, or complains about being alone and deserted. The dreamer feels in the grip of conflicting emotions and alternates between pure joy about the reunion and remorse and guilt for having stayed away from the dead, neglected him, etc. He wakes up, usually, with anxiety and finds it difficult to realize that the whole experience has 'only been a dream.'

It seems to me that the latent content of these dreams has much in common with the mental processes ascribed above to the person who loses a material possession. Here too a part is played by the interference of two opposite tendencies with each other, the simultaneous wishes to retain and to discard being replaced in this instance by the simultaneous urges to remain loyal to the dead and to turn toward new ties with the living. Here, as in the former examples, the survivor's desolation, longing, loneliness are not acknowledged as his own feelings, but displaced onto the dream image of the dead, where they are experienced in identification with the dead. As above, it can be shown here, when the dream is submitted to interpretation, that identification with the 'lost object,' the deserted person, is derived from specific infantile experiences when the dreamer, as a child, felt unloved, rejected, and neglected.

There is no doubt of the dream wish here, of course, since its fulfill-ment is brought about openly by the reappearance of the dead and accompanied by the positive emotions which characterized the lost relationship. The painful accusations, regrets, etc., in the manifest content correspond to the dreamer's realization that he is on the point of becoming disloyal to the dead and his guilt about this. The anxiety which interrupts the dream corresponds to the defense against the opposite wish: to yield to the dream image's invitation, turn away from life altogether, and follow the lost object into death.

Loyalty conflicts with regard to the dead are frequent motifs, not only in dream life but equally in fairy tales, myths, and folklore in general.

Many popular beliefs, for example, are concerned with the figure of a dead person who reappears, usually at nighttime, and beckons to the living. Such figures are invested with dread, obviously to the degree to which the survivor has to ward off the wish to accept the invitation.

Further, we are familiar with innumerable ghost stories, which have a different origin. In these tales, the spirit of the dead person appears in the role of avenger, threatening punishment. Analytic interpretation suggests that tales of this kind are based on the survivor's ambivalence and that such large measures of anxiety are aroused by them because this corresponds to the intensity of the warded-off death wishes which had been directed toward the former love object in life.

The connection is still closer between our subject of losing and another common myth, that of the 'lost,' 'poor,' or 'wandering' soul. Such lost souls are depicted as being unable to rest in their burial places and condemned instead to wander aimlessly, especially at nighttime, when they moan, sigh, and complain, and beseech the living to help them find release. Some act — often left indefinite — needs to be performed to bring this about.

'Lost souls' are pitiable rather than threatening and uncanny rather than outrightly frightening. They are 'poor,' since they symbolize the emotional impoverishment felt by the survivor. They are 'lost' as symbols of object loss. That they are compelled to 'wander' reflects the wandering and searching of the survivor's libidinal strivings which have been rendered aimless, i.e., deprived of their former goal. And, finally, we understand that their 'eternal rest' can be achieved only after the survivors have performed the difficult task of dealing with their bereavement and of detaching their hopes, demands, and expectations from the image of the dead.

Notes

1. According to a term introduced by W. Hoffer (1952).
2. 'Projective identification,' a concept introduced by Melanie Klein (1932).

9

The Symptomatology of Childhood: A Preliminary Attempt at Classification (1970)

The purpose of this paper is to bridge the gap between the classification of symptoms and diagnostic entities on the one side and the hypothesized, unconscious mental processes believed to account for them on the other. The psychoanalytic investigation and treatment of abnormal mental states has shown that the presence of identical symptoms in different patients may have a different psychopathology. Equally, dissimilar symptoms may spring from an identical psychopathology.

Anna Freud differentiates between 'symptomatology proper' and 'other signs of disturbance and other reasons for a child's clinical referral'. Under each heading she illustrates the connections between the 'symptoms proper' and their unconscious determinants. These may spring from a lack of differentiation between somatic and psychological processes; from compromise formation between id and ego, as in neurotic symptomatology; as a result of an eruption of id derivatives into the ego, as in the psychoses and from other changes in the mental economics of the libido and aggression; and lastly, symptoms can result from undefended regressions and from organic causes.

The 'other signs of disturbance' which lead to referral are understood by Anna Freud as being due to interferences with the normal processes of mental development. This developmental approach takes account of the quantitative differences that exist between the mental lives of the healthy and of the abnormal child. She details the chronology of fears and anxieties and their manifest and latent content. She reviews the delays and failures of development which lead to difficulties in schooling and social adaptation.

Important as a child's symptoms and aberrant behaviour may be, the aim of the psychoanalytic diagnostician is to try to provide an assessment of the child's developmental status and total personality.

'The Symptomatology of Childhood: A Preliminary Attempt at Classification' was first presented to the Western New England

Psychoanalytic Society, New Haven, Conn., on 18 April 1970. It was first published in *The Psychoanalytic Study of the Child*, 25: 19–41, 1970.

The Misleading Quality of Manifest Symptomatology

Analysts have always been proud of the distinction that theirs is a causal therapy, aiming directly at the conflicts and stresses which are hidden in the patients' personalities and underlie their symptomatology. Inevitably, with this approach they find themselves at cross-purposes with many of the adult neurotics under analysis who are intent only on being relieved of the suffering caused by painful anxieties and crippling obsessions, and who regard these as the only logical starting point for investigation; or with the parents of child patients who are concerned only with removing the disturbing manifestations in the child and completely disregard the pathological turn in the child's development which is revealed by the disturbances that trouble them.

Naturally, neither the adult neurotics themselves nor the parents of these endangered children possess the analyst's knowledge of the deceiving nature of overt symptomatology. They lack the experience of how quickly anxieties can be shifted from one apparently all-important object to another; or how easily one particular compulsion can be substituted for by a different one. Therefore, they cannot appreciate that symptoms are no more than symbols, to be taken merely as indications that some mental turmoil is taking place in the lower strata of the mind. Many symptoms, important and unassailable as they seem if untreated, give way fairly easily to many types of therapy. But if they are removed by measures which do not reach to their roots, their place may be taken almost instantaneously by other pathological formations which, although overtly different, express the same latent content and may be no less aggravating for the individual's life.

On the other hand, symptoms are negligible in the analyst's view only for the purposes of the technique of therapy; in their eyes, too, symptoms have retained full significance so far as diagnostic classification is concerned. Whether a patient is assessed as a hysteric or phobic subject, as suffering from an obsessional neurosis or a paranoid state, is decided wholly on the basis of his manifest symptomatology, i.e., on the overt evidence of bodily conversions, anxiety attacks, avoidance mechanisms, compulsive acts, ruminations, projections, etc.

There is an incongruity here between the analyst's therapeutic thinking, which is metapsychological, i.e., directed toward the dynamic, economic, genetic, and structural aspects of psychic functioning, and his thinking as a diagnostician, which proceeds on the basis of concepts and categories which are descriptive.[1] The difference between these viewpoints is so fundamental that it has caused many analysts to withdraw their interest altogether from diagnostic assessment as from an area which is neither essential nor very significant for their field of work, and has caused some others to regard all their patients' abnormalities as mere variations of the many vagaries and complexities of human behavior.[2]

But before subscribing to a diagnostic nihilism of this extreme kind, the attempt seems worthwhile to bridge the gap between the two contrasting approaches and to use the vast array of overt symptoms themselves for the purpose of forging links between them. There is no reason, after all, why the very classification of symptomatology should not go beyond enumeration and description and why probing into dynamic clashes and genetic antecedents should be excluded from it, to be reserved for scrutiny within the analytic procedure. It is inevitable, of course, that such a different mode of classification will sacrifice the neatness and order of any system based on phenomenology.

It is only to be expected that in many instances there will be no one-to-one correlation between underlying unconscious constellation and manifest symptom. The former, as shown in Part I of this paper, can give rise to a variety of manifestations; the latter, as demonstrated in Part II, are the result of a variety of causes. Far from this being confusing for the analyst, it can only help to sharpen his diagnostic acumen.

When one is dealing with the psychopathology of childhood, a descriptive survey of symptomatology is even less rewarding. As is well known, in the immature personality isolated symptoms are no reliable guide to any specific type of underlying pathology, nor are they a measure of its severity. Symptoms may be no more than the child's answer to some developmental stress and as such transitory, i.e., liable to pass away together with the maturational phase which has given rise to them. Or symptoms may represent a permanent countercathexis against some threatening drive derivative and as such be crippling to further development. Or symptoms, though pathological in origin, may nevertheless be ego-syntonic, and merged with the structure of the child's personality to a degree which makes it difficult to distinguish between such manifestations as outward evidence of ongoing pathological involvement or as more or less normal, stable features of the individual's character. There is no doubt that in any classification system based on phenomenology, these widely different classes of symptom appear as if on a par.

Moreover, if we scrutinize what children's clinics list under the heading of 'referral symptoms,' we feel doubtful whether in all instances these manifestations deserve to be classified as symptomatology, or whether the meaning of the term 'symptom' is not extended here beyond its proper use. What is grouped together in such surveys are, on the one hand, the true signs or residues of present or past pathological processes; on the other hand, such complaints by parents and disruptions of the child's life as, for example, multiplicity of fears; disturbances of intake, digestion, and elimination; sleep, respiratory or skin disturbances; aches and pains, motor disturbances; unusual sexual behavior; self-injurious acts and habits; disturbances of mood, affect, and object relatedness; failure of learning processes and/or poor quality of other ego functions; behavior disorders including antisocial reactions; moral indifference; failures of adaptation; failure to comply with parental demands or to fulfill parental expectation in general; etc.

Although an enumeration of this kind promises a first orientation in the field, and seems to satisfy the clinicians' immediate need at the stage of intake of cases, what it does, in fact, is to defeat its own purpose. By remaining strictly on the descriptive level, regardless of genetic roots, dynamic, structural, and economic complications, such an initial approach discourages analytic thinking and blocks the road to diagnostic assessment proper instead of facilitating it. Last but not least, it provides no clue for the diagnostician with regard to the choice of adequate therapeutic method.[3]

There is no warning implied in such a phenomenological survey that many of the items listed in it may belong genetically to any one of two, three, or more analytic categories. A *behavior disorder,* such as lying, for example, may be rooted in the child's stage of ego development, i.e., express the immature individual's inability to distinguish between reality and fantasy, or may signify a delay in acquiring and perfecting this important ego function. But, equally, lying may betray the level and quality of the child's object relations and express his fear of punishment and loss of love. As fantasy lying, it may be evident of persistent denial of unpalatable realities, with the function of reality testing fundamentally intact. As a feature of the child's character, it may denote weakness or failure of superego function.[4]

Disturbance of elimination such as extreme withholding of feces may have its roots in a very early vulnerability of the digestive system (i.e., psychosomatic); or it may be symbolic of the child's imitation of and identification with a pregnant mother (hysterical); or it may signify his revolt against inappropriate forms of toilet training (behavioral); or it may express phallic sexual needs and fantasies on a regressed anal level (obsessional).

Similarly, *enuresis* may be the sign either of simple failure of control in a generally impulsive personality structure,[5] or a highly complex reaction on the level of penis envy and castration anxiety.

Learning failures may point to developmental arrest or, conversely, to blocking and inhibitions interfering with basically intact intellectual functions.

Antisocial reactions, such as aggressive outbursts, may be the mark of defusion or insufficient fusion between libido and aggression; or of insufficient control of drives in an impulsive character; or of a violent defensive reaction against underlying passive-feminine leanings in boys striving overtly for masculinity.

In short, manifest symptoms may be identical so far as their appearance is concerned, but may differ widely in respect to latent meaning and pathological significance. According to the latter, they may require very different types of therapeutic handling.

Ideally, the solution for the analytic clinician in the children's field is a classification of symptoms which, on the one hand, embodies consideration of the various metapsychological aspects, while, on the other hand, maintains links with and pointers to the descriptive diagnostic categories as they are in common use. It is obvious, nevertheless, that no complex system of this kind will lend itself to the quick, almost automatic application to which diagnosticians are used so long as they remain within the framework of phenomenology. What is needed to make such a new classification of symptomatology profitable is, already at the diagnostic stage, a thorough investigation of the child's personality which makes it possible to pinpoint each symptom's relevance with regard to developmental level, structure, dynamic significance, etc.

I. Symptomatology Proper

As indicated above, for a first attempt of ordering the clinical material, it seems useful to separate symptoms, in the narrow sense of the term, from other signs of disturbance and other reasons for a child's referral for diagnosis and treatment. In this restricted field it becomes more possible to survey the relevant range of pathological processes and to correlate them with the various forms of mental illnesses which correspond to them.

1. Symptoms Resulting from Initial Nondifferentiation between Somatic and Psychological Processes: Psychosomatics

At the beginning of life, before somatic and psychological processes are separated off from each other, bodily excitations such as hunger, cold, pain, etc., are discharged as easily via mental pathways in the form of unpleasure, anxiety, anger, rage, as mental upsets of any kind are discharged via disturbances of the body surface, of intake, digestion, elimination, breathing, etc. Such 'psychosomatic' reactions are developmentally determined at this time of life. It is important for later events which particular bodily outlets are given preference by the individual since this choice gives rise to increased sensitivity and vulnerability in the organ system concerned, i.e., the skin, the respiratory system, the intestinal system, the sleep rhythm, etc.

Normally, this easy access from the mind to body (and vice versa) diminishes with advancing ego development and the opening up of new, purely mental pathways of discharge by means of action, thought, speech. Where it remains more than usually open, on the other hand, it accounts directly for the range of *psychosomatic symptomatology*, i.e., for *asthma, eczema, ulcerative colitis, headaches, migraine*, etc.

It is also responsible for the creation of the so-called 'somatic compliance' which, in later and more complex hysterical symptom formation, facilitates the conversion of mental processes into physical manifestations with symbolic meaning.

2. Symptoms Resulting from Compromise Formations between Id and Ego: Neurotic Symptomatology

Since basic psychoanalytic training takes place in the area of theory and therapy of the neuroses, analysts feel most knowledgeable about the specific structure of neurotic symptomatology. In fact, so far as the neuroses are concerned, the term 'symptom' has become synonymous with the conception of the ego acting as intermediary and finding solutions for the clashes between drive derivatives on the one hand and other, rational or moral, claims of the individual on the other hand. The complex route of symptom formation along a line of danger-anxiety-regression-defense-compromise has become familiar.

The resulting symptomatic structures may prove ego-dystonic and continue to produce mental pain and discomfort; or they may be accepted as ego-syntonic and become part of the individual's character. The latter outcome depends largely on economic factors, i.e., on the varying degrees to which elements from id, ego, and superego sides are embodied in the final symptomatic result. It depends also on the ego's willingness to become distorted itself by accommodating the pathological manifestation within its structure. This last-mentioned solution, not to treat the symptoms as a foreign body, is one often adopted by children.

Since compromise formations of this kind depend for their existence on established boundaries between id and ego, unconscious and conscious, we do not expect to find neurotic symptoms in the unstructured personality, i.e., in early infancy. Neurotic symptom formation waits until the ego has divided itself off from the id, but does not need to wait until ego and superego also have become two independent agencies. The first id-ego conflicts, and with them the first neurotic symptoms as conflict solutions, are produced with the ego under pressure from the environment, i.e., threatened not by guilt feelings arising internally from the superego but by dangers arising from the object world such as loss of love, rejection, punishment.

The neurotic manifestations of this phase are *hysterical* in nature so far as the body areas involved have oral or oral-aggressive value and the symptom implies a primitive defense against these drive representatives (*affection of single limbs, motor disturbances, aches and pains, food fads and avoidances, vomiting*). They are *obsessional* in nature so far as they defend against anal-sadistic strivings (first appearance of *compulsive cleanliness, orderliness, repetitiveness, avoidance of touch*).

With the emergence and dissolution of the phallic-oedipal strivings and the superego as an independent source of guilt these isolated symptoms become organized into the syndromes which form the familiar infantile neuroses, i.e., the full-blown *phobias* (of animals, of separation, of doctor, dentist, of the lavatory, of school, etc.) as well as the true *obsessional neuroses*, complete with *doubting, repeating, rituals,* bedtime *ceremonials, ruminations, compulsive actions*. Crippling *inhibitions, ego restrictions*, and *self-injurious tendencies* appear as character defenses against aggression at this time.

3. Symptoms Resulting from the Irruption of Id Derivatives into the Ego

Neurotic symptomatology comes about only where the border between id and ego is intact. This may be lacking for a variety of reasons: the ego may be constitutionally weak; or the id strivings may be constitutionally increased in intensity; damage may have been done to the ego through traumatic events which have put it out of action; or through phase-determined alterations of the inner equilibrium. In any case, the result will be failure to control id content and the entrance of id elements into the ego organization, with disruptive consequences for the latter.

Where the irrupting elements are part of primary process functioning and take the place of the rational secondary process thinking which is characteristic for the ego otherwise, the corresponding manifest symptoms such as *disturbances of thought and language, misidentifications, delusions*, etc., are significant for the differential diagnosis between neurosis and psychosis; if only partially in evidence, they are a hallmark of the borderline states between the two diagnostic categories.

Where the irrupting elements are from the area of the drives, the resulting symptoms consist of the *undefended* (or unsuccessfully defended) *acting out of drive derivatives* with disregard for reality considerations which is characteristic for certain types of delinquency and criminality.

The combination of both leakages from the id produces those ominous types of abnormal behavior which, on the one hand, carry the individual beyond the confines of what is legally permissible and, on the other hand, characterize him as mentally ill and for this reason absolved from responsibility for his actions.

4. Symptoms Resulting from Changes in the Libido Economy or Direction of Cathexis

Although all symptom formation implies pathological upsets to the dynamics and structural aspects of the personality, these may be secondary to alterations in the economy of the libido and the direction of its employment.

Where, for example, the narcissistic cathexis of the self is increased unduly, the corresponding symptomatic results are *egotism, self-centeredness, overvaluation* of the self, in extreme cases *megalomania*. Where such cathexis is decreased unduly, the symptoms are *bodily neglect, self-derogation, inferiority feelings, depressive states, depersonalization* (in childhood).

Direction of cathexis may be altered in three respects with corresponding symptomatology. Narcissistic libido may move from the individual's mind to his body, where the increased cathexis of specific body parts creates *hypochondriacal* symptoms. Object libido may be withdrawn from the external world, changed into narcissistic libido, and employed wholly in cathexis of the self. Or, conversely, all narcissistic libido may be added to the existing object libido and become concentrated on an external love object with consequences for its overvaluation; in extreme cases, for complete *emotional surrender* to it.

5. Symptoms Resulting from Changes in the Quality or Direction of Aggression

What is significant for symptomatology in this respect are the changes in intensity as well as the frequent changes in aim direction, from mind to body, from self to object, and vice versa.

The former, the quantitative changes, are brought about mainly by the vagaries within the defense organization, in childhood by the varying quality of the defense mechanisms which are employed, from crudely primitive to highly sophisticated. These decide about the availability or non-availability of the necessary aggressive contributions to ego functioning and to sublimations. Some of the resulting symptomatic manifestations are *inhibitions* and *failure* in play, learning, and work.

The type of defense used against aggression is also responsible for the swings between *self-injurious behavior*, which corresponds to aggression turned against the self, and violent *aggressive-destructive outbursts* against animate and inanimate objects in the environment.

6. Symptoms Resulting from Undefended Regressions

In our work with children we have become alerted to a type of pathological manifestation which equals a prestage of neurotic symptom formation, but remains abortive so far as the infantile neuroses are concerned. Its point of origin is the phallic phase, its precipitating cause is danger and anxiety arising from the oedipus and castration complexes, followed by regression to oral and anal fixation points.

While in neurotic symptom formation such regressions are rejected by the ego and defended against, in these cases they are accepted and treated as ego-syntonic; i.e., they do not give rise to further conflict. The result is a lowering of all aspects of the personality (drive activity as well as ego functioning). The clinical pictures which correspond to this are *infantilism* and a form of *pseudodebility*, accompanied by behavioral symptoms such as *whining, clinging*, prolonged *dependency, passive-feminine traits* in boys, *inefficiency*, etc.

7. Symptoms Resulting from Organic Causes

The foregoing enumeration leaves to the last those disturbances of psychic function which have an organic origin such as brain damage due to prenatal influences or birth injury or to later inflammatory processes or to traumatic accidents. A whole range of symptoms is attributable to these causes such as a *delay in developmental milestones*, *difficulties in locomotion*, difficulties with *speech, poor* quality of *intellectual functions, interference with concentration, flatness or lability of affect, distractability*, etc. Many of these symptoms bear a close resemblance to the results of inhibitions, compromise formations, or any other of the categories described above, and the correct diagnosis is difficult in those cases where the neurological tests prove inconclusive. Doubtless, mistakes in differential diagnosis occur here in both directions, either mental or organic damage being discounted unjustifiably, or a combination between both factors being overlooked.

What should also be added here are those symptomatic manifestations or deviations from the norm which are the direct or indirect consequence of physical handicaps, whether inborn or acquired ones. It is well known by now that where vision is missing, ego development is thrown into confusion, the balance between autoerotism and object relatedness disturbed, aggression inhibited, passivity enhanced, etc. Where hearing is absent or grossly defective, not only speech development but secondary process thinking and, with it, higher development of the personality are interfered with. Missing limbs, spasticity bring with them their own psychopathology which needs to be explored further.

II. Other Signs of Disturbance and Other Reasons for a Child's Clinical Referral

As discussed before, not all the manifestations which lead to a child's clinical examination are evidence of true pathology, nor do they all form part of recognized clinical pictures. There are other disturbances, upsets, and malfunctions, and, consequently, other reasons for referral. What they all have in common is that they represent interferences with normal processes, with adequate growth and development, with reasonable behavior, with contentment and enjoyment of life, with adaptation to environmental conditions and requirements. Since the causes for them are diffuse, and the same overt manifestation may be due to a variety of underlying constellations, the attempt seems justified to approach their classification from a different angle. The method adopted before consisted of following certain psychic processes ongoing in the depth to their various expressions on the surface of the mind. The procedure applied to what follows is the opposite one, namely, to start out from the surface signs of disturbance and, from there, to trace back the links to whichever upheaval, involvement or failure may be responsible for them.

1. The Fears and Anxieties

The mere number of children who are referred to clinics with fears and anxieties of all kinds and intensities justifies the attempt to classify these manifestations as such, i.e., apart from the active role which they play in the formation of a variety of clinical syndromes.

It is well known to analysts, of course, that anxiety, experienced by the ego, is a regular accompaniment to development in childhood, occasioned on the one hand by the helplessness of the immature being, on the other hand by the structuralization, higher development, and the resultant rising tension between the inner agencies. Its absence rather than its presence in the picture is considered an ominous sign. Nevertheless, even although anxiety is normal and the disturbance in many instances no more than a quantitative exacerbation of expectable reactions, anxiety states remain one of the most common and potent causes of suffering in childhood.

To arrive at their understanding, these manifestations have to be viewed from a number of angles. For example, their classification can be, and has been, attempted from the *developmental* point of view, by creating a chronological sequence according to which the common fears and anxieties are allocated to the various instinctual phases in which they arise and, connected with these, the external or internal dangers toward which they are directed. Classification has also been carried out from the aspect of *dynamic* vicissitudes, i.e., from the side of the defenses employed to keep fear and anxiety in check, and the *economic* factors which determine the success or failure of these coping mechanisms. What has been done most frequently by analytic authors, without doubt, is to explore the role played by the various kinds of anxiety in *structural* conflict and the responsibility which has to be ascribed to them for the swings between mental health and illness, since it is at their instigation that the ego's defensive mechanisms and, following on them, the ego's compromises with the id are put into action.

Obviously, it is the diagnostician's task to explore each of these avenues in greater detail.

(i) The Chronology of Fears and Anxieties

Where the clinician arrives at ordering the child's manifest fears and anxieties according to the developmental stages in which they arise and according to the dangers represented by these stages, many of the quantitative increases in them can be understood as due to unsatisfied developmental needs or to unjustifiable developmental interferences (see Nagera, 1966).

The initial stages of ego development, in this view, become correlated with the so-called *archaic fears* of the infant. These are inevitable while the ego has no resources of its own to cope either with the massive stimuli which arrive from the environment or with the equally disturbing tensions in the inner world. These fears increase in intensity and range when a child's ego is unusually sensitive or when a child's mother is unusually unable to provide the comfort and reassurance to which the infant is entitled at this stage. Where ego development is slow, the archaic fears last beyond infancy. Their undue persistence and prominence can be taken as diagnostic indicators for retardation or arrest in the area of ego functioning.

The symbiotic stage, i.e., the phase of biological unity between infant and mother, is relevant for the arousal of *separation anxiety*, i.e., fear of object loss, whenever this unity is threatened. Separation anxiety becomes overwhelming if the infant experiences actual separations from the mother, or if in other ways the mother proves unreliable as a stable object. Separation anxiety can be prolonged unduly, which points diagnostically to fixation in the symbiotic phase or arrests in it.[6]

When the parental objects become representatives of the demand for drive control, the child's difficulty of complying with this arouses *fear of rejection* by the object and fear of loss of the object's love. As such, these fears are signs of beginning moral adjustment and positive prestages of superego development; their nonemergence points to developmental failure in these respects. They become excessive for environmental reasons if the parents commit errors in either the timing or the harshness of their demands. But even where no blame can be attached to the environment in this respect, oversensitivity of the ego or excessive dependency on being loved can bring about the same result for internal reasons.

The arrival of a boy in the phallic phase, which as such is a welcome event, commonly reveals itself at the same time in a heightened fear for the intactness of his sex organ, i.e., in *castration anxiety*. The frequent exacerbations of this correspond directly to the strivings of the oedipus complex and depend on the defenses and compromise formations which the ego employs to deal with them. Castration anxiety represents a specific threat for development owing to the drive regressions initiated by it and their further role for neurosis and character formation.

The child's first moves from family to community and his new dependency on the opinions of his peers give rise to an additional *fear*, that of *social disgrace*, which is especially experienced in school.

According to the individual child's structural development, i.e., with the establishment of the superego's independence and authority (whenever this happens), the advance from anxiety to *guilt* is made as the crowning step in this chronology of infantile fears.

Obviously, such a chronology of fears and anxieties is helpful as a diagnostic tool since observation of the presenting disturbance leads directly to the corresponding phase of development in which the child's mental upset is rooted. Nevertheless, it fails to serve the diagnostician in other respects, since it does not include an important anxiety which neither originates in any particular phase nor bears the characteristics of any one, but persists through the whole period of development and reappears at all times of later life, not for reasons of fixation or regression but whenever the inner structural balance is upset. This anxiety denotes the ego's concern for the intactness of its own organization, at whatever level; it is due to economic reasons, i.e., to the uneven distribution of energy between id and ego; and it gains in intensity whenever the strength of the drive derivatives increases or ego strength diminishes for some reason.

In contrast to other anxieties, this *fear of the id* is not favorably influenced by the lightening of external pressure. Much to the parents' disappointment, it is increased rather than decreased by excessive educational leniency or by educational nihilism.

When fear of the id is more than usually in evidence, it arouses the diagnostic suspicion of a borderline or prepsychotic state.

(ii) The Manifest and Latent Content of Fears and Anxieties

While in the childhood cases described, the affect of anxiety is manifest and brought directly to the clinician's notice, the latent meaning of the fear is obscured by the fact that almost any type of anxiety can find symbolic expression in almost any mental representation, or can remain free-floating and unattached. Nevertheless, in most instances it is possible to correlate fear and symbol as follows:

Archaic fears: of darkness, noise, strangers, solitude, etc.

separation anxiety: of annihilation, starvation, loneliness, helplessness, etc.

fear of loss of love: of punishment, rejection, desertion, earthquakes, thunderstorms, death, etc.

castration anxiety: of operation, mutilation, doctor, dentist, illness, poverty, robbers, witches, ghosts, etc.

On the whole, these symbols are also interchangeable, and by themselves, an insufficient guide to diagnosis.

(iii) Defense Against Anxiety, Absence of Defense, Its role Within the Structure

So far as a classification of the various fates of anxieties is concerned, the study of childhood cases is more productive than that of adult ones since the defensive moves against anxiety are more often incomplete, i.e., partly unsuccessful. This allows both sides to be visible on the conscious surface, on the one hand the manifest expression of the anxiety affect, on the other hand the ego's attempts to deal with the danger situations and their affective consequences by means of denial or avoidance, displacement or projection, repression, reaction formation, or any other available defense mechanism or defensive move, or a combination of several of them.

There is also the possibility for defense against anxiety to be lacking altogether, or to be wholly unsuccessful, in which case the affect reigns supreme in the form of *panic states* and full-blown *anxiety attacks*.[7] The occurrence of these is indicative that the child's ego has failed to acquire the important ability to reduce harmful panic anxiety to structurally useful signal anxiety, i.e., to the much smaller amount which is necessary to set defense in motion. Panics and anxiety attacks are not only extremely painful for the total personality of the child; they are, in fact, actually harmful for the ego which is swamped by them. Similar to true traumatic events, they temporarily put ego functioning out of action and thereby constitute a threat to the stability of the ego organization.

Classification of anxiety according to defense activity also provides clues for predicting the direction in which the child's further course is set: toward more or less normal adjustment; toward social or dissocial character formation; toward hysterical, or phobic, or obsessional or paranoid symptom formation or character development, etc.

2. The Delays or Failures in Development

It is well known by now that the developmental age of a child does not need to coincide with his chronological age and that fairly wide discrepancies in this respect are within the normal range. Children may be either fast or slow developers throughout. One also frequently sees that they change their rate of growing between one developmental phase and the succeeding one.

Nevertheless, a large number of children arrive in the clinic with the 'referral symptoms' of unsatisfactory development, which, on clinical examination, may be found to range from the merest delay to complete cessation of all forward movement on the lines of progress.

A child's failure to reach the expected level of growth may show up anywhere within the structure of his personality. It may concern the so-called milestones in the first year of life, i.e., the advances in motor development, the beginning of speech, etc. On the side of the drives it may concern a lagging behind on the prephallic libidinal and aggressive stages; in extreme instances, a failure to reach the phallic-oedipal level at all.

So far as the ego is concerned, arrest may reveal itself in the quality of object relatedness, for example, in the persistence of anaclitic relationships at a time of life when object constancy is to be expected; or in the retardation of functions such as control of motility, reality testing, memory, learning capacity which remain below par; or in the defense organization which may remain at a primitive level of functioning via somatization, denial, projection, avoidance, etc., instead of advancing to repression, reaction formations, and sublimations.

The superego may be retarded either with respect to its autonomy, or its effectiveness, or with regard to the quality of its content, i.e., the crudeness of the internalized commands and prohibitions.

Developmental irregularities and failures of this kind confront the clinician with many problems, foremost among them the need to differentiate between the causes for them. Retardation of milestones in the first year of life raises the suspicion of *organic* damage (see Part 1, 7). Delay in drive development either may be due to *constitutional* factors or may be determined *environmentally* by inadequate response from the parental objects. Ego retardation is frequently due to poor *endowment* but, as the study of many underprivileged children has revealed, equally often the consequence of lack of proper *environmental* stimulation. Arrested superego development may be part of general ego retardation (and share its causations); or it may be due to the lack of adequate objects in the child's *environment*; or to separations from them; or to *internal* failure to form relations to objects; or to the *qualities* of the parental personalities with whom the child identifies. Traumatic experiences may at any time endanger progress in any direction or, at worst, bring forward development to a complete standstill.

It remains as a task then to distinguish between these developmental delays and failures and another type of damage to development which, though superficially similar, is different in kind. While the former refer to expected developmental steps not being taken, the latter represents the undoing of developmental achievements after they have been acquired and is due to regressions and inhibitions, i.e., based on conflict (see Part 1, 2, neurotic symptomatology). Although the differential diagnosis here is important, and becomes all-important when the choice of therapy comes into question, confusion – especially between the effects of arrest and regression – is frequent.

There are few criteria to guide the clinician when, for example, he has to decide whether a boy has retreated from the phallic to the anal level (due to castration anxiety), or whether he has never reached the phallic phase; whether a child's superego has never proceeded beyond a primitive, crude level or whether it has become so at a later, more sophisticated stage of development, due to aggression turned inward and/or sexualization of its demands, etc. The most reliable hallmarks of neurosis are anxiety, guilt, and conflict, while in contrast to this the various types of developmental arrest may remain internally undisputed, especially in those cases where the arrest affects more than one sector of the personality. But this diagnostic indicator, too, cannot be trusted in all instances. Retarded children frequently react with anxiety and a semblance of guilt to the disapproval of their disappointed parents, while neurotic children are well able to deny conflict and guilt and thereby make them disappear from the manifest picture.

3. The School Failures

While all developmental failures are apt to arouse the parents' concern, usually they seek clinical advice most urgently when the child lags behind in age-adequate intellectual achievement and becomes a school failure. While the parents' concern exists regardless of the origin of the defect, in clinical examination it proves most important to distinguish between the different types of causation which can be subsumed under almost any of the different diagnostic categories discussed above.

Thus, learning difficulties, although they may be identical in their manifest appearance, may have to be allocated to any of the following categories:

> to *arrested development*, affecting either the person of the child as a whole, or the ego in general, or the ego's intellectual function in particular;

to *undefended ego regression*, either global or in particular to the intellect;

to *sexualization or aggressive symbolization*, either of the learning process as such, or of the particular subject to which the learning difficulty is attached;

to *defense* against the symbolic dangers implied, especially by means of inhibition and ego restriction;

to *symptom formation* of the neurotic types and its crippling effect on ego activity in general and sublimation in particular.

4. Failures in Social Adaptation

In this respect, as in the previous one, there is a marked discrepancy between the parents' concern which is easily alerted when a child fails to respond to moral standards, and their ignorance with regard to the causes which, either singly or combined, lead to asocial, or dissocial, or delinquent or even criminal behavior which is produced.

On the basis of reasoning which has gone before, failures in social adaptation can be seen in the following lights:

as the logical outcome of adverse environmental circumstances such as neglect, lack of stability in object relations, separations and other traumatic events, undue parental pressure, failure of parental guidance, etc.;

as the result of defects in the ego functions and the defense organization due to developmental arrests or neurotic regressions;

as the result of economic alterations in the balance between id and ego;

as the result of defects in the superego, caused by failures in object relatedness, identifications, internalizations, or by aggression used in its entirety against the external world instead of being in part at the disposal of the superego;

as the result of faulty ego ideals, due to deviant parental models for identification.

In fact, causation of social failure is extremely varied in its nature, ranging, as it does, from the purely environmental to the near-psychotic.

This has led to doubts among clinicians and some law teachers whether it is permissible at all to use the terms 'dissociality' or 'delinquency' as diagnostic labels, instead of merely speaking of dissocial or delinquent actions committed by individuals who may belong to any number of diagnostic categories.[8]

5. Aches and Pains

What remains are the multiple aches and pains of childhood for which no organic cause can be found in physical examination. They alarm the parents, and distress the child. Incidentally, they also lead to innumerable absences from school and, if massive, may constitute a serious threat to formal education. They are also the most frequent reason for a child's medical referral to a child guidance clinic or, in general, for a pediatrician's interest in the intricacies of child psychology.

According to the metapsychological classification of symptoms in Part 1 of this paper, the various aches and pains of nonorganic origin can be traced back to three or four of the categories enumerated there:

> to category 1, so far as they are the direct somatic expression of mental processes;
> to category 2, so far as the affected body parts are symbolic of mental content and as such involved in mental conflict;
> to categories 3 or 4, so far as the affection of the body part is due to changes of cathexis, either qualitative or quantitative.

The diffuse aches and pains of childhood can be characterized as either psychosomatic, or hysterical, or hypochondriacal. It hardly needs stressing that these different origins have a significant bearing on the evaluation of the presenting symptom, on the therapeutic approach to it, as well as on the prognosis with regard to its transience or permanency.

Conclusions

The Diagnostic Profile, as it is used in the Hampstead Child-Therapy Clinic at present, is intended to draw the diagnostician's contribution away from the child's pathology and to return it instead to an assessment of his developmental status and the picture of his total personality. The present attempt at classifying the symptomatology of childhood may serve to amend and amplify this procedure by returning to the symptoms themselves a measure of diagnostic significance. If symptoms are viewed merely as manifest phenomena, dealing with them remains arid so far as analytic interest is concerned. If the clinician is alerted to see opening up behind these the whole range of possible derivations, causations, and developmental affiliations, the field becomes fascinating, and scrutinizing a child's symptomatology becomes a truly analytic task.

Besides, so far as work with children is concerned, diagnostic assessment is more than a mere intellectual exercise for the clinician. It is, in fact, the only true guide to the choice of therapeutic method.

As matters stand now, the form of treatment available for a disturbed child depends usually not on the specific category of his disorder but on the resources of the department or clinical facility to which he has been referred: institutional or foster parent provision if he is taken in care; residential treatment if, legally, found out of control; weekly psychotherapy if referred to a child guidance clinic; family psychiatry, where this is the clinic's orientation; full-scale child analysis in a psychoanalytic clinic. It is only too frequent that the specific type of treatment applied is insufficiently matched with the specific type of disorder which should have been ascertained. Where this happens, children find themselves in institutions while they are in urgent need of individual, one-to-one relationships to develop their libidinal potentialities. Or they find themselves adopted, or in foster care, in spite of being far removed from the possibility of producing the child-to-parent attitudes which are an indispensable requirement of these situations. Or they receive analysis when education and guidance are needed; or guidance, when only analysis can solve their internal conflicts.

It is also futile to expect that any single method, whether superficial or deep, educational or therapeutic, will prove effective with disorders which are as different from each other as, for example, the neurotic compromise formations and the developmental arrests; or, so far as the learning failures are concerned, those caused by arrest, by undefended regression, and by inhibitions. Arrested children have to be treated educationally on their own mental level, an approach which fails disastrously where the therapeutic need is for the undoing of regressions or of lifting conflicts to consciousness, i.e., of freeing in the child an existing intellectual potentiality. Where the diagnostician remains on the phenomenological level and remains oblivious of the underlying fundamental differences, such therapeutic misapplications become inevitable.

The same plea for therapeutic differentiation (following diagnostic differentiation) is justified where the child's fears and anxieties are concerned. It is as futile therapeutically to reassure a child in the throes of castration anxiety and guilt as it would be futile to approach separation anxiety at the symbiotic stage with analytic efforts. Fear of loss of love can be diminished by removal of external pressure, but only in those instances where its origin is due largely to environmental causes; not in others. Where fear of the id is present, as said before, parental leniency acts as an aggravating factor, not as a relieving one.

Where children commit delinquent acts, it is perhaps more obvious than with other disturbances that treatment has to be selected according to the cause either environmental, or developmental, or neurotic, or psychotic. No single type of therapy, however elaborate, or costly, or easily available, can possibly fit these widely different circumstances.

It is reasonable to expect that any step forward in the refinement of diagnostic assessment will, in the long run, lead to improvements in matching disorder and therapy in the children's field. The present paper is meant to represent a move in this direction.

Appendix

The Symptomatology of Childhood

I. Symptomatology Proper

1. Symptoms resulting from initial nondifferentiation between somatic and psychological processes=psychosomatic manifestations.
2. Symptoms resulting from compromise formations between id and ego=neurotic manifestations.
3. Symptoms resulting from the irruption of id derivatives into the ego=infantile psychosis, borderline states, delinquent states.

4. Symptoms resulting from changes in the libido economy or direction of cathexis=upsets in self and object valuation, depressive states, autism, emotional surrender.

5. Symptoms resulting from changes in the quality or direction of aggression=inhibition of functioning, accident proneness, self-injury, aggressive outbursts.

6. Symptoms resulting from undefended regressions=infantilisms, pseudodebility.

7. Symptoms resulting from organic causes:
    (a) from brain damage=delay of milestones, reduced quality of ego functioning, affective changes, etc.;
    (b) from sensory or anatomical handicaps=deviations in drive and ego development, multiple upsets of inner equilibrium.

II. Other Signs of Disturbance

1. The fears and anxieties (origin, content, defense, bearing on pathology).

2. The delays and failures in development (organic, constitutional, environmental, traumatic; differentiation from regression).

3. The school failures (developmental arrest, undefended ego regression, sexualization or aggressive symbolisation and defense against it, neurotic inhibition, ego restriction, neurotic symptom formation).

4. Failures in social adaptation (environmental, developmental, economic, structural, neurotic, psychotic).

5. Aches and pains (psychosomatic, hysterical, hypochondriacal).

Notes

1. Or, at best, on the basis of unconscious content converted into conscious symbols.

2. An outstanding example of the latter is Karl Menninger who is known to condemn all psychiatric labels and classifications as unjustified offenses against the patient's human dignity, i.e., as 'name-calling.'

3. This may be the explanation why many clinics for children provide only one type of treatment, i.e., once weekly psychotherapy.

4. See also Hedy Schwarz, 'On lying' (unpublished manuscript).

5. See J.J. Michaels (1955).
6. There are fears of object loss in later childhood which manifest themselves as difficulties in separating from the parental objects, especially the mother. Although phenomenologically identical, they are different in dynamic and structural respects, i.e., due to internal rejection of aggression and death wishes directed against the parents.
7. For the clinician it is important to differentiate between such states and the common temper tantrums of childhood, which are manifestly similar but different as regards origin.
8. See, for example, Joseph Goldstein of the Yale Law School who opposes violently the use of 'delinquency' as a meaningful diagnostic term.

10

A Psychoanalytic View of Developmental Psychopathology (1974 [1973])

Working with children led Anna Freud to appreciate the importance of abnormal mental development as primarily causative of manifest psychopathology. This resulted in her turning to the study of healthy mental development in order to acquire criteria for its different stages. It would then be possible to gauge the extent to which the disturbed child deviated from these criteria. To achieve this aim she introduced the concept of the developmental lines. She describes a number of such lines along which the child proceeds. How far the child succeeds in advancing along one or other of the lines depends on innate and environmental influences as well as on the interaction between the lines.

By using the concept of the developmental lines as a means of identifying where and at what point disturbed children are arrested in their development Anna Freud came to realize that it is possible to differentiate two types of childhood psychopathology. One type, based on conflict, is responsible for anxiety states, phobic, hysterical and obsessional symptoms. The other, based on developmental defects, is responsible for atypical and borderline states. Clearly the same therapeutic measures cannot be effective in both types. In the case of developmental defects, interpretation cannot undo the damage as happens in the case of symptoms due to conflict. This hypothesis of two types of childhood psychopathology provides a much more realistic approach to prognosis and the possibilities of treatment.

'A Psychoanalytic View of Developmental Psychopathology' was first delivered as the twentieth Freud Memorial Lecture, Philadelphia in 1973. It was first published in the *Journal of the Philadelphia Association for Psychoanalysis*, 1: 7–17, 1974. An Italian translation followed in 1979: 'Un'opinione psicoanalitica sulla psicopatologia evolutiva', *Opere*, 3: 1137–52. Turin: Paolo Boringhieri, 1979. It was translated into German as 'Entwicklungs-Psychopathologie aus psychoanalytischer Sicht'. *Die Schriften der Anna Freud*, Volume 10. Munich: Kindler Verlag, 1980.

I am grateful to Dr. Ecker for his gracious introduction as well as to Governor Shapp for the official honor conferred on me by his welcoming letter. I wish to thank the inaugurators of this annual event in memory of my father and those members of the audience who regularly take part in it.

As you have heard from Dr. Ecker, this is the twentieth lecture in the series of Freud Memorial Lectures, of which I have given the first in 1954. Nineteen years is a long time measured in terms of personal life or the life of a psychoanalytic society. It is an astonishingly short period when applied to the study of a specific subject. Progress in psychoanalytic inquiries especially is of necessity slow since many individual cases need to be examined and analyzed before new knowledge emerges and allows for general application. It is all the slower if the subjects under investigation are not adults but children whose alliance with the analyst's work is frequently minimal. I cite this fact to explain why title and content of my paper tonight are not significantly different from the one offered here before, i.e., why I and my co-workers in the Hampstead Clinic are still concerned predominately with the assessment of infantile psychopathology.

Comparison Between Past and Present

I begin by listing for myself and the audience some of the happenings during the intervening years. There is one respect where matters have remained unchanged. We were asked then why as child analysts we were so concerned with the problem of diagnosis before treatment, that is, with a topic considered of little importance by the analysts of adults and, moreover, one not even included in the curriculum of our psychoanalytic institutes. Our answer is now, as it was then, that the child analysts' responsibility when deciding for or against therapy is much greater than the corresponding one in the case of adults. The adult sufferer from a neurosis or allied disorder does not present himself for analysis before he has convinced himself that his disturbance is severe enough to justify this course; above all, that without therapeutic help it would remain permanent. Also, usually, he has tried all manners of external measures before deciding on internal interference. This is different with children. Even with increasing experience of assessing their psychopathology, we always remain in doubt how far their symptoms remain influenceable by external management or how far they are open to spontaneous cure via developmental alterations, i.e., how far they are transitory. Thus, we are faced by the dilemma whether, by suggesting treatment, we are perhaps involving child and parents in much discomfort, trouble, time, and expense which might be unnecessary; or whether, by refusing it, we are perhaps condemning the child to a lifetime of suffering and failure.

Sufficient as this reason for early assessment may be by itself, a further motive for pursuance of the problem has appeared in recent years. We now believe that errors in the understanding of childhood abnormality are widespread and also that they exert an impact on our view of adult psychopathology. Improvement of insight into the early processes may rectify the situation, as will be shown later.

To continue with the comparison of past and present. What has, quite obviously, remained unchanged are the *sources of information* about the children who are presented to us at the Clinic. As before, we have to take account of what we are told by the *parents*, however biased and unreliable their descriptions are in many cases. We still note with regret that young children have little or no *insight* into their own mental state and tend to obscure rather than reveal their need for therapeutic help. We rely on *diagnostic interviews*, knowing full well that the picture emerging from them is open to distortion by the parents' anxiety imparted to the child and by the child's own distrust and fear of the stranger's intervention. We gather samples of *behavior* at home and in school and of the child's general functioning or malfunctioning. A list of *symptoms* is provided for us in the form of parental complaints. As before, we use a variety of intelligence and projective tests to furnish circumscribed knowledge about different aspects of the child's personality.

Nevertheless, it is only the quality and extent of information at our disposal which have remained the same. What has progressed significantly is the use to which we are able to put it.

We have learned more than we did in the past about the *translation of behavior* patterns into their unconscious motivations. We have made ourselves increasingly *independent of psychiatric categories* used for diagnosing the mental disorders of adult patients, and have established our own series of diagnostic entities, based on *developmental* considerations. We have trained ourselves to compose comprehensive character images of our children, so-called *Profiles*, in which the diagnostician's thinking is directed away from purely symptomatic aspects and toward the genetic, dynamic, economic, and adaptive modalities of the child's personality. More important than all that is another advance: we have broken with the tradition according to which every mental difficulty is seen and explained by comparison with severe pathological patterns and, instead, try to see it against the background of the *norm*, expectable for the particular child's age, and to measure its distance from it. We have thus redirected the main bulk of our inquiries from interest in pathology toward a study of the norm.

A Psychoanalytic Study of the Norm

As analysts of adults, we have taken the path from inquiry into the pathological manifestations to a gradual understanding of the normal ones and of decreasing the alleged gap between them. As child analysts we may do better by taking the opposite road, i.e., by getting a firm grasp of the facts of normal development and by viewing the abnormal outcomes as more or less significant deviations from this course. Not that this recommendation is by any means a popular or generally accepted one. Not unlike their colleagues in the adult field, child analysts too feel the urge to widen the scope of their therapeutic efforts and to proceed from the more benign to the severest manifestations, i.e., from the infantile neuroses to the borderline, the autistic and psychotic states.

Moreover, those who manage to turn in the suggested direction, toward the norm, are faced by the disappointing realization that the existing analytic knowledge about normal child development is much more scant than they had estimated. There is, of course, a wealth of single facts unearthed from the beginnings of psychoanalysis up to the present day: the sequence of libidinal stages as the normal precursor of mature sexuality; the ubiquity of the oedipus and castration complexes; the legitimacy of narcissism as forerunner of and adjunct to object love;

the developmental stages of the ego with its mechanisms, functions, and contents; the stages of the aggressive drive; the overriding general impact of the mother–infant relationship, etc.

Nevertheless, these acquisitions, as by-products of therapeutic analyses, are more or less isolated facts, not fully interrelated with each other. Also, they are global rather than circumstantial, spanning, as the libidinal phases do, for example, periods as long as a year or more. For these reasons, they do not really satisfy our need for a detailed, orderly picture of the growth of the child's integrated personality.

There are, though, two notable exceptions from this picture in the psychoanalytic literature. René Spitz (1965), in his study of the first year of life, does not content himself with tracing the infant–mother relationship on the one hand and ego growth on the other, but demonstrates step by step how every single advance in ego functioning and awareness is placed in the service of the infant's libidinal processes to alter and shape them, both libido and ego interacting at the same time with the responses of the mother. Margaret Mahler (1968), in her turn, when faced in her work with infants with the stage of biological unity between mother and child, subdivides what appears at first glance as an entity into a significant sequence of developmental phases: the symbiotic, the autistic, and the separation–individuation phases.

The Concept of Developmental Lines

The principles of interaction of agencies and subdivision of stages, applied by these two authors to infancy, can, I believe, with profit be carried further and used to shed light on the child's whole path from immaturity to maturity. I have attempted to do this by introducing the concept of Lines of Development. What these lines represent are ladders leading up to every one of the expected achievements of the child's personality, each step on them being the result of interaction between id, ego, and environment, the way leading upward in the course of normal, progressive growth, or downward whenever regression occurs.

I repeat here briefly what I described previously (1965) as examples of such lines.

On the line from *Biological Unity with the Mother to the Adolescent*

Revolt against parental influence, we expect the normal child to negotiate a large number of libidinal and aggressive substations such as: the symbiotic, autistic, separation–individuation phases (Mahler); the part-object (Melanie Klein), need-fulfilling, anaclitic relationship; the stage of object constancy; anal–sadistic ambivalence; the triangular phallic–oedipal relationship; the latency extension of ties to peers, teachers, the community, and impersonal ideals; preadolescent regressions; adolescent struggle against infantile ties and search for objects outside the family.

What has to accompany these forward moves of the drives on the ego side are an increase of awareness and understanding of environmental happenings, expanding empathy with fellow beings, progress in identifications and internalizations, in secondary process thinking, in appreciation of cause and consequence, of the reality principle in general, of adaptation to community standards, etc.

What the environment is expected to contribute are the provision of appropriate human objects, their accepting, promoting, stimulating, and controlling attitudes toward the child.

On the line from *Being Nursed to Rational Eating*, the substations are: food equals mother; food symbolizes oral, anal, sadistic, impregnation, poisoning, and birth fantasies; the mother's handling of the feeding situation has a far-reaching influence on eating and appetite becoming gradually free from these irrational concomitants.

The advance from *Wetting and Soiling to Bowel and Bladder Control* shows most clearly its determination from three sides: on the instinctual side, the child has to pass beyond his urethral and anal interests; on the environmental side, training for cleanliness has to be handled gently and gradually to prevent breakdowns and regressions; the child's ego has to outgrow its original high valuation of the body products; the superego has to incorporate the adult's devaluation of them into its own structure.

The previously described lines toward *Body Management*, toward *Companionship with Peers*, and toward the capacity to *Work* are characterized similarly as the result of interaction between the id, the maturing ego, the rudimentary superego, and the stimulating, encouraging, and controlling influences of the environment. But the list given was by no means considered to be complete; rather, it was in fact meant as an invitation to the readers of the book to make their own additions to it. Since this challenge has so far not been taken by any other author, I offer in what follows some supplementary prototypes, constructed on the basis of the same principle.

From Physical to Mental Pathways of Discharge

At the beginning of life, every excitation, whether physical or mental, takes its path through the body and is discharged via processes in the area of sleep, food intake, intestinal movement. Also, during the whole of the first year, while psychological life expands, the access between body and mind remains an easy one. Every upheaval in the bodily sphere causes mental distress, crying, etc., while every mental upset such as shock, frustration, anxiety causes physical upheaval. This truly psychosomatic period comes to an end as, with advancing age, more and more mental pathways open up for the child and the discharge of mental tension is allocated to them. In the second year the use of the mind for the purpose of tension discharge increases considerably until, approximately in the third year, due to the perfection of secondary process thinking and speech, the division becomes decisive, mental excitation from then onward being discharged mentally and bodily excitation physically.

There are, though, some important flaws as well as frequent regressions which affect the smooth advance on this vital line. I allude here to the familiar fact that not all mental content is accepted by the ego and allowed discharge via consciousness; i.e., that repressed libidinal fantasies and aggressive impulses find the way blocked to psychological expression and for this reason continue with, or regress to, physical discharge in the form of psychosomatic or hysterical manifestations.

From Animate to Inanimate Objects

To construct any developmental line in its entirety is an arduous task; and even where great attention is paid to detail, as for instance in the advance toward emotional independence (first line of the previous enumeration), complications and offshoots are easily neglected.

I turn here to Winnicott's (1953) concept of the 'transitional object' as characterization of a stage when the infant, after concentrating his libidinal and aggressive impulses on the mother, accepts a toy, partly as an addition, partly as symbolic substitute for her. While the child's love—hate relationship to human beings develops further through the stages described above, there branches off here, it seems to me, a normal sideline which carries varying quantities of libido and aggression away from their targets in the human environment and attaches them otherwise. We realize that this move is greatly encouraged by the provision of appropriate toys, cuddly animals such as teddy bears and dolls. We also know that these substitutes are gladly accepted by the child for two reasons: as libidinal objects, they are more under the child's possessive control than the living ones; as objects of aggression, they do not take offense or retaliate. Both qualities are shared to some degree by certain animals, especially placid dogs who are 'good with children.' What we do not know is why specific persons, from childhood onward, change what should normally be a sideline into the main channels for their libido and aggression. We are left with guesses as to the reasons for this deviation. Contributions to it from the environmental side may be lack of appropriate objects for emotional attachment and/or rejection of the child, and these may interact with a child's specially low tolerance for frustration and specially great need for impulse discharge in the anal-sadistic phase. In any case, the result could be two distortions visible in the developmental line. With respect to the libido, the steps would lead to a greater role played by animals in the individual's life; or, more frequently, to the overvaluation of material goods, their acquisition, collection, and possession. With respect to aggression, the line would lead from the child's maltreatment of his own toys to the torturing of defenseless animals and from there to massive destructiveness turned against inanimate objects.

From Irresponsibility to Guilt

This particular line traces the child's path from his original state of happy irresponsibility in moral matters to the experience of painful guilt feelings whenever the moral code has been infringed. It is our analytic understanding that this happens by way of identification with the controlling and prohibiting influences in the external world, an explanation which covers the total road toward the expected end result.

We are well aware of some of the substations through which the child passes on his way after the first open clashes between his primitive id impulses and the external barriers to their unhindered fulfillment. We are alerted to the compliance enforced on the infantile ego by the child's physical and emotional dependency on the object world, i.e., by his fear of losing the object, or the object's love, or of incurring punishment. We can follow the changed ego attitudes toward the id which are produced first by imitation of the objects and their demands, then by the identifications with and internalizations of them which structure the superego. What we tend to miss is an intermediate stage which owes its existence to the young child's unwillingness to submit to the painful experience of internal conflict, i.e., to acknowledge the simultaneous presence within the structure of his personality of impulsive wishes and their condemnation. Since the critical faculties of his superego already are, at this time, inescapable, he resorts to the defenses of denying awareness of his own wish and allocating it via externalization to another person, usually a child. This makes him critical and censorious of his peers, until he matures sufficiently to take the final step, that is, to admit that both wish and prohibition are his own and that there is reason to feel guilt.

As with all developmental lines, it is important for our view of the adult personality that any stage of the sequence, instead of being transitory, can become a point for permanent arrest, and that the progressive steps upward can also be taken in the downward direction regressively. Thus, individuals, due to arrest or regression on this particular line, may obey the moral code only when compelled by external authority; or when observed or supported by authority; or they may remain censorious of others, i.e., hypocritical, instead of self-critical.

Early Development Seen From the Aspect of Developmental Lines

Taking the totality of developmental lines as described to date and as to be constructed in the future, we arrive at a new view of child development. We can imagine an ideal norm, according to which each such line proceeds unhindered and at an even pace and reaches its highest point at the age appropriate for it, in some instances before age five years, in others not before the end of childhood, i.e., in adolescence. With complete temporal balance and harmony between the various lines, the result could not fail to be a completely harmonious, well-balanced personality.

We know, of course, that such states of ideal normality do not exist except in our imagination and that what happens in reality is different. In fact, progress on any line is subject to influence from three sides: the variation in innate givens, which provide the raw material out of which id and ego are differentiated; the environmental conditions and influences, which only too often differ widely from what is appropriate and favorable for normal growth; the interactions between internal and external forces, which constitute the individual experience of each child. According to the impact of each of these, progress on any one line may be slow and obstructed, while being fast and unhindered on another. There may be slow forward movement on all lines, i.e., generally reduced but fairly balanced growth. There may be slight or grave temporal unbalance or, at worst, multiple failure on several of the most vital lines.

In any case, whatever happens in the individual picture, we are left with the impression that it is this variety of progress on the lines, i.e., developmental failures and successes, which can be held responsible for the innumerable variations in human characters and personalities.

Two Types of Early Psychopathology

We are, by now, alerted to the contributions made by what happens on the developmental lines to childhood psychopathology. What we have been most familiar with in the analytic literature so far are the abnormalities caused by the incidence of trauma, and of conflict between the internal agencies followed by anxiety, defense, and compromise formation. What have received much less attention[1] and are added here are the defects in the personality structure itself which are caused by the aforementioned developmental irregularities and failures. We can thus differentiate between two types of infantile psychopathology. The one based on conflict is responsible for the anxiety states and the phobic, hysterical, and obessional manifestations, i.e., the infantile neuroses; the one based on developmental defects, for the psychosomatic symptomatology, the backwardness, the atypical and borderline states.

It would be convenient to take the point of view that success or failure on the developmental lines primarily shapes the personalities which secondarily become involved in internal conflict. But any statement of this kind would be a gross falsification once the infant ceases to be an undifferentiated, unstructured being. It would ignore the temporal relations between the two processes which occur simultaneously, not subsequent to each other. Progress on the lines is interfered with constantly by conflict, repression, and consequent regression, while the conflicts themselves and quite especially the methods available for their solution are wholly dependent on the shape and level of personal development which has been reached.

However different in origin the two types of psychopathology are, in the clinical picture they are totally intertwined, a fact which accounts for their usually being treated as one.

Implications

If, by the foregoing, I have encouraged colleagues to tackle the difficult task of disentangling the two pathogenic processes from each other, I have done so because of its relevance for every analyst's diagnostic, technical, and theoretical concerns.

So far as the *assessment of cases* before, during, and after therapy is in question, lack of distinction between developmental and conflictual pathology leads to errors which are only too common at the present time: neurotic symptoms in either children or adults are linked directly with the earliest events in the infant's first year of life, an assumption which, in my view, constitutes a serious short-cut. What actually happens at this early date, owing to the interplay between infant and mother, is the laying of the groundwork for personality building, i.e., the more or less successful starting off of a number of developmental lines. Whatever clashes occur at that time proceed externally between the infant and his environment, not internally within a not yet existing structure. Where deprivation and frustration are excessive, this leads not to symptom formation but to developmental setbacks. It is only in the later course of differentiation and structuralization that the resultant deviations from normal growth become involved in the phase-adequate internal conflicts as they are known to us.

With regard to the *technique* of child analysis, we come up against some unexpected questions. If we accept the view that childhood psychopathology has a twofold causation, one rooted in conflicts, defense, and compromise formations, the other in the developmental processes, we have no reason to believe that the same therapeutic measures will be equally effective for both. We are on familiar analytic ground with the conflictual-neurotic pathology where interpretation lifts repressed or otherwise defended material into consciousness and helps the child's ego to find solutions for his internal struggles, which are no longer based on anxiety, panic, and infantile misapprehensions of reality. We also realize that, so far as the pathologies are interlocked, the analytic work will undo regressions and lift crippling conflicts off the developmental lines. But so far as the developmental progress itself is defective or unbalanced due either to innate or to environmental conditions, we cannot expect interpretation to undo the damage, even if it clarifies the past and may help the child toward better ways of facing and coping with its consequences. If, in spite of that, children also profit from analysis in this respect, such success may be due not to the truly analytic work but to admixtures to the technique such as new positive object attachment, new superego identification, suggestive influence, or even corrective emotional experience which with the very young can set arrested developmental lines going again.

So far as the *theoretical* thinking of the analyst is concerned, a closer look at the lines of development may help toward answering three open questions.

For one, we have always wondered what determines the *pathogenic impact* of an event. To mention examples: for some children, the birth of a sibling becomes a turning point in development to which all later pathology can be connected; others take this in their stride. Moving to another home can be traumatic for some and a pleasurable experience for others. Bodily illness, separation from a playmate, death of a parent have very different consequences for different individuals and different ages. We arrive at a better understanding of this if we connect the event with the particular point on the particular developmental line which is affected by it. We realize then that the arrival of a sibling has different meaning before or after the stages of object constancy or of ambivalence have been reached on the line toward emotional independence; that the impact of bodily illness depends not only on the age adequateness of castration fear but also on the station reached on the line toward independent body ownership and management; that loss of a parent changes its meaning altogether according to the time of occurrence and has different pathogenic value at the stages of biological unity, of infantile ambivalence, of need for oedipal involvement, or in adolescence when withdrawal from the parent is a developmental task which does not bear to be interfered with by the actual removal of the object. Moving house, even though all the human objects remain present, may prove traumatic in cases where the young child has deviated too far on the line away from human to material objects.

Secondly, the same reasoning, if applied to the *defense mechanisms*, may shed some light on the question of their chronology. We know, of course, that repression cannot come into action before division of the undifferentiated personality into id and ego has taken place; or that projection and introjection in their defensive use depend similarly on the ego's capacity to distinguish between self and nonself. We can now add that somatization and its later use in conversion (somatic compliance) become more understandable when we see them as predominately based on the line from physical to mental discharge, in fact, caused by the arrests and regressions which occur on it. Regression as a defense is resorted to most readily by individuals whose entire progression on the lines has been halting and shaky. The obsessional mechanisms cannot come into use before two of the developmental lines have reached their climax, i.e., the line from physical to mental discharge as well as the line from irresponsibility to moral guilt.

Finally, we may hope that the further study of these connections will also provide some hints toward answering a question which has troubled workers in the field since the beginnings of psychoanalysis, namely, the *choice of neurosis*. What we can make out so far is that the type of pathology which an individual child presents is as closely tied up with the intricacies of his developmental processes as are his character and personality.

Note

1. Exceptions to be mentioned are Augusta Alpert and Peter Neubauer in the U.S., and Michael Balint in England, who has introduced the concept of 'basic faults.'

11

Psychopathology Seen Against the Background of Normal Development (1976 [1975])

This paper is included in the series because it supplements the contents of the last paper. Its title speaks for itself, once again emphasising the principle that psychopathology has its roots in deviations affecting the processes of healthy mental development. As the paper was presented to an audience of psychiatrists, Anna Freud describes how adult symptomatology can be understood as resulting from a failure of developmental achievements. She presents a number of examples of developmental deviations resulting from an abnormal endowment, abnormal external conditions and disturbances in the 'rates of internal structualization', i.e., individual children differ with respect to the timing of the appearance of the ego and superego. Recognition of developmental disturbances has important consequences for the treatment of adults. As in the case of children, the developmental deviations of childhood can lead to a non-conflictual psychopathology which is not amenable to an interpretative type of analytical psychotherapy.

'Psychopathology Seen Against the Background of Normal Development' was first delivered as the 49th Maudsley Lecture before the Royal College of Psychiatrists on 21 November 1975. It was published in 1976 in the *British Journal of Psychiatry*, 129: 401–6, 1976. It was translated into French in 1977: 'La Psychopathogie envisagée à partir du développement normal', *Revue Française Psychanalyse*, 41: 429–38, 1977. An Italian translation ('La psicopatologia considerata sullo sfondo dello sviluppo normale'. *Opere*, 3: 1153–4. Turin: Paolo Boringhieri, 1979) and a German translation ('Die Beziehungen zwischen Psychopathologie und Normalentwicklung'. *Die Schriften der Anna Freud*, Volume 10. Munich: Kindler Verlag, 1980) followed in 1979 and 1980 respectively.

When choosing a title for this paper, I hesitated between two possible ones, the one above which I finally selected, and another, termed 'Links between Adult Psychiatry and Child Psychiatry.' Although in wording they seem different enough from each other, I hope to show in what follows where the two subject matters meet.

The First Object of Psychoanalytic Investigation

To begin with a look at the history of psychoanalysis. The first object of psychoanalytic study was the neuroses. This was due not to any predilection of the originator of the new discipline but to the exigencies of his private practice. Nevertheless, the nature of the matter under investigation proved decisive for many characteristics of the evolving theory. Since the neurotic manifestations emanate from the depth, psychoanalysis embarked on the study of the unconscious. Since they are due to conflict between internal forces, it became a dynamic psychology. Since conflicts are solved according to the relative strength of these forces, the economic viewpoint was developed. Since the roots of every neurosis reach back to the early years of the individual's life, the genetic aspects of the theory played a paramount part. Incidentally, this last-mentioned point also represented the first opportunity for bringing infantile psychopathology within the orbit of the therapist of adults.

The Widening Scope of Psychoanalysis

All this, of course, was only the beginning of the story. It did not take long for psychoanalytic exploration to widen its scope, with therapeutic efforts always in its wake. Its path went from the neuroses to the psychoses; from sexual inhibitions to the perversions; from character disorders to the delinquencies; from adult psychopathology to adolescence; from adolescence to childhood. As early as 1925, Freud can be read to say: 'children have become the main subject of psycho-analytic research and have thus replaced in importance the neurotics on whom its studies began' (1925, p. 273). Although at the date when it was written, this statement may have been prophetic rather than factual, child analysts today will be glad to claim it as the motivation and justification governing their work. In fact, it is less the increasing dissection of the adult's personality and more child analysis and the analytic observation of young children which are responsible for two important results: (1) for a chart of normal personality development; (2) for pointing out the relevance of its details for the assessment of adult psychopathology.

Reconstruction Versus the Direct View

As regards the developmental chart, it would be unjustified, of course, if child analysts claimed major credit for its setting up. It was reconstruction from the analyses of adults and not the direct analytic study of the child which established the fact of an infantile sex life with its sequence of libidinal phases; the existence of the oedipus and castration complexes; the developmental line of anxiety from separation anxiety, fear of object loss, fear of loss of love, castration anxiety to guilt; the division of the personality into id, ego, and superego, each inner agency pursuing its own purposes; the advance from primary process to secondary process functioning; the gradual building up of a defense organization. What was left to the child analysts was to make amendments wherever the direct contact with infantile functioning did not seem to confirm what had been glimpsed from the distance. There was the point, for instance, that in reconstruction no early developmental stage ever appears in its true colors, since it invariably is overlaid by characteristics which belong to later phases, even where regression in the transference has taken place; or that what appears in later analysis as a one-time traumatic event may in reality have been a series of such happenings, telescoped into one in the individual's memory. But besides and beyond these minor corrections, one major assumption emerged, namely, that reconstruction from adult analysis inevitably is weighted toward pathology to the neglect of normal developmental happenings; that it is always the conflictual and unsolved which does not come to rest in the individual's mind, which welcomes the opportunity to reestablish itself in the transference situation and thus captures and monopolizes the analyst's attention. In contrast, the satisfied impulses, the successful adaptive conflict solutions disappear from view by entering the fabric of the personality. They are outgrown with little incentive left for revival at a later date.

Thus, while the analysts of adults become expert in tracing psychopathology back to its early roots, only the child analysts appear to hold the key to the description of the course taken by normal infantile development.

The Child Analyst's Picture of Normal Development

The 'Abnormal' Aspects of the Norm

It may be necessary to stress that normal growth and development, as seen by the child analyst, do not appear as a smooth, unbroken line leading from early infancy via the latency period, preadolescence, and adolescence to a healthy adulthood. On the contrary, every single developmental phase as well as every single forward move can be shown to contain disturbing concomitants which are characteristic for them.

To take the first year of the child as an example. What belongs to this period of life are the diffuse distress states to which all infants are subject. We regard them as the normal forerunners of later anxiety and as such inevitable. Nevertheless, unlike the affect of anxiety which is psychologically caused and felt, they can be aroused and experienced on the physical as well as on the mental side, and they demand from the mothering person the utmost in care, comfort, and attention to the infant's body and mind. They are thus an instructive illustration of the double regime which governs functioning at this early date when the individual's body and mind interact freely: physical excitation such as pain or discomfort can be discharged via mental upset, while mental excitation such as frustration, impatience, or longing can find its outlet via the body, in disturbances of sleep, food intake, or elimination. This double source and experience of distress is disturbing to infant and environment alike. But nothing can prevent it from existing until developmental growth itself alters the situation by creating new mental pathways for the discharge of mental stimuli via the maturing ego (thought, speech, etc.).

On the other hand, these new developments, beneficial as they are in one respect, contain their own hazards in another. Evidence for this is the sleeping disorders which appear frequently at the border between the first and second year and cause distress to both infant and mother, usually in the form of inability to fall asleep. As analytic observers we ascribe these upsets to the child's reluctance to renounce recently acquired functions such as his emotional hold on the object world and his ego interest in his surroundings. Both militate against the body's need for rest and interfere with the return to narcissistic withdrawal and to renunciation of ego interests which are the preconditions for sleep.

There are other examples of difficulties which arise due to developmental progress. Motor skills advance in leaps and bounds at the toddler stage but are not equaled on the ego side by similar advances in motor control and/or appreciation of danger from heights, water, fire, traffic, etc. Consequently, the young child becomes accident-prone, a developmental occurrence which makes formidable demands on environmental protection. Simultaneously, the increasing complexities in the infant–mother relationship affect food intake. Since food and mother are still equated by the child, every hostile or ambivalent feeling toward her leads to food refusal and further to the endless and developmentally harmful battles at mealtimes. Other 'normal' developmental manifestations are the upsetting temper tantrums which, before the acquisition of speech, are the growing toddler's typical mode of discharge for anger, frustration, and rage, with major involvement of the motor apparatus. There also is the excessive and distressing clinging which accompanies the fading out of the biological unity between child and mother, i.e., the upsets within the separation–individuation phase as described by Margaret Mahler (1968).

The upsetting upheavals of the next phases are even more familiar in their characteristics. Obviously, the child in the anal-sadistic stage cannot be expected to deal with his instinctual tendencies on the one hand and the environmental demands on the other without experiencing conflict, extreme distress, and emotional turmoil, resulting in occasional regression with accompanying loss of acquired functions or with sullenness, rebelliousness, obstinacy, or with phase-bound obsessional characteristics such as insistence on sameness and routine, and anxiety outbreaks whenever the self-imposed order and regularity are infringed by the environment.

As regards the phallic–oedipal development, we do not expect the child to cope with the accompanying emotional complications and anxiety increases without pathological by-products. Long before the advent of child analysis, it was one of the accepted psychoanalytic tenets that this is the time when the whole turmoil of anxieties, affects, and conflicts is organized into the clinical picture of one of the infantile neuroses. Whatever the fate of the latter, whether transitory or permanent in its impact on developmental progress, it represents the individual child's crowning achievement in his struggle for simultaneous adaptation to the inner and outer world.

Relevance of This Developmental Chart for Adult Psychopathology

There are several items in the chart of normal growth which therapists in the adult field may find relevant for their assessments of symptomatology.

The psychosomatic illnesses in adult life, for instance, may be easier to understand when seen as the survival of the psychosomatic regime which is legitimate in infancy. Although the communicating doors between body and mind are never completely closed for anybody, as evidenced by headaches after mental upset, the physical accompaniments of anxiety, etc., they are more open in some individuals than in others, and this becomes responsible for the mental contributions to such severe afflictions as migraine, asthma, high blood pressure, and stomach ulcers.

Furthermore, the pattern of some sleep disorders in adult life has something in common with those described for early childhood. Even though the sleepless adult's depressed or agitated state of mind differs in its content from the child's, what is identical in both instances is the painful struggle between a tired body longing for relaxation and a restless mind unable to rid itself of excitation.

There are some other characteristics of normal child development which serve as patterns for later pathology. One is the forerunner of object love proper, i.e., the infant's tie to the mother which is based on the satisfactions received from her. Certain disturbances of adult love life, such as shallowness and promiscuity, are understood better when seen as residues of this early stage of which too large a proportion has remained.

Similarly, the anxiety attacks of hysterical patients can be likened to the panic states of young children before the ego has acquired the mental mechanisms which defend against anxiety and reduce debilitating panic to the adaptive form of signal anxiety.

The Prerequisites of Normal Development

Describing the chain of events leading from the infant's complete immaturity to the comparative maturity of the mental apparatus at latency age, I stressed the fact that progress — even if normal — is interspersed with conflicts, emotional upsets, and distress states; that it is also interrupted by regressive setbacks and halted by temporary arrests; in short, that it is neither smooth, nor unimpeded, nor effortless, nor painless. What has not been emphasized sufficiently so far is the experience that even this checkered advance is extremely vulnerable and open to a variety of threats. We see the developmental process as dependent on the interaction of three factors: endowment; environment; rate of structuralization and maturation within the personality. Provided that all three are within the expectable norm, the child will arrive in every crucial developmental phase with the right inner equipment and meet the right environmental response, i.e., have a chance of normal growth. If, however, any of the three deviates too far from the average, the developmental result will become distorted in one direction or another.

Examples of Normal Developmental Advance

That developmental achievements are not due to single factors but are multiply based is illustrated for certain instances in the child analytic literature. René Spitz (1965) traced in detail the origins of the infant's first tie to the mother and pinpointed three prerequisites for it: an adequate advance in the infant's libidinal capacity; normal maturation of the perceptive apparatus, which enables interest to be turned from the infant's own body to the environment; the mother's sufficient libidinal involvement with the child, expressed in comforting and satisfying handling. Provided that in the life of a normally born infant these various influences are at work and interact, the first step on the ladder toward mature object love will be taken.

Similarly, Margaret Mahler (1968), exploring the complexities of the separation–individuation phase in the second year of life, makes us realize how many elements are needed for its successful negotiation: sufficient maturation of motility to enable the child to run away from the mother as well as toward her; in the ego, the unfolding of inquisitive-ness and curiosity; on the libidinal side, some advance toward object constancy and 'basic trust' to allow for temporary separation without distress; on the mother's side, her readiness to release the child from the close union with her own person, to accept and even enjoy his status as a separate person.

Similar combinations of forces can be seen at work behind any further developmental advance, whether from one of the major libidinal stages to the next, or from one small step to the next on one of the long developmental lines leading toward mature object love; to companionship with peers; to independent body management; to the ability to work. Even to achieve reliable sphincter control, beyond mere reflex action, depends on a multiplicity of intact factors, such as: maturation of the muscular apparatus; adequately timed and exerted maternal intervention; the child's compliance due to his object tie; the process of identification with the environmental demand leading finally to the individual's own so-called sphincter morality.

Examples of Developmental Deviations

None of these positive developmental results can be expected if either endowment, or environmental conditions, or the rate of personality structuralization depart too far from the average.

First, as regards *endowment*, our child analytic studies of the blind, deaf, and mentally deficient show that any single defect in the individual's inborn equipment suffices to throw the entire developmental course into disarray, far beyond the sphere where the damage itself is located. With the blind, attachment to the object world is delayed; once formed, it remains longer on primitive levels; motility matures later than normal and remains restricted; prolonged dependence interferes with the unfolding of aggression; verbalization suffers from a gap between words and their meaning; superego formation bears the mark of the initial differences in object relationship (Burlingham, 1972, 1979). With the deaf, the absence of acoustic elements affects the thought processes and the important step from primary to secondary process functioning. The mentally deficient miss out, not only as regards understanding the environment, i.e., intellectually, but vitally as regards the ego's defense organization, i.e., impulse and anxiety control.

Secondly, concerning abnormal *environmental conditions*, their harmful impact on development has always been recognized, even without the added evidence from child analyses. What needs emphasis, though, is the fact that there is no one-to-one, invariable relationship between the fact of parents being absent, neglecting, indifferent, punitive, cruel, seductive, overprotective, delinquent, or psychotic and the resultant distortions in the personality picture of the child. Cruel treatment can produce either an aggressive, violent, or a timid, crushed, passive being; parental seduction can result either in complete inability to control sexual impulses ever after, or in severe inhibition and abhorrence of any form of sexuality. In short, the developmental outcome is determined not by the environmental interference per se, but by its interaction with the inborn and acquired resources of the child.

The third important influence on personality building, namely, the *rate of internal structuralization*, has received comparatively little attention so far. The facts are that individual children differ considerably with regard to the timing when their ego emerges from the undifferentiated ego—id matrix, or when their superego emerges from the ego; when they advance from the primary process to secondary process functioning; when the borders between unconscious and conscious are set up; when signal anxiety replaces panic attacks; when defenses change from the primitive to the sophisticated. Normally, this sequence of achievements matches the sequence of internal instinctual and external parental pressures and enables the child to find more or less adaptive solutions for the arising conflicts. However, when ripening of the mental apparatus is either delayed or accelerated, there is no such match between conflict situations and the appropriate means for coping with them.

Child analytic studies yield various examples of the developmental confusion which ensues.

For instance, during the boy's phallic stage, there occurs an age-adequate conflict between active and passive strivings. This is dealt with by repression of passivity, compensating masculine fantasies, heroic daydreams, and so forth provided that the mental structure is up to date. But in cases where the latter is delayed in its unfolding, no such sophisticated mechanisms are available and their place is taken by muscular action (as in the infantile tantrums) resulting in aggressive outbursts, self-injury, atypical or borderline manifestations.

In the girl's age-adequate emotional move toward the oedipal father, there occurs the need to free herself by whatever means from her ties to the mother. This healthy advance is interfered with where the superego precociously upholds moral demands which forbid rivalry, hostility, death wishes, etc.

Precocious understanding of the difference between the sexes may involve a little girl in the throes of penis envy before there are adequate means at her disposal for defense against massive unpleasure.

Relevance for Adult Psychopathology

Knowledge of these developmental complications is relevant for the psychotherapist of adults so far as they affect the therapeutic possibilities.

Analytic and analytically oriented therapy is directed toward the patient's ego and attempts to widen its controlling powers. It is a radical therapy so far as it deals with damage which the ego has inflicted on itself by excessive repression which limits its sphere of influence; by unsuitable other defense mechanisms which distort it; by regressions which lower its functioning; by arrests which prevent further unfolding. However, with regard to harm inflicted on the ego by endowment, environment, and vagaries of internal maturation, i.e., by influences beyond its control, it is no more than an alleviating therapy, dealing not with causes but with their aftereffects and working toward better integration of the latter. A distinction of this kind may help to explain some of the therapeutic limitations which patients as well as analysts deplore.

Summary

It was the object of this paper to pursue some links between mental health and illness, immaturity and maturity. It was its further aim to convince psychiatrists of adults that there is much to be learned from child psychiatry, and to convince child psychiatrists that infantile psychopathology should be assessed against the background knowledge of normal development.

12

Problems of Pathogenesis: Introduction to the Discussion (1983 [1981])

Anna Freud takes the opportunity in this paper to warn against an oversimplified theory of causation (psychopathogenesis) of mental disorders in childhood and adults. To attribute vulnerability to mental illness to real and psychical events of infancy alone fails to take account of the multiplicity of external and internal events which occur during a child's development. As in her paper, 'The Concept of the Rejecting Mother' (1955), she rejects the idea of the unempathetic mother as a pathogenic agent. As she says: 'even the most perfect mother–infant interaction and developmentally successful first year are no guarantee of future mental health and certainly no safeguard against neurotic symptomatology'.

The emphasis on interaction with an object (the mother) has led to a devaluation of the role of internalized conflict in psychopathogenesis. The conflict which arises from the growing child's battle for impulse control can be seriously weakened by developmental disharmonies of the kind which she describes in the papers, 'A Psychoanalytic View of Developmental Psychopathology' (1974) and 'Psychopathology Seen Against the Background of Normal Development' (1976). When a developmental defect arises from a disharmonious evolution of ego, id and superego, the soil is prepared for severe mental conflict. This predisposes to neurotic symptomatology and behavioural disorders in childhood.

'Problems of Pathogenesis: Introduction to the Discussion' was first published in *The Psychoanalytic Study of the Child*, 38: 383–88. New Haven: Yale University Press, 1983. It is a modified version of a paper presented to the International Scientific Study Colloquium on 'The Psychoanalytic Approach to the Nature and Location of Pathogenesis,' held at the Hampstead Child-Therapy Clinic on 30 and 31 October 1981.

When, at the end of last year's symposium on the superego I suggested 'Problems of Pathogenesis' as a further subject for discussion, I did so under the misapprehension that we stood more or less isolated with our distrust of many of the current conceptions in this respect. Since then, however, I had the privilege of reading a paper on the same subject by Arlow (1981), which gave me the feeling that we have a potent ally, and that this should encourage us all the more to bring forward our own data derived from the observations and analyses of children.

What I and many others had been waiting for is the kind of insight and objective appraisal of the many theories which dominate the analytic field at present. What worried us, as evidently it worried Arlow, is the present trend to place single pathogenic determinants at ever earlier phases of life – a quest which invalidates or ignores every element of Freud's original, broad, developmental view. It is the essence of this view that the onset of mental disturbance, and especially of neurotic disorder, is due to conflicting forces within the personality; that it is nonspecific, i.e., that it has multiple causes; and that it can be located in all phases of development. In contrast to this view, many authors today regard the events of the early mother–infant relationship as the main pathogenic agents, thereby either ignoring the role of conflict or assuming its existence at a time of life when the personality, according to our views, still is unstructured. In addition, they ascribe to a single stage of development the power to determine on its own the individual's future health and pathology, thereby diminishing the importance of all further stages, preoedipal or oedipal, in this respect.

The Interdependence of the Development Stages

Not that on the grounds of our own material we have reason to doubt the significance or impact of early happenings. However, we regard them primarily as laying the base from which further development proceeds. If anything, we go further in our expectations than those authors who regard the outcome of mother–infant interaction above all in the light of the vicissitudes of narcissism and object relationship. We, too, assign to this phase a beginning capacity to distinguish between an inner and an outer world; the first establishment of a balance between pleasurable and painful experience; the first beginnings of the body ego; ego nuclei emerging from the more or less differentiated id. We consider success in these advances essential for initiation of the next phase when with the step from oral to anal sexuality the further humanization of the infant should take place. What needs to be negotiated by the individual at this time is an impressive list of new achievements, such as temporary separation from the mother and individuation as a replacement of the former biological unity; object constancy in the place of transient need-directed relationships; mental instead of physical outlets for excitation; the beginnings of secondary process thinking; division between id and ego which allows for organization of the earliest, even if still primitive defense mechanisms; beginning control of body functions; building up of a reality sense; etc. As formidable as these accomplishments are, however, in a longitudinal study of young children they take on the aspect of mere underpinning for the moves due to appear together with the step from anality to phallic sexuality: object constancy as the precursor of the emotional entanglements of the oedipus complex; denial replaced by repression and other sophisticated defenses; structuralization increased to make room for the addition of the superego; reality sense extended to include a time sense; and objective instead of subjective appraisal of the happenings in the external world.

If these very well-known facts are listed here, it is done to give weight to the argument that the demands made on the individual by development are countless, ongoing, extensive, complex, and that at all times they contain numerous possibilities for failure, delay, disharmony, and consequently for pathological involvement. No step forward can be taken without the ground being prepared for it by previous achievement. To name only a few examples: object constancy will not occur if, in the first year of life, in the anaclitic relationship to the mother, frustration rather than need fulfillment has been the order of the day; control of sexual and aggressive impulses will remain defective if in the anal phase the fear of loss of love, i.e., the toddler's attachment needs, have not urged him toward compliance with the mother's wishes; identification and superego formation in the phallic phase will be effective only commensurate with the strength and validity of the child's object relationships during orality and anality.

The Concept of the Inadequate Mother as Pathogenic Agent

I criticize above all the lack of data to support the concept of the unempathetic mother as pathogenic agent. There are too many diagnostic statements which take the mere fact of later pathology as evidence that the mother must have failed in her task of empathy with the infant – in spite of no relevant evidence being available, or even when the available data speak against it. Equally, if a child shows healthy adaptation in later life, the mother's adequateness is automatically taken for granted, sometimes in the face of an available history which points to the contrary. From our own observations, we can quote the impressive example of a child who was exposed to potentially traumatic abandonment and lack of care in infancy but who nevertheless developed pleasing normal characteristics and adapted healthily to nursery school and school; as well as of children who developed more or less severe pathology, even though in infancy their successful interaction with a concerned and empathic parent had been open to our view.

The statement that an inadequate mother causes pathology by halting or distorting progress may be erroneous or correct, but in any case it is not reversible. Any longitudinal observation shows that even the most perfect mother–infant interaction and developmentally successful first year are no guarantee of future mental health and certainly no safeguard against neurotic symptomatology. There are countless ways in which such early gains can be lost or, even worse, where the initial benefit of the mother–infant harmony can turn into a threat.

To quote from our own data:

1. In our Baby Clinic we have observed more than one infant who developed in an all-around satisfactory manner during part of the first year while cared for by a concerned, empathic mother, but lost all of his gains irretrievably when, prematurely, she returned to full-time work, leaving the child to a less than adequate substitute.

2. We can cite at least a similar number of instances of the opposite kind, i.e., of mothers whose narcissistically based empathy with the

infant failed to change into the normally more distant and flexible object relationship and thus outlasted its appropriate time. When this happens, the bond interferes drastically with the separation–individuation moves which are normal for the child in the second year of life.

3. We are seeing infants who, on their side, cannot tolerate an ending to the period of biological unity with their mothers, quite especially in cases where the interaction with their mothers was a total one. Typically after the birth of a sibling with its natural consequences or after the return of a father following a prolonged absence, the drop in intimacy with the mother is experienced as traumatic; this may lead to a with-drawal of object libido, increased narcissistic cathexis of the body or the self, and in some instances to long-lasting damage to the growing individual's capacity to form valid object relationship.

4. We, like all other child analysts, are familiar with instances where a girl's exclusive bond with her mother is prolonged from infancy and proves an obstacle to her turn to the father in the phallic phase, i.e., prevents oedipal attachment. It is well known that the child's ambivalent battle against this crippling tie – her conflict with the repressed death wishes against the mother – forms the background of many of the most persistent school phobias.

5. For the analyst of adults, any revival of the mother–infant attachment in the transference – even if it is only approximate – should be immensely instructive. It reveals that during this early phase the individual is insatiable, totally egocentric, and exclusively governed by the urge for pleasurable need and wish fulfillment. There is no doubt that these primitive characteristics by themselves cause pathological involvement and character distortion if in any form they persist longer than the time normally allotted to them.

The Role of Conflict in Pathogenesis

There are serious problems which arise when, as a reason for pathology, interaction with an object is put in place of clashes between contrasting forces within the personality. In fact, our own efforts have gone in a direction opposite to the authors named by Arlow [1981]. Instead of playing down the significance of internal conflict, we have gone out of our way to demonstrate the inevitableness and ubiquity.

1. We have tried to show that in the growing child's battle for impulse control 'developmental defect' can take the place of the regressive processes which initiate neurosis. A different rate of growth, or a different endowment in the relative strength of the drives and the ego, creates internal disharmonies which the individual resolves via compromises. These at least resemble neurotic symptomatology, and are, by the way, a fertile breeding ground for future true neurotic development. The best examples of this are certain obsessional manifestations which occur as early as the anal phase and are not due to regression from the phallic stage, as is the case in true obsessional neuroses. This happens if ego maturation is premature, compared with a much slower development of the drives. In contrast, uncontrollable impulsiveness occurs in cases where ego development lags behind drive development or where, for constitutional reasons, ego strength is minimal with an increased, constitutionally given urgency of the drives. In all the instances mentioned, it is disharmony which leads to conflict, and in turn conflict which leads to pathology.

2. We have made, and tried to substantiate, the assertion that conflict governs the entire process of personality development. That id, ego, and superego are at cross-purposes with each other in the sphere of drive control is basic knowledge. It is less recognized that the same may also be true for the whole range of gradually unfolding ego achievements. I have described this process in detail under the term 'developmental lines,' i.e., sequences which lead from immaturity to maturity concerning characteristics such as emotional self-reliance, adult object relations, peer relations of equality, control of body functions and motility, development of signal anxiety, secondary process functioning, working ability, etc. (A. Freud, 1965). To look at such developmental gains as

the result of smooth maturation seems to me a fallacy. On the contrary, I believe, and have tried to prove, that each step forward in any of these respects represents a hard-won victory in a battle of influences which emanate simultaneously from the inherited constitution, the environment, and the three different agencies within the mind. Thus, in this ego area, too, I see progress as based on compromise formations between conflicting forces. So far as these compromises (fashioned with the help of the synthetic function) are adaptive, they serve progress toward adulthood and mental health. However, as often as not they are nonadaptive in the sense that they halt or limit forward movement. In the latter instance, they give rise, if not to symptomatology, at least to pathological distortions of character and personality (A. Freud, 1981).

Conclusion

I am offering this compressed and abbreviated statement of my own position on pathogenesis to invite discussion. Any contribution which further adds to, widens, or clarifies the subject will be more than welcome.

PART 3

Preadolescence and Adolescence

13

On Certain Difficulties in the Preadolescent's Relation to His Parents (1949)

This paper, and the following paper on adolescence, are included here because of the importance Anna Freud attached to this period of life. Concentration on early childhood events has tended to overshadow the fact that the final formation of an individual's personality is significantly shaped by events in these later years.

Preadolescence is characterized by personality changes of varying degrees of intensity which contrast sharply with the steadier and predictable behaviour of the previous few years (the latency period). Parental influences have less impact. There is a revolt against authority. While the preadolescent has started to turn away from her parents she has not as yet made the new attachments which will characterize adolescence. Anna Freud attributes the rejection of the parents to the return of repressed phantasies of the preoedipal and oedipal periods when the mother and father are the first objects of the young child's love. The preadolescent's revolt against the parents is an attempt to prevent the parents of the present becoming confused with the parents of early childhood. The preadolescent requires help and understanding to help her deal with 'this conflict-laden period' of her life.

> 'On Certain Difficulties in the Preadolescent's Relation to His Parents' (1949b) was first published in German: 'Über bestimmte Schwierigkeiten der Elternbeziehung in der Vorpubertät', in *Die Psychotherapie*, M. Pfister-Amende, ed. Bern: Huber, 1949, pp. 10–16. It appeared in English for the first time in Volume 4 of *The Writings of Anna Freud*, published by International Universities Press, New York, 1968.

The application of psychoanalytic principles and methods to the study of children has left no doubt in our minds as to the overwhelming significance of early developmental happenings and early experiences. Following the new discoveries, many parents and workers in the field have shifted the weight of their efforts, which used to be directed toward the older children, to the understanding and sympathetic handling of the infant and the preschool child. Beneficial as this change of front is, we should not let ourselves be misled into thinking that later events in the individual's life contribute nothing to the final formation of his personality and to its potential abnormalities. While the events of the first five years lay the foundation of neurotic development, it is the experiences in the second decade of life which determine how much of the infantile neurosis will be reactivated or retained and will become, or remain, a permanent threat to mental health. To guide the individual through the anxieties and conflicts of the preadolescent and adolescent periods remains therefore meaningful and rewarding for the educator or psychologist – a task only second in importance to that of guiding the infant through the first difficulties of his instinct and ego development.

The Breakdown of Infantile Morality in Preadolescence

The transition from the latency period to preadolescence is marked in the child's life by a series of upsets. Parents and teachers who are accustomed to assess the child's state only on the basis of his behavior experience these happenings as regressive rather than as progressive steps in development. They are alarmed when all the educational achievements laboriously established in the preceding years are threatened one after the other. Whereas the latency child (approximately from five to eleven, twelve years) had begun to show definite and well-circumscribed character and personality traits, the preadolescent (approximately eleven, twelve to fourteen years) is once more unpredictable. Where the latency child has become modest, reasonable, and well mannered with regard to food, the preadolescent reacts with greed and demandingness; insatiableness in preadolescence frequently leads to thefts of food and sweets. Similar changes occur in almost all the spheres of the child's life. Preadolescent boys in particular are known to be dirty in their lavatory habits and negligent in their clothing. Cruel and bullying actions are regular occurrences; so are mutual masturbation, the seduction of younger children, and sexual compliance toward older playmates; destructive acts, thefts, and robberies are carried out alone or in company with others. Within the family the preadolescent causes disharmony by his selfishness and inconsiderateness; in school he is frequently in trouble because of his lack of interest in the school subjects, his inability to concentrate, his irresponsibleness and insubordination. In short, the whole promising process of adaptation to the environment seems to have stopped short. What parents and teachers are confronted with is once again the full, undiminished impact of the instinctual forces within the child.

The Return of the Repressed in Preadolescence

The writings of Freud (1905), Jones (1922), Aichhorn (1925), Meng (1934, 1943), Pfister (1920, 1922), Zulliger (1935, 1950, 1951) (see also A. Freud, 1936, Chapters 11 and 12) have made us familiar with the psychoanalytic conception according to which this breakdown of infantile morality as the child approaches puberty is an inevitable occurrence, determined by the developmental processes themselves.

During the latency period the instinctual side of the child's personality had been comparatively little in evidence owing to the usual decrease in the libidinal and aggressive urges at this time. This state of affairs ends in preadolescence when a quantitative increase in the drives takes place, serves to reactivate every single one of the component instincts of infantile sexuality and aggression, and creates an overwhelming need for the fulfillment of these wishes. The preadolescent's ego is not equipped to deal with these increased demands from within and under their pressure fails to maintain the previously established equilibrium of the personality. The results are outbreaks of anxiety with increased efforts at ego defense which lead to neurotic behavior and symptom formation or, failing this, to breakthroughs from the repressed instinctual life in the form of either perverse sexual manifestations or dissocial actions.

Thus the preadolescent finds himself in inner disharmony, anxious, inhibited, depressed, and at variance with his environment. This state of mind is not only painful and unfavorable in itself but foreshadows

167

disturbances of adolescence proper by establishing attitudes which may leave more permanent marks, such as a tendency to dissociality, to homosexual object choice, etc.

The Failures of Educational Guidance in Preadolescence

There is no other period in life when the growing child is more in need of help and guidance than in this transitional stage with its almost overwhelming inner and outer struggles. Yet, there is no other time when parents and teachers find themselves equally powerless to help. The methods of guiding the child which had been potent enough with regard to the infant have by this time lost their effectiveness. The preadolescent cares little for praise or criticism, rewards or punishments. He is no longer exclusively dependent on the adult figures in his life for the fulfillment of his needs; nor is his opinion of himself dependent on parents and teachers. His self-criticism and the appreciation or rejection on the part of his contemporaries are more important to him than the signs of approval or disapproval from the adults.

The parents' power over the child is, as we know, based on the child's emotional attachment to them and varies with the strength of this attachment. In preadolescence the child begins to shed these old ties on the one hand, while on the other hand he has not yet made the new attachments which will characterize and stabilize the adolescent years to come: the attachments to heroes and leaders of his own choice, to congenial friends, to impersonal ideals, etc. The preadolescent child is characteristically weak and wavering in his allegiances, lonely, narcissistic, self-centered. It is precisely this impoverishment of his object attachments which renders him less accessible to help and influence from the environment than he has ever been in the past or will be again in the future.

Rejection of the Parents Owing to the Return of the Repressed

The component instincts of infantile sexuality which return from repression bring with them the fantasies of the preoedipal and oedipal period which are directed toward the mother and father as the first objects of the young child's love. These fantasies contain oral, anal, and phallic elements, aggressive wishes, memory traces of satisfactions, of disappointments, frustrations, rivalries, and longings connected with the person of the parents. This medley of emotions, instinctual urges, and affects had filled the consciousness of the young child who had reacted to them with anxiety and guilt, projected them into the environment, repressed them, turned them into the opposite – in short, done everything in his power to deny that they existed in his own mind.

It is only natural that the preadolescent cannot with equanimity face a revival of these repressed fantasies. Their contents fill him with the same horror and anxiety which he felt before, all the more so since his ego has, if anything, grown more intolerant toward infantile strivings in the intervening period. The preadolescent is unable to prevent a rising up of these dreaded early wishes; all he can do is to prevent their linking up with the persons of the parents, who were their objects in the past. It is a characteristic fact that the manifest dreams of this period frequently contain intimate sexual scenes with the parents, barely disguised or distorted by the dream work. In contrast to this, the waking life of the preadolescent is dominated by the opposite tendencies: he avoids the parents, retreats from their company, distrusts their opinions, belittles their interests and achievements, revolts against their authority, feels repelled by their personal appearance and bodily characteristics – in short, he gives evidence in all his actions of his wish to free himself by force from the emotional bondage of which the infantile fantasies are the dreaded survivors. These fears will subside much later when the adolescent has succeeded in attaching his mature genital strivings to an object outside the family. The relations to the parents will then become positive once more and the parents may even regain some remnants of their former role and rights. But at the stage of preadolescence the child cannot conceive of or anticipate this later development.

Parents err, therefore, when they consider themselves as the natural helpmates and advisors of their growing children. Their person is at the very center of the child's conflict, a symbol of the very danger against which the child's ego strives to defend itself. Every approach on the part of the parents, well meant as it may be, merely serves to increase the instinctual danger and therefore the anxieties and the negative responses of the child. Any outsider has a better chance to help, unless a quick transference relationship develops and renders his person as dangerous as that of the parents themselves.

It is poor comfort for the parents to be told that the child's behavior toward them is no more than a reaction against his deep and passionate attachment to them. This alters neither their feeling of helplessness nor the very real disturbance of peace in their family life.

Other Reasons for Rejecting the Parents: The Family Romance

Open revolt against the parents and hostile reactions to their approaches are not the only factors in the parent–child relationship of this period, although they may dominate the surface picture. Other, more subtle developments take place simultaneously. During the whole of the latency period the growth of the critical function of the child's intellect has paved the way toward a new and more realistic assessment of the parents, based no longer on the child's emotions toward them but on a more objective comparison of their personalities with that of other adults.

Seen with new eyes, the parents look so different from the images created in the child's mind during the early years that there gradually emerges a conscious daydream of the existence of two sets of parents, one of them rich, noble, powerful, resembling the figures of kings and queens in fairy tales (the parents of the past); the other, humble, ordinary, subjected to all the common hardships, deprivations, and restrictions (the parents as they are seen in the present). The child's fantasy asserts that he himself is really of noble birth, deserted by his glamorous parents for some reason, and given into the care of the humble ones from whom he will be rescued and reinstalled into his rights and privileges at some later date. This so-called family romance, which originates soon after the passing or breakdown of the oedipus complex, reflects the progressive process of 'outgrowing the parents' combined with the deep regressive longing for the return of the reassuring, comforting relationship of early childhood days, when the parents were thought to be all-powerful, omniscient, unrivaled in perfection, in short, the measure of all things.

The family romance is the forerunner of the more complete, more ruthless disillusionment concerning the parents which characterizes preadolescence. The preadolescent not only sees the father's social position and his professional achievements in a realistic light which reduces the formerly outsize figure to ordinary human proportions. He also revenges himself on the father for the disappointment and disillusionment caused by this transformation, and his overcritical attitude, his contemptuous hurtful remarks, and his modes of behavior bear witness to the depth of disappointment.

To outgrow the infantile dependence on the parents and their overestimation is inseparable from the normal process of ego and superego formation and, assessed from the developmental point of view, it is a purely progressive step. It is merely a by-product of the situation that it also intensifies the existing bitterness by adding some realistic elements to the fantastic criticisms and accusations leveled by the children against their parents at this stage. It is easy to understand why the parents, now doubly devalued, have little or no authority left which they could exercise for the child's benefit.

Further Reasons for the Difficulties in the Child–Parent Relationship: The Fantasy of Changing Roles

There are by now many reasonable parents, with good insight into the inevitableness and painful nature of these problems, who try to meet the child halfway by adapting their own behavior to the growing individual's needs. From early days onward they discourage the child's belief in their omnipotence and perfection, they freely admit their own weaknesses and mistakes and welcome in the growing child every sign of beginning independence and self-reliance. Without waiting for the child's claims in this respect, they renounce much of their position of authority in favor of an attitude of equality with the child and accept the young individual's qualities, attitudes, and idiosyncrasies.

It is worth noting that this tolerant behavior on the part of the parents does not go a long way toward reducing the difficulties of preadolescence, though it may mitigate some of their expressions to a slight degree. It becomes apparent that the preadolescent claims more than even the most accommodating parent can concede. His drive for future independence, realistic as it may appear on the surface, simultaneously serves to hide fantastic motives which stem from the past and represent repressed, unconscious tendencies.

Our analytic investigations of adults and children have taught us that the wish 'to be big' begins in the earliest years and originates in the libidinal relationship to and identification with father and mother, the 'big' people of this period of life. In his fantasy activity the child takes the place of one or the other of these people, usurps their rights, and plays their part.

The direct observation of children of two or three years reveals a particular addition to this fantasy of substitution, or identification. During the mother relationship which precedes the oedipus complex, children frequently play the following game: they change roles with the mother, act the mother's part, while the mother has to be the child; then they carry out on the person of the mother all those activities to which they have to submit passively in real life (such as feeding, washing, undressing, being put to bed, etc.). In a similar game with the father, the child divests him of the articles which are the symbols of his power and strength (such as hat, walking stick, watch, etc.), appropriates them himself, and leaves it to the father to play the part of the child, symbolically weakened and impoverished. Sayings as well as actions of children in this developmental phase betray that 'to be big' means to them to change places with the adult. According to the child's reasoning, he will have to be small while the parents are big; when he has grown up, the parents will have become small, will in fact be his children.

The following are examples taken from the direct observation of young children in the Hampstead Nurseries:

A boy of three years said to his nurse: 'When I am big, I shall push you in the pram.'

A boy aged three and three quarter years said to his favorite nurse when saying good night: 'When I am your nurse, I shall sit with you a long time in the evening ... I shall be so big then that my head touches the ceiling and you will be quite small ... When I am big, I shall always let you have your bath in the big tub.'

Another boy, also aged three and three quarter, said: 'Do you still remember when you were a baby and I was big? You were a good boy and you never spilled your cocoa.'

A boy of four years, in a rage, screamed at his nurse: 'You will get smaller and smaller until you are no higher from the floor than this little bit!'

It is wishes of this kind which the child reactivates in preadolescence and which add peculiar aggressive and, for the parents, intolerable elements to the relationship, which is in any case precarious. On the basis of these infantile tendencies the growing child demands more than equality with the parents. To grow in strength, to mature, to become clever is automatically translated by him into the fall and decline of the parents. When he feels grown up, father and mother appear childish to him; when he feels proud of his own knowledge, the parents seem stupid; the boy's masculinity is synonymous for him with the father's impotence, his social success with seeing the father as a failure.

According to the imaginings which govern the relationship between infant and adult, only one of them can be big, powerful, clever, either the parent or the child. On the basis of this fantasy the growing child expects the parents to renounce their status of mature, reasonable adults altogether, so that he may invest himself with these same attributes instead. It is understandable that even the least rigid and authoritarian parents may find it difficult to meet the child's wishes to that degree.

Conclusion

Parents and teachers will approach the conflicts of preadolescence in a different way when they have insight into their unconscious determinants. The child does not deliberately intend the decline of his morality, poor school performance, and troubled adjustment to family and community; the child suffers, far more than his environment, from the re-emergence of his old, repressed instinctual wishes. What he needs in this conflict-laden period of life is help with and understanding of his inner processes, not rebuke, strictness, or punishment, which will merely further increase his isolation and bitterness. For the reasons presented above, this help should be given by analytically trained educators, and not by the parents, who themselves are at the core of the conflicts.

14

Adolescence (1958 [1957])

This paper is a continuation and expansion of the chapters entitled 'The Ego and the Id at Puberty' and 'Instinctual Anxiety During Puberty' which appeared in The Ego and the Mechanisms of Defence *(1936). There, puberty and adolescence were taken to illustrate the defensive processes which arise to deal with the upsurge of instinct which occurs at that time.*

In this paper on adolescence Anna Freud draws attention to the difficulties of 'fact finding'. Analytic work with adolescents encounters many obstacles which appear to be caused by the individual's difficulty in establishing a therapeutic alliance with the analyst. Like the unhappy lover or the mourner, the adolescent has temporarily lost the capacity to find a new love object to replace the parents. Thus adolescence is characterized by attempts to repair this loss. This leads to rapidly changing relationships with others – idealized at one time and then rejected. This occurs pari passu with a heightened egocentrism. In technical terms, adolescence is a period when there is an instability of libido distribution between self and objects. Adolescent upheavals reflect psychical (unconscious) adjustments which are in progress.

It follows that adolescence is a fertile breeding ground for mental pathology. Emotionally disturbed adolescents reveal vividly what is only to be discerned faintly in a healthy young person. There is disillusionment with the parents. There is either over-evaluation of the self or it is despised or hated. The body is both exciting and distasteful. These manifestations, albeit in a grossly exaggerated form, are to be found in psychoses which have their onset in early and middle adolescence. In these states, the immediate cause of the illness lies in a miscarriage of those developmental processes which enable the young person to loosen her attachment to her parents, consolidate her sense of personal and sexual identity and establish satisfying and stable relationships with others. Anna Freud details the different psychical dangers which confront the adolescent and the means by which the adolescent counters them.

'Adolescence' was read on the occasion of the Thirty-fifth Anniversary of the Worcester Youth Guidance Center on 18 September 1957. It was first published in *The Psychoanalytic Study of the Child*, 13: 255–78 in 1958 and also appeared in *Recent Developments in Psychoanalytic Child Therapy*, Joseph Weinreb, ed., New York: International Universities Press, 1960, pp. 1–24. A German translation followed in 1960 in 'Probleme der Pubertät', *Psyche*, 14: 1–14. The paper was partially reproduced in *The Family and the Law* by Joseph Goldstein and Jay Katz. New York: Free Press, 1965, pp. 907–8.

Adolescence in the Psychoanalytic Theory

I return to the subject of adolescence after an interval of twenty years. During this time much has happened in analytic work to throw added light on the problems concerned and to influence the conditions of life for young people, whether normal or abnormal. Nevertheless, in spite of partial advances, the position with regard to the analytic study of adolescence is not a happy one, and especially unsatisfactory when compared with that of early childhood. With the latter period, we feel sure of our ground, and in possession of a wealth of material and information which enables us to assume authority and apply analytic findings to the practical problems of upbringing. When it comes to adolescence, we feel hesitant and, accordingly, cannot satisfy the parents or educational workers who apply for help to us and to our knowledge. One can frequently hear it said that adolescence is a neglected period, a stepchild, where analytic thinking is concerned.

These complaints, which come from two sides, from the parents as well as from the analytic workers themselves, seem to me to warrant closer study and investigation than they have received so far.

Adolescence in the Psychoanalytic Literature

The psychoanalytic study of adolescence began, as is well known, in 1905 with the relevant chapter of the *Three Essays on the Theory of Sexuality*. Here, puberty was described as the time when the changes set in which give infantile sexual life its final shape. Subordination of the erotogenic zones to the primacy of the genital zone; the setting up of new sexual aims, different for males and females; and the finding of new sexual objects outside the family were listed as the main events. While this exposition explained many features of the adolescent process and behavior which had been unexplained before, the newly developed notion of the existence of an infantile sex life could not but lower the significance of adolescence in the eyes of the investigators. Before the publication of the *Three Essays*, adolescence had derived major significance from its role as the beginning of sex life in the individual; after the discovery of infantile sexuality, the status of adolescence was reduced to that of a period of final transformations, a transition and bridge between the diffuse infantile and the genitally centered adult sexuality.

Seventeen years later, in 1922, Ernest Jones published a paper on 'Some Problems of Adolescence' which dwelt on a 'correlation between adolescence and infancy' as its most distinctive point. Following the pronouncement in the *Three Essays* that the phase of development corresponding to the period between the ages of two and five must be regarded as an important precursor of the subsequent final organization, Jones showed in detail how 'the individual *recapitulates and expands* in the second decennium of life the development he passed through during the first five years . . .' (p. 398). He ascribed the difference in 'the circumstances in which the development takes place' but went as far as propounding 'the general law . . . that adolescence recapitulates infancy, and that the precise way in which a given person will pass through the necessary stages of development in adolescence is to a very great extent determined by the form of his infantile development' (p. 399). In short: 'these stages are passed through on different planes at the two periods of infancy and adolescence, but in very similar ways in the same individual' (p. 399).

Jones's important but isolated contribution to the problem coincided with a peak in the publications of Siegfried Bernfeld in Vienna, a true explorer of youth, who combined work as a clinical analyst and teacher of analysis with the unceasing study of adolescence in all its aspects of individual and group behavior, reactions to social influences, sublimations, etc. His most significant addition to the analytic theory was the description of a specific kind of male adolescent development (1923), the so-called 'protracted' type which extends far beyond the time limit normal for adolescent characteristics, and is conspicuous by 'tendencies toward productivity whether artistic, literary or scientific, and by a strong bent toward idealistic aims and spiritual values . . .' As the solid background for his assumptions, Bernfeld published, in cooperation with W. Hoffer, a wealth of material consisting of self-observations of adolescents, their diaries, poetic productions, etc.

While Bernfeld accounted in this manner for the elaborations of the normal adolescent processes by the impact of internal frustrations and external, environmental pressures, August Aichhorn, also in Vienna, approached the problem from the angle of dissocial and criminal development. His work lay with those young people who respond to the same pressures with failure to adapt, faulty superego development, and revolt against the community. His book *Wayward Youth* (1925) acquired world renown as the outstanding pioneering attempt to carry psychoanalytic knowledge into the difficult realm of the problems of the young offender.

Familiar with Bernfeld's views, and having been intimately connected with Aichhorn's studies, I contributed in 1936 two papers under the titles 'The Ego and the Id at Puberty' and 'Instinctual Anxiety during Puberty.'[1] In my case, interest in the adolescent problems was derived from my concern with the struggles of the ego to master the tensions and pressures arising from the drive derivatives, struggles which lead in the normal case to character formation, in their pathological outcome to the formation of neurotic symptoms. I described this battle between ego and id as terminated first by a truce at the beginning of the latency period and later breaking out once more with the first approach of puberty, when the distribution of forces inside the individual is upset by quantitative and qualitative changes in the drives. Threatened with anxiety by the drive development, the ego, as it has been formed in childhood, enters into a struggle for survival in which all the available methods of defense are brought into play and strained to the utmost. The results, that is, the personality changes which are achieved, vary. Normally, the organization of ego and superego alter sufficiently to accommodate the new, mature forms of sexuality. In less favorable instances, a rigid, immature ego succeeds in inhibiting or distorting sexual maturity; in some cases, the id impulses succeed in creating utter confusion and chaos in what has been an orderly, socially directed ego during the latency period. I made the point that, more than any other time of life, adolescence with its typical conflicts provides the analyst with instructive pictures of the interplay and sequence of internal danger, anxiety, defense activity, transitory or permanent symptom formation, and mental breakdown.

Interest increased in the postwar years and brought a multitude of contributions, especially from the United States. Fortunately for the student of the subject, Leo A. Spiegel published in 1951 a lengthy 'Review of Contributions to a Psychoanalytic Theory of Adolescence.' Although his attempt to construct an integrated theory out of often widely divergent parts could hardly be successful, the paper serves a most useful purpose by abstracting, reviewing, and classifying the material. He grouped the publications under headings such as:

'Classification of Phenomenology' (Bernfeld, Hartmann, Kris, and Loewenstein, Wittels)

'Object Relations' (Bernfeld, Buxbaum, H. Deutsch, Erikson, Fenichel, A. Freud, W. Hoffer, Jones, A. Katan, Landauer)

'Defense Mechanisms' (Bernfeld, H. Deutsch, Fenichel, A. Freud, Greenacre, E. Kris)

'Creativity' (Bernfeld, A. Freud)

'Sexual Activity' (Balint, Bernfeld, Buxbaum, H. Deutsch, Federn, Ferenczi, S. Freud, Lampl-de Groot)

'Aspects of Ego Functioning' (Fenichel, A. Freud, Harnik, Hoffer, Landauer)

'Treatment' (Aichhorn, K. R. Eissler, A. Freud, Gitelson, A. Katan, M. Klein, Landauer, A. Reich).

A detailed bibliography attached to the review contained altogether forty-one papers by thirty-four authors, covering apparently every theoretical, clinical, and technical aspect of the subject.

But in spite of this impressive list of contributors and contributions the dissatisfaction with our knowledge of the field remained unaltered, nor did our own, or the parents', confidence in our analytic skill with adolescent patients increase. There was now much published evidence to the contrary; nevertheless, adolescence remained, as it had been before, a stepchild in psychoanalytic theory.

Some Difficulties of Fact Finding Concerning Adolescence

There are, I believe, two different causes which may, possibly, account for our bewilderment when faced with all the intricacies of the adolescent process.

When, in our capacity as analysts, we investigate mental states, we rely, basically, on two methods: either on the analysis of individuals in whom that particular state of mind is in action at the moment, or on the reconstruction of that state in analytic treatment undertaken at a later date. The results of these two procedures, used either singly or in combination with each other, have taught us all that we, as analysts, know about the developmental stages of the human mind.[2]

It happens that these two procedures which have served us well for all other periods of life, prove less satisfactory and less productive of results when applied to adolescents.

Reconstruction of Adolescence in Adult Analysis

As regards reconstruction, I am impressed how seldom in the treatment of my adult cases I succeed in reviving their adolescent experiences in full force. By that I do not mean to imply that adult patients have an amnesia for their adolescence which resembles in extent or in depth the amnesia for their early childhood. On the contrary, the memories of the events of the adolescent period are, normally, retained in consciousness and told to the analyst without apparent difficulty. Masturbation in preadolescence and adolescence, the first moves toward intercourse, etc., may even play a dominant part in the patients' conscious memories and, as we know well, are made use of to overlay and hide the repressed masturbation conflicts and the buried sexual activities of earlier childhood. Further, in the analyses of sexually inhibited men who deplore the loss of erective potency, it is fairly easy to recover the memories of the bodily practices carried out in adolescence – frequently very crude and cruel ones – which served at that time to prevent erections or to suppress them as soon as they occurred.

On the other hand, these memories contain no more than the bare facts, happenings, and actions, divorced from the affects which accompanied them at the time. What we fail to recover, as a rule, is the atmosphere in which the adolescent lives, his anxieties, the height of elation or depth of despair, the quickly rising enthusiasms, the utter hopelessness, the burning – or at other times sterile – intellectual and philosophical preoccupations, the yearning for freedom, the sense of loneliness, the feeling of oppression by the parents, the impotent rages or active hates directed against the adult world, the erotic crushes – whether homosexually or heterosexually directed – the suicidal fantasies, etc. These are elusive mood swings, difficult to revive, which, unlike the affective states of infancy and early childhood, seem disinclined to re-emerge and be relived in connection with the person of the analyst.

If this impression, which I gathered from my own cases, should be confirmed by other analysts of adults, such a failure – or partial failure – to reconstruct adolescence might account for some of the gaps in our appraisal of the mental processes during this period.

Analysis During Adolescence

Discussing the contributions dealing with the analytic therapy of adolescents, Spiegel (1951) deplored what seemed to him an undue pessimism on the part of some authors. He pointed to the need of adapting the analytic technique to the adolescent patients' particular situation and expressed surprise at the absence of explicit discussion of an introductory phase 'analogous to the one used with children and delinquents'.

Actually, since 1951, some further papers on the subject of technique appeared in print. Two of them dealt with the opening phase (Fraiberg, 1955; Noshpitz, 1957), a third with the terminal one (Adatto, 1958). (See also Eissler, 1958; Geleerd, 1958.)

While these authors brought material to highlight the special technical difficulties encountered in the beginning and ending of therapy, work on adolescents done in our Hampstead Child-Therapy Clinic emphasized special technical difficulties met with in the very center of it, i.e., at the critical moment when preadolescence gives way to adolescence proper, when the revolt against the parents is anticipated in the transference and tends to lead to a break with the analyst, i.e., to abrupt and undesirable termination of treatment from the patient's side.

Thus, according to experience, special difficulties are encountered in the beginning, in the middle, and in connection with the end of treatment. Put in other words, this can only mean that the analytic treatment of adolescents is a hazardous venture from beginning to end, a venture in which the analyst has to meet resistances of unusual strength and variety. This is borne out by the comparison of adolescent with adult cases. In adult analysis, we are used to handle the difficult technical situations with certain hysterical patients who cannot bear frustration in the transference and try to force the analyst to enact with them their revived love and hate feelings in an actual personal relationship. We are used to guard against the obsessional patients' technique of isolating words from affect and of tempting us to interpret unconscious content while it is divorced from its emotional cathexis. We attempt to deal with the narcissistic withdrawal of the borderline schizophrenics, the projections of the paranoid patients who turn their analyst into the persecuting enemy, the destructive hopelessness of the depressed who claim disbelief in any positive outcome of the analytic effort; the acting-out tendencies and the lack of insight of the delinquent or psychopathic characters. But in the disturbances named above, we meet either the one or the other of these technical difficulties, and we can adapt the analytic technique to the resistance which is specific to the type of mental disorder. Not so in adolescence where the patient may change rapidly from one of these emotional positions to the next, exhibit them all simultaneously, or in quick succession, leaving the analyst little time and scope to marshal his forces and change his handling of the case according to the changing need.

Obstacles in the Libido Economy: Comparison with the States of Mourning and Unhappy Love

Experience has taught us to take a serious view of such major and repeated inadequacies of the analytic technique. They cannot be explained away by individual characteristics of the patients under treatment or by any accidental or environmental factors which run counter to it. Nor can they be overcome simply by increased effort, skill, and tact on the part of the analyst. They have to be taken as indications that something in the inner structure of the disturbances themselves differs markedly from the pattern of those illnesses for which the analytic technique was originally devised and to which it is most frequently applied (Eissler, 1950). We have to gain insight into these divergences of pathology before we are in a position to revise our technique. Where the analyses of children, of delinquents, and of certain borderline states are concerned, this has already happened. What the analytic techniques had to provide for in these cases were the immaturity and weakness of the patients' ego; their lower threshold for the toleration of frustration; and the lesser importance of verbalization with increased importance of action (acting out) for their mental economy. It remains to be pointed out what corresponding factors are characteristic of the adolescent disorders, i.e., to what specific inner situation of the patients our technique has to be adjusted to make adolescents more amenable to analytic treatment.

So far as I am concerned, I am impressed by a similarity between the responses of these young patients and those of two other well-known types of mental upset, namely, the reactions to treatment during unhappy love affairs and during periods of mourning. In both these states, there is much mental suffering and, as a rule, the urgent wish to be helped; in spite of this, neither state responds well to analytic therapy. Our theoretical explanation of this comparative intractability is the following: being in love as well as mourning are emotional states in which the individual's libido is fully engaged in relation to a real love object of the present, or of the most recent past, the mental pain being caused by the difficult task to withdraw cathexis and give up a position which holds out no further hope for return of love, that is, for satisfaction. While the individual is engaged in this struggle, insufficient libido is available to cathect the person of the analyst, or to flow back regressively and reinvest former objects and positions. Consequently, neither the transference events nor the past become meaningful enough to yield material for interpretation. The immediate object (of love, or of mourning) has to be given up before analytic therapy can become effective.

To my mind, the libidinal position of the adolescent has much in common with the two states described above. The adolescent too is engaged in an emotional struggle – moreover, in one of extreme urgency and immediacy. His libido is on the point of detaching itself from the parents and of cathecting new objects. Some mourning for the objects of the past is inevitable; so are the 'crushes,' i.e., the happy or unhappy love affairs with adults outside the family, or with other adolescents, whether of the opposite or of the same sex; so is, further, a certain amount of narcissistic withdrawal which bridges the gap during periods when no external object is cathected. Whatever the libidinal solution at a given moment may be, it will always be a preoccupation with the present time and, as described above, with little or no libido left available for investment either in the past or in the analyst.

If this supposition as to the libido distribution in the adolescent personality can be accepted as a correct statement, it can serve to explain some of our young patients' behavior in treatment, such as: their reluctance to cooperate; their lack of involvement in the therapy or in the relationship to the analyst; their battles for the reduction of weekly sessions; their unpunctuality; their missing of treatment sessions for the sake of outside activities; their sudden breaking off treatment all together. We learn here by contrast how much the continuity of the average adult analysis owes to the mere fact of the analyst being a highly cathected object, quite apart from the essential role played by the transference in the production of material.

There are, of course, those cases where the analyst himself becomes the new love object of the adolescent, i.e., the object of the 'crush,' a constellation which will heighten the young patient's keenness to be 'treated.' But apart from improved attendance and punctuality, this may mean merely that the analyst is brought up against another of the specific difficulties of the analyses of adolescents, namely, the urgency of their needs, their intolerance for frustration, and their tendency to treat whatever relationship evolves as a vehicle for wish fulfillment and not as a source of insight and enlightenment.

Under these conditions it is not surprising that besides analytic therapy many alternative forms of treatment for adolescents have been evolved and practiced, such as manipulation of the environment, residential treatment, the setting up of therapeutic communities, etc. Valuable as these experimental approaches are from the practical point of view, they cannot, of course, be expected to contribute directly to our theoretical insight into the unconscious contents of the adolescent's mind, the structure of his typical disturbances, or into the details of the mental mechanisms by which these latter are maintained.

Clinical Applications

What follows is an attempt to apply at least some of our hard-won insights to three of the most pressing problems concerning adolescence.

Is the Adolescent Upset Inevitable?

There is, first, the ever-recurrent question whether the adolescent upheaval is welcome and beneficial as such, whether it is necessary, and, more than that, inevitable. On this point, psychoanalytic opinion is decisive and unanimous. The persons in the child's family and school who assess his state on the basis of behavior may deplore the adolescent upset which, to them, spells the loss of valuable qualities, of character stability, and of social adaptation. As analysts, who assess personalities from the structural point of view, we think otherwise. We know that the character structure of a child at the end of the latency period represents the outcome of long-drawn-out conflicts between id and ego forces. The inner balance achieved, although characteristic of each individual and precious to him, is preliminary only and precarious. It does not allow for the quantitative increase in drive activity, or for the changes of drive quality which are both inseparable from puberty. Consequently, it has to be abandoned to allow adult sexuality to be integrated into the individual's personality. The so-called adolescent upheavals are no more than the external indications that such internal adjustments are in progress.

On the other hand, we all know individual children who as late as the ages of fourteen, fifteen, or sixteen show no such outer evidence of inner unrest. They remain, as they have been during the latency period, 'good' children, wrapped up in their family relationships, considerate sons of their mothers, submissive to their fathers, in accord with the atmosphere, ideas, and ideals of their childhood background.

Convenient as this may be, it signifies a delay of normal development and as such is a sign to be taken seriously. The first impression conveyed by these cases may be that of a quantitative deficiency of drive endowment, a suspicion which will usually prove unfounded. Analytic exploration reveals that this reluctance to 'grow up' is derived not from the id but from the ego and superego aspects of the personality. These are children who have built up excessive defenses against their drive activities and are now crippled by the results, which act as barriers against the normal maturational processes of phase development. They are, perhaps more than any others, in need of therapeutic help to remove the inner restrictions and clear the path for normal development, however 'upsetting' the latter may prove to be.

Is the Adolescent Upset Predictable?

A second question which we are frequently asked to answer concerns the problem whether the manner in which a given child will react in adolescence can be predicted from the characteristics of his early infantile or latency behavior. Apart from the more general affirmative answer given by Ernest Jones (1922), only one among the authors named above has made clear and positive assertions in this respect. Siegfried Bernfeld (1923), discussing the protracted type of male adolescence and its characteristics, established the links between this form of puberty and a specific type of infantile development based on the following three conditions: (a) that the frustration of infantile sexual wishes has been shattering for the child's narcissism; (b) that the incestuous fixations to the parents have been of exceptional strength and have been maintained throughout the latency period; (c) that the superego has been established early, has delineated sharply from the ego, and that the ideals contained in it are invested with narcissistic as well as with object libido.

Other and less precise answers to the same question are scattered through the literature. We find the opinion that, in the majority of cases, the manifestations of the adolescent process are not predictable since they depend almost wholly on quantitative relations, i.e., on the strength and suddenness of drive increase, the corresponding increase in anxiety causing all the rest of the upheaval.

I suggested in 1936 that adolescence occasionally brings about something in the nature of a spontaneous cure. This happens in children whose pregenital activities and characteristics remained dominant throughout latency until the increase in genital libido produces a welcome decrease in pregenitality. This latter occurrence, on the other hand, can be matched by a corresponding one which produces the opposite effect: when phallic characteristics have remained dominant during latency, the increase in genital libido produces the effect of an exaggerated and threatening aggressive masculinity.

It seems to be generally accepted that a strong fixation to the mother, dating not only from the oedipal but from the preoedipal attachment to her, renders adolescence especially difficult. This latter assertion, on the other hand, has to be correlated with two recent findings of a different nature which we owe to our work done in Hampstead Child-Therapy Clinic. One of these findings is derived from the study of orphaned children who were deprived of the relationship to a stable mother figure in their first years. This lack of a mother fixation, far from making adolescence easier, constitutes a real danger to the whole inner coherence of the personality during that period. In these cases adolescence is frequently preceded by a frantic search for a mother image; the internal possession and cathexis of such an image seem to be essential for the ensuing normal process of detaching libido from it for transfer to new objects, i.e., to sexual partners.

The second finding mentioned above is derived from the analyses of adolescent twins, in one case children whose twin relationship in infancy had been observed and recorded in minute detail (Burlingham, 1951a). In their treatments it transpired that the 'adolescent revolt' against the love objects of infancy demands the breaking of the tie to the twin in no lesser degree than the breaking of the tie to the mother. Since this libidinal (narcissistic as well as object-directed) cathexis of the twin is rooted in the same deep layer of the personality as the early attachment to the mother, its withdrawal is accompanied by an equal amount of structural upheaval, emotional upset, and resulting symptom formation. Where, on the other hand, the twin relationship survives the adolescent phase, we may expect to see a delay in the onset of maturity or a restrictive hardening of the character of the latency period similar to the instances mentioned above in which the childhood love for the parents withstands the onslaught of the adolescent phase.

187

To return to the initial question: it seems that we are able to foretell the adolescent reactions in certain specific and typical constellations but certainly not for all the individual variations of infantile personality structure. Our insight into typical developments will increase with the number of adolescents who undergo analysis.

Pathology in Adolescence

This leaves us with a third problem which, to my mind, outweighs the preceding ones so far as clinical and theoretical significance is concerned. I refer to the difficulty in adolescent cases to draw the line between normality and pathology. As described above, adolescence constitutes by definition an interruption of peaceful growth which resembles in appearance a variety of other emotional upsets and structural upheavals.[3] The adolescent manifestations come close to symptom formation of the neurotic, psychotic, or dissocial order and merge almost imperceptibly into borderline states, initial, frustrated, or fullfledged forms of almost all the mental illnesses. Consequently, the differential diagnosis between the adolescent upsets and true pathology becomes a difficult task.

For the discussion of this diagnostic problem I leave most other authors in the field to speak for themselves and summarize my own impressions based on past and present clinical experience.

In 1936, when I approached the same subject from the aspect of the defenses, I was concerned with the similarity between the adolescent and other emotional disturbances rather than with the differences between them. I described that adolescent upsets take on the appearance of a neurosis if the initial, pathogenic danger situation is located in the superego with the resulting anxiety being felt as guilt: that they resemble psychotic disturbances if the danger lies in the increased power of the id itself, which threatens the ego in its existence or integrity. Whether such an adolescent individual impresses us, then, as obsessional, phobic, hysterical, ascetic, schizoid, paranoid, suicidal, etc., will depend on the one hand on the quality and quantity of id contents which beset the ego, on the other hand on the selection of defense mechanisms which the latter employs. Since, in adolescence, impulses from all pregenital phases rise to the surface and defense mechanisms from all levels of crudity or complexity come into use, the pathological results – although identical in structure – are more varied and less stabilized than at other times of life.

Today it seems to me that this structural description needs to be amplified, not in the direction of the similarity of the adolescent to other disorders but in that of their specific nature. There is in their etiology at least one additional element which may be regarded as exclusive to this period and characteristic of it: namely, that the danger is felt to be located not only in the id impulses and fantasies but in the very existence of the love objects of the individual's oedipal and preoedipal past. The libidinal cathexis of them has been carried forward from the infantile phases and was merely toned down or inhibited in aim during latency. Therefore, the reawakened pregenital urges, or – worse still – the newly acquired genital ones, are in danger of making contact with them, lending a new and threatening reality to fantasies which seemed extinct but are, in fact, merely under repression.[4] The anxieties which arise on these grounds are directed toward eliminating the infantile objects, i.e., toward breaking the tie with them. Anny Katan (1937) has discussed this type of defense, which aims above all at changing the persons and the scene of conflict, under the term of 'removal.' Such an attempt may succeed or fail, partially or totally. In any case, I agree with Anny Katan that its outcome will be decisive for the success or failure of the other, more familiar line of defensive measures which are directed against the impulses themselves.

A number of illustrations will serve to clarify the meaning of this assumption.

Defense Against the Infantile Object Ties

Defense by Displacement of Libido: There are many adolescents who deal with the anxiety aroused by the attachment to their infantile objects by the simple means of flight. Instead of permitting a process of gradual detachment from the parents to take place, they withdraw their libido from them suddenly and altogether. This leaves them with a passionate longing for partnership which they succeed in transferring to the environment outside the family. Here they adopt varying solutions. Libido may be transferred, more or less unchanged in form, to parent substitutes, provided that these new figures are diametrically opposed in every aspect (personal, social, cultural) to the original ones. Or the attachment may be made to so-called 'leaders,' usually persons in age between the adolescent's and the parents' generation, who represent ideals. Equally frequent are the passionate new ties to contemporaries, either of the same or of the opposite sex (i.e., homosexual or heterosexual friendships) and the attachments to the adolescent groups (or 'gangs'). Whichever of these typical solutions is chosen, the result makes the adolescent feel 'free' and revel in a new precious sense of independence from the parents who are then treated with indifference bordering on callousness.

Although the direction taken by the libido in these instances is, in itself, on lines of normality, the suddenness of the change, the carefully observed contrast in object selection, and the overemphasis on the new allegiances mark it as defensive. This course represents an all-too-hasty anticipation of normal growth rather than a normal developmental process.

It makes little further difference to the emotional situation whether the libidinal flight is followed by actual flight, i.e., whether the adolescent also 'removes' himself bodily from his family. If not, he remains in the home in the attitude of a boarder, usually a very inconsiderate one so far as the older and younger family members are concerned.

On the other hand, the withdrawal of cathexis from the parents has most decisive consequences for the rest of the defensive processes. Once the infantile objects are stripped of their importance, the pregenital and genital impulses cease to be threatening to the same degree. Consequently, guilt and anxiety decrease and the ego becomes more tolerant. Formerly repressed sexual and aggressive wishes rise to the surface and are acted on, the actions being taken outside the family in the wider environment. Whether this acting out will be on harmless, or idealistic, or dissocial, or even criminal lines will depend essentially on the new objects to whom the adolescent has attached himself. Usually, the ideals of the leader of the adolescent group or gang are taken over wholeheartedly and without criticism.

Adolescents of this type may be sent for treatment after their actions have brought them into conflict with their schools, their employers, or the law. As far as psychoanalytic therapy is concerned, they seem to offer little chance for the therapeutic alliance between analyst and patient without which the analytic technique cannot proceed. Any relationship to the analyst and, above all, the transference to him would revive the infantile attachments which have been discarded; therefore, the adolescent remains unresponsive. Moreover, the escape from these attachments has suspended the feeling of internal conflict, at least temporarily; consequently, the adolescent does not feel in need of psychological help. Aichhorn had these points in mind when he maintained that adolescents of the dissocial and criminal type needed a long period of preparation and inner rearrangement before they could become amenable to analytic treatment. He maintained that the latter would be successful only if, during this preparation in a residential setting, the adolescent made a new transference of object love, reawakened his infantile attachments, internalized his conflicts once more – in short, became neurotic.

To try and analyze an adolescent in this phase of successful detachment from the past seems to be a venture doomed to failure.

Defense by Reversal of Affect: A second typical reaction to the same danger situation is, although less conspicuous outwardly, more ominous in nature inwardly.

Instead of displacing libido from the parents – or, more likely, after failing to do so – the adolescent ego may defend itself by turning the emotions felt toward them into their opposites. This changes love into hate, dependence into revolt, respect and admiration into contempt and derision. On the basis of such reversal of affect the adolescent imagines himself to be 'free,' but, unluckily for his peace of mind and sense of conflict, this conviction does not reach further than the conscious surface layer of his mind. For all deeper intents and purposes he remains as securely tied to the parental figures as he has been before; acting out remains within the family; and any alterations achieved by the defense turn out to his disadvantage. There are no positive pleasures to be derived from the reversed relationships, only suffering, felt as well as inflicted. There is no room for independence of action, or of growth; compulsive opposition to the parents proves as crippling in this respect as compulsive obedience to them can prove to be.[5] Since anxiety and guilt remain undiminished, constant reinforcement of defense is necessary. This is provided in the first place by two methods: denial (of positive feeling) and reaction formations (churlish, unsympathetic, contemptuous attitudes). The behavioral picture that emerges at this stage is that of an uncooperative and hostile adolescent.

Further pathological developments of this state of affairs are worth watching. The hostility and aggressiveness, which in the beginning serve as a defense against object love, soon become intolerable to the ego, are felt as threats, and are warded off in their own right. This may happen by means of projection; in that case the aggression is ascribed to the parents, who as a consequence become the adolescent's main oppressors and persecutors. In the clinical picture, this appears first as the adolescent's suspiciousness and, when the projections increase, as paranoid behavior.

Conversely, the full hostility and aggression may be turned away from the objects and employed inwardly against the self. In these cases, the adolescents display intense depression, tendencies toward self-abasement and self-injury, and develop, or even carry out, suicidal wishes.

During all stages of this process, personal suffering is great and the desire to be helped intense. This in itself is no guarantee that the adolescent in question will submit to analytic therapy. He will certainly not do so if treatment is urged and initiated by the parents. Whenever this happens, he will consider analysis as their tool, extend his hostility or his suspicions to include the person of the analyst, and refuse cooperation. The chances are better if the adolescent himself decides to seek help and turns to analysis, as it were, in opposition to the parents' wishes. Even so, the alliance with the analyst may not be of long duration. As soon as a true transference develops and the positive infantile fantasies come into consciousness, the same reversal of affect tends to be repeated in the analytic setting. Rather than relive the whole turmoil of feelings with the analyst, many adolescent patients run away. They escape from their positive feelings, although it appears to the analyst that they break off treatment in an overwhelmingly strong negative transference.

Defense by Withdrawal of Libido to the Self: To proceed in the direction of increasing pathology: Withdrawal of libido from the parents, as it has been described above, does not itself determine its further use or fate. If anxieties and inhibitions block the way toward new objects outside the family, the libido remains within the self and may be employed to cathect the ego and superego, thereby inflating them. Clinically this means that ideas of grandeur will appear, fantasies of unlimited power over other human beings or of major achievement and championship in one or more fields. Or the suffering and persecuted ego of the adolescent may assume Christlike proportions with corresponding fantasies of saving the world.

On the other hand, the cathexis may become attached only to the adolescent's body and give rise to the hypochondriacal sensations and feelings of body changes that are well known clinically from the initial stages of psychotic illness.

In either case, analytic therapy is indicated as well as urgent. Treatment will dispel the appearance of severe abnormality if it reopens a path for the libido, either to flow backward and recathect the original infantile objects, or to flow forward, in the direction described above, to cathect less frightening substitutes in the environment.

What taxes the analyst's technical skill in these cases is the withdrawn state of the patient, i.e., the problem of establishing an initial relationship and transference. Once this is accomplished, the return from narcissistic withdrawal to object cathexis will relieve the patient, at least temporarily.

I believe that there are many cases where the analyst would be wise to be content with this partial success without urging further treatment. A further and deeper involvement in the transference may well arouse all the anxieties described above and again lead to abrupt termination of the analysis due to the adolescent's flight reaction.

Defense by Regression: The greater the anxiety aroused by the object ties, the more elementary and primitive is the defense activity employed by the adolescent ego to escape them. Thus, at the extreme height of anxiety, the relations with the object world may be reduced to the emotional state known as 'primary identification' with the objects. This solution, with which we are familiar from psychotic illnesses, implies regressive changes in all parts of the personality, i.e., in the ego as well as in the libido organization. The ego boundaries[6] are widened to embrace parts of the object together with the self. This creates in the adolescent surprising changes of qualities, attitudes, and even outward appearance. His allegiance to persons outside himself betrays itself in these alterations of his own personality (i.e., his identifications) rather

than in an outflow of libido. Projections, together with these identifications, dominate the scene and create a give-and-take between the self
and the object which has repercussions on important ego functions.
For example, the distinction between the external and internal world
(i.e., reality testing) becomes temporarily negligible, a lapse in ego
functioning which manifests itself in the clinical picture as a state of
confusion.

Regression of this kind may bring transitory relief to the ego by
emptying the oedipal (and many of the preoedipal) fantasies of their
libidinal cathexis,[7] but this lessening of anxiety will not be long-lived.
Another and deeper anxiety will soon take its place, which I have
characterized on an earlier occasion [A. Freud, 1952a] as the fear of
emotional surrender, with the accompanying fear of loss of identity.

Defense Against the Impulses

Where the defenses against the oedipal and preoedipal object ties fail
to achieve their aim, clinical pictures emerge which come nearest to
the borderline of psychotic illness.

The 'Ascetic' Adolescent: One of these, the 'ascetic' adolescent, I have
previously described as fighting all his impulses, preoedipal and oedipal,
sexual and aggressive, extending the defense even to the fulfillment of
the physiological needs for food, sleep, and body comfort. This, to me,
seems the characteristic reaction of an ego driven by the blind fear of
overwhelming id quantities, an anxiety which leaves no room for the
finer distinctions between vital or merely pleasant satisfactions, the
healthy or the morbid, the morally permitted or forbidden pleasures.
Total war is waged against the pursuit of pleasure as such. Accordingly,
most of the normal processes of instinct and need satisfaction are
interfered with and become paralyzed. According to clinical observation, adolescent asceticism is, with luck, a transitory phenomenon. For
the analytic observer it provides precious proof of the power of defense,
i.e., of the extent to which the normal, healthy drive derivatives are
open to crippling interference by the ego.

On the whole, analytic treatment of the ascetic type does not present
as many technical difficulties as one would expect. Perhaps, in these

individuals, defense against the impulses is so massive that they can permit themselves some object relationship to the analyst and thus enter into transference.

The 'Uncompromising' Adolescent: Another, equally abnormal adolescent is described best as the 'uncompromising' type. The term, in this instance, does refer to more than the well-known conscious, unrelenting position adopted by many young people who stand up for their ideas, refuse to make concessions to the more practical and reality-adapted attitudes of their elders, and take pride in their moral or aesthetic principles. 'Compromise,' with these adolescents, includes processes which are as essential for life as, for example, the cooperation between impulses, the blending of opposite strivings, the mitigation of id strivings by inter-ference from the side of the ego. One adolescent whom I observed in analysis did his utmost, in pursuit of this impossible aim, to prevent any interference of his mind with his body, of his activity with his passivity, his loves with his hates, his realities with his fantasies, the external demands with his internal ones, in short, of his ego with his id.

In treatment, this defense was represented as a strong resistance against any 'cure,' the idea of which he despised in spite of intense suffering. He understood correctly that mental health is based in the last resort on harmony, i.e., on the very compromise formations which he was trying to avoid.

The Concept of Normality in Adolescence

Where adolescence is concerned, it seems easier to describe its patholo-gical manifestations than the normal processes. Nevertheless, there are in the above exposition at least two pronouncements which may prove useful for the concept: (1) that adolescence is by its nature an interruption of peaceful growth; and (2) that the upholding of a steady equilibrium during the adolescent process is in itself abnormal. Once we accept for adolescence disharmony within the psychic structure as our basic fact, understanding becomes easier. We begin to see the upsetting battles which are raging between id and ego as beneficient attempts to restore peace and harmony. The defensive methods which are employed either against the impulses or against the object cathexis begin to appear legitimate and normal. If they produce pathological results, this happens not because of any malignancy in their nature, but because they are overused, overstressed, or used in isolation. Actually, each of the abnormal types of adolescent development, as it is described above, also represents a potentially useful way of regaining mental stability, normal if combined with other defenses, and if used in moderation.

To explain this statement in greater detail: I take it that it is normal for an adolescent to behave for a considerable length of time in an inconsistent and unpredictable manner; to fight his impulses and to accept them; to ward them off successfully and to be overrun by them; to love his parents and to hate them; to revolt against them and to be dependent on them; to be deeply ashamed to acknowledge his mother before others and, unexpectedly, to desire heart-to-heart talks with her; to thrive on imitation of and identification with others while searching unceasingly for his own identity; to be more idealistic, artistic, generous, and unselfish than he will ever be again, but also the opposite: self-centered, egoistic, calculating. Such fluctuations between extreme opposites would be deemed highly abnormal at any other time of life. At this time they may signify no more than that an adult structure of personality takes a long time to emerge, that the ego of the individual in question does not cease to experiment and is in no hurry to close down on possibilities. If the temporary solutions seem abnormal to the onlooker, they are less so, nevertheless, than the hasty decisions made in other cases for one-sided suppression, or revolt, or flight, or withdrawal, or regression, or asceticism, which are responsible for the truly pathological developments described above.

While an adolescent remains inconsistent and unpredictable in his behavior, he may suffer, but he does not seem to me to be in need of treatment. I think that he should be given time and scope to work out his own solution. Rather, it may be his parents who need help and guidance so as to be able to bear with him. There are few situations in life which are more difficult to cope with than an adolescent son or daughter during the attempt to liberate themselves.

Summary

In the foregoing paper I have reviewed and summarized some of the basic literature on adolescence[8] as well as my own views on the subject. My former description of the defensive processes in adolescence has been amplified to include specific defense activities directed against the oedipal and preoedipal object ties.

Notes

1. See Chapters 11 and 12 in *The Ego and the Mechanisms of Defence* (1936).
2. It may be worthwhile to remind the reader in this connection that our knowledge of the mental processes of infancy has been derived from reconstructions in the analyses of adults and was merely confirmed and enlarged on later by analyses or observations carried out in childhood.
3. Adolescence is, of course, not the only time in life when alterations of a physiological nature cause disturbances of mental equilibrium. The same happens in later years in the climacterium; and recently Grete L. Bibring (1959) has given a convincing description of similar damage to the equilibrium of mental forces during pregnancy.
4. An important clinical instance of this can be found in adolescent girls with anorexia nervosa. Here the infantile fantasies of oral impregnation receive added impetus from the new real possibilities of motherhood opened up by genital development. Consequently, the phobic measures adopted against the intake of food on the one hand and identification with the mother on the other hand are overemphasized to a degree which may lead to starvation.
5. Ferenczi pointed to this effect of 'compulsive disobedience' many years ago.
6. See Federn (1952) and, following him, Freeman *et al.* (1958).
7. See in this connection M. Katan (1950).
8. [Since this paper was written, several psychoanalytic studies of adolescence have been published. See Eissler (1958), Geleerd (1958), Hellman (1958), Erikson (1959), Solnit (1959), Lampl-de Groot (1960), Jacobson (1961, 1964), Blos (1962), Lorand and Schneer (1962), Sprince (1962), Frankl (1963), Rosenblatt (1963), Laufer (1964, 1965, 1966, 1968), Rexford (1966), H. Deutsch (1967), Kestenberg (1967–1968).]

PART 4

Technique and the Scope of Psychoanalysis

15

Indications for Child Analysis (1945)

Written in 1945, this paper includes more than the title indicates. Most significantly, it anticipates many of Anna Freud's later developmental hypotheses. The selection of children for analysis is not to be based on symptomatology, but seen from the perspective of the child's developmental status. The criteria which are of value in the case of adult patients – 'neurotic suffering' and 'disturbances of normal capacities' – do not apply in the case of children. The decision as to whether or not a child requires analysis is made more difficult by the fact that neurotic symptoms in childhood are often transitory in nature. This makes an assessment of the child's developmental status, i.e., her instinctual and ego development, more important than the symptomatology itself. This is explicated by the detailed description which Anna Freud gives, earlier in the paper, of the evolution of the libido and the ego and the influences which can render this development anomalous.

The paper is also of interest because Anna Freud turns to the problems and controversies which have characterized the history of child analysis. At first, there was the resistance of the general public to the idea of subjecting children to analysis. Then there was the controversy about the technique of treatment. Could the child's play be regarded as the equivalent of an adult patient's free associations? There were those who maintained that analysis could be conducted with children whose verbal capacity was still limited. Anna Freud was sceptical about this. Play, as important as it is, is only one of the means by which an insight into a child's psychopathology becomes possible.

'Indications for Child Analysis' was first published in *The Psycho-analytic Study of the Child*, 1: 127–49, 1945; also in *The Psycho-Analytical Treatment of Children*. London: Imago Publishing Co., 1946; New York: International Universities Press, 1959, pp. 67–93. French translation: 'Indications pour le traitement psychanalytique des enfants', *Revue Française de Psychanalyse*, 13: 70–96, 1949. German translation: 'Indikations-stellung in der Kinderanalyse', *Psyche* (Heidelberg), 21: 233–53, 1967.

Since 1905, when a phobia in a five-year-old boy was first treated by psychoanalysis, the father acting as intermediary between child and analyst (see Freud, 1909), child analysis as a therapeutic method has had a stormy and checkered career. There is hardly a detail that has remained uncontested, that has not at some time become the starting point for controversy.

Controversies

In some respects child analysis revived the same objections that the psychoanalytic treatment of adults had to meet and overcome a full decade earlier.

The Sexual Prejudice

At the end of the last century the conception of a sexual origin of adult neurosis ran counter to all the prevalent prejudices. However, no one went so far as to deny altogether the existence of adult sexuality, although medical and lay opinion failed to concede it the importance it deserved. On the other hand, everyone violently objected to the possible existence of a sexual life in childhood. Psychoanalysis had laid itself open to the reproach of overestimating the role of sexuality in the adult and to a similar charge of inventing an infantile sex life, contrary to the facts then known and accepted by physicians and educators. Thus the existence of an infantile sexuality had to be established and proved at the same time that its importance in the development of the neuroses of childhood had to be demonstrated (Freud, 1905).

The Fear of Immorality as a Consequence of Psycho-analytic Treatment

A second argument originally used against the analytic treatment of adult neurotics was based on a misconception of the psychoanalytic process itself. It was thought that the constant preoccupation with instinctual tendencies which is inherent in the analytic work, the release of these tendencies from repression, and their consequent emergence in consciousness could have only the one effect of their expression in actions, i.e., the fulfillment of the instinctual (sexual and aggressive) wishes which had been kept under repression before the treatment. According to this argument, psychoanalytic treatment would lead directly to immorality and licentiousness. It needed much patient and lengthy demonstration to convince the public that this was not the case; that, on the contrary, unconscious tendencies were deprived of most of their power when an outlet into conscious thought was opened up for them: relegated to the unconscious, these instinctual urges had been out of reach; uncovered, and lifted to the conscious level, they automatically came under the patient's control and could be dealt with according to his best ideas and ideals.

The same objections that had been successfully refuted with regard to adult patients arose again in full force when child analysis made its first appearance. The argument was now advanced that the child could certainly not be trusted with the same discretion in dealing with his reawakened instinctual tendencies as the adult. Surely the child would want to make full use of the license offered him in the analytic situation and would give free rein to his instinctual urges inside and outside of the analytic hour. Or even if his intentions were otherwise, his attempts at restraint and adaptive behavior would be entirely overrun by the instinctual forces let loose through the agency of analytic treatment. Fears of this kind were expressed not only by doctors, teachers, and parents, but were shared to some extent by certain analysts who thought it quite possible that child analysis might need some special form of educational guidance as its constant implement and counterpart. But, as experience proved, this was not necessary as often as had been expected. It was demonstrated repeatedly that when a child's ego and superego were both severe enough to produce an infantile neurosis, they could also, with some help, be relied on to deal with the sexual and aggressive impulses that emerged from repression after the neurosis had been analyzed successfully. Fears of this nature are more justified when the object of child analysis is not a neurotic, but a dissocial, delinquent, or otherwise deficient character.

Controversies about the Technique of Child Analysis

It immediately became obvious that the classical analytic technique was not applicable to children, at least not before the age of puberty, or at best prepuberty. Free association, the mainstay of analytic technique, had to be counted out as a method; young children are neither willing nor able to embark on it. This fact affects dream interpretation, the second main approach to the unconscious. Children tell their dreams freely; but without the use of free association, the interpretation of the manifest dream content is less fruitful and convincing. The child analyst frequently has to supply the links between the manifest dream content and the latent dream thoughts according to his own intimate knowledge of the child's inner situation at the time of dreaming. Furthermore, it is impossible to establish the same outward setting for the analytic hour. Children placed on the analytic couch for the purpose of relaxed concentration are usually completely silenced. Talk and action cannot be separated from each other in their case. Nor can the patient's family be wholly excluded from the analysis. Insight into the seriousness of the neurosis, the decision to begin and to continue treatment, persistence in the face of resistance or of passing aggravations of the illness are beyond the child, and have to be supplied by the parents. In child analysis, the parents' good sense plays the part which the healthy part of the patient's conscious personality plays during adult analysis to safeguard and maintain the continuance of treatment.

Appropriate substitutes for free association were accordingly the prime necessity in establishing techniques suitable to the varying needs of different phases of childhood. The first divergence of opinion between child analysts arose about this matter. Certain child analysts (Hug-Hellmuth in Vienna, Melanie Klein in Berlin and later in London) developed the so-called play techniques of child analysis, a method that promised to give more or less direct access to the child's unconscious.

According to this technique, the child's spontaneous play activity with small toys, offered by the analyst for free use within the analytic hour, was substituted for free association. The individual actions of the child in connection with this material were considered to be equivalent to the individual thoughts or images in a chain of free associations. In this manner the production of material for interpretation became largely independent of the child's willingness or ability to express himself in speech.

Other child analysts (on the European continent and in the United States) were reluctant to employ this play technique to the same extent. Although such a method of interpretation allowed certain flashes of direct insight into the child's unconscious, it seemed to them open to objections of various kinds. Like all interpretation of symbols (for instance, purely symbolic dream interpretations), it had a tendency to become rigid, impersonal, and stereotyped, without being open to corroboration from the child; it aimed at laying bare the deeper layers of the child's unconscious without working through the conscious and preconscious resistances and distortions. Furthermore, these analysts refused to accept such activities as actual equivalents of free associations. The free associations of the adult patient are produced in the set situation of analytic transference and, although they are freed from the usual restrictions of logical and conscious thought, they are under the influence of the patient's one governing aim to be cured by analysis. The play activity of the child is not governed by any similar intention. This leads to the further open and controversial question whether the relationship of the child to the analyst is really wholly governed by a transference situation. Even if one part of the child's neurosis is transformed into a transference neurosis, as happens in adult analysis, another part of the child's neurotic behavior remains grouped around the parents, who are the original objects of this pathogenic past.

Considerations of this nature led a large number of child analysts to evolve techniques of a different kind. They worked on the various derivatives of the child's unconscious in dreams and daydreams, in imaginative play, in drawings, etc., including the emotional reactions of the child, both in and outside of the analytic hour. As in adult analysis, the task was to undo the various repressions, distortions, displacements, condensations, etc., that had been brought about by neurotic defense mechanisms until, with the active help of the child, the unconscious content of the material was laid bare. Such cooperation with the child naturally presupposes the extensive use of speech.[1]

The method of symbolic interpretation of play activity that Melanie Klein devised for her technique was later taken over by psychotherapists and widely used in England and America under the name of 'play therapy.' But in these instances it was deprived of its full original meaning, since it was used without reference to an analytic transference situation.

Controversies Concerning the Appropriate Age for Child Analysis

Differences in the manner in which child analysis was practiced inevitably led to differences in opinion concerning the age at which the therapeutic method was applicable. The decisive factor in this respect was the use of speech. Melanie Klein and her followers repeatedly expressed the opinion that with the help of play technique, children can be analyzed at almost any age, from earliest infancy onward. When the faculty of speech in the child is of major importance for the treatment, it is hardly possible to contemplate analysis before the age of two or three. The majority of cases treated with the Vienna-Prague-Berlin techniques (as distinguished from the Kleinian techniques) were considerably older than that; many of them were analyzed at the height of the oedipus complex (four or five years) or in the latency period.

Controversies Concerning the Range of Application of Child Analysis

Here again a wide difference of opinion exists between the school of Melanie Klein and the former Vienna school of child analysts, many of whom are at present working in America. Child analysts of the Kleinian school express the view that every child passes through phases of grave abnormality (psychotic states, depressions, etc.) in infancy, and that normal development in later stages can best be safeguarded by early child analysis, by analyzing the psychotic residues of the earliest stage whenever outward circumstances permit. The former Vienna school, on the other hand, is of the opinion that the application of child analysis should be restricted to the most severe cases of the infantile neurosis which every child experiences at one time or another before entering the latency period. With all other children, the application of analytic knowledge to their educational handling may prove sufficient to guide them through the intricacies of their instinctual and emotional development.

The Evaluation of Infantile Neuroses

Selection of Cases

Those who do not share the opinion that analysis should be universally applied to all children are faced with the task of selecting their cases, that is, of assessing the seriousness of the various manifestations of infantile neurosis. In practice, child analysts today have little opportunity to determine this matter by their own judgement. The question whether or not a child should be analyzed is usually decided for them, and not infrequently for inadequate reasons. Children who are severely ill are often withheld from treatment because their parents, with whom the decision lies, know too little about analysis, or are frightened by the little they do know; because the parents are reluctant to have the intimacies of their own lives exposed to the analyst; because they fear the sexual enlightenment of the child; because they, especially the mothers, are unwilling to see a stranger succeed with their child when they themselves have failed. Sometimes the reasons given are very superficial: analytic hours would clash with school hours; would take up the time otherwise given to sport, handicraft, or some other occupation, from which the child usually has ceased to benefit because of his neurotic disturbance. The most decisive factor is frequently the matter of time and distance. To accompany a child to and from a daily analytic hour is a heavy burden on the mother; if long distances aggravate the issue, this factor is often prohibitive.

On the other hand, a number of children are sent into analysis not because they suffer from an excessive form of infantile neurosis, but because their parents, either as analytic patients themselves, or as practicing analysts, are more apt than others to detect and evaluate signs of neurotic behavior whenever they appear. They readily decide upon analytic treatment at an early stage to avoid for their child the graver forms of neurotic suffering which they know only too well from personal experience. Their positive decision for treatment, like the above-mentioned negative decision against treatment, is based on a personal attitude rather than on an objective assessment of the child's disturbance.

The child cases actually in treatment in our day, either in child departments of psychoanalytic clinics or in private practice, are thus a more or less chance selection, not a representative selection of infantile neuroses that are most in need of therapeutic help. It is to be expected that these conditions will change when knowledge about the mental development of the young child becomes more widespread, that is, when parents and physicians understand at least as much about the importance of instinctual, emotional, and intellectual setbacks in the child's development as they understand now about his bodily illnesses. The assessment of the disturbance and the decision whether treatment is indicated or not will then be left to the psychiatrist or psychoanalyst, as it is nowadays left to the pediatrician in all cases of organic disturbance.

The Factor of Neurotic Suffering

The question whether or not an adult neurotic seeks treatment is in the last resort dependent on the amount of suffering his neurotic symptoms cause him. For this reason neurotics undergo treatment more willingly than, for instance, perverts. A perversion disrupts normal life as much as a neurosis; but the perversion brings satisfaction, whereas neurotic symptoms are painful.

This statement can be maintained in spite of the fact that every neurosis is also a source of pleasure to the individual who is afflicted with it. The pleasure that the patient derives from the distorted gratification of repressed wishes, that is, from his symptoms, is not experienced as pleasure by his conscious system. The conscious pleasure, on the other hand, that neurotics often enjoy owing to the consideration they receive from their environment, a sense of importance, etc., is of a secondary nature and not really inherent in the illness. Whenever this secondary gain from the illness becomes greater than the neurotic suffering itself, the patient will be unfit for treatment, or will in most cases quite openly refuse to be treated. The existence of neurotic suffering is an important prerequisite, if it is not indispensable, for the attitude of persistence and determination that a patient needs to carry him through the difficulties of analytic treatment.

In dealing with cases of infantile neurosis, one realizes that neurotic suffering is not present in the child to the same extent; and that whatever the amount of suffering may be, it is equally divided between the child and the parents. In some instances, it is only the reaction of the parents to the symptom that brings home to the child, secondarily, that he suffers from a symptom. Such is the case, for instance, in the frequent feeding disturbances of childhood. Children become bad eaters for reasons that originate in their early mother relationship, in their reactions against their oral—sadistic tendencies, etc. The normal intake of food is thus made difficult or impossible for neurotic reasons. The child, left to himself, would gladly put up with this symptom and eat less. Mothers, on the other hand, suffer acutely from anxiety caused by this behavior of the child and, in their turn, inflict suffering on the bad eater through reproaches, scoldings, forcible measures, etc. The same occurs in the neurotic bed wetting of childhood. Children under a certain age tend to show indifference toward this symptom, while the adult environment suffers badly on its account; the amount of pain it causes the child depends on the reaction of the environment. The night terrors of children (pavor nocturnus) usually cause consternation and anxiety to the parents, while the afflicted child himself remains unmindful of them. Temper tantrums are disturbing to the family; for the child himself, they are often a welcome outlet. Neurotic displays of aggression and destructiveness, as they occur in the initial stages of an obsessional neurosis, are the most disturbing symptoms to the family; the child rather indulges in them. His attitude in this respect resembles that of an adult pervert more closely than that of an adult neurotic.

Acute neurotic suffering is felt by the child in all states of anxiety before a consistent defense against it has become established. Once anxiety has been warded off, either by phobic or obessional mechanisms, the amount of the child's suffering again depends on the reactions of the environment. Many mothers fear the child's anxiety as much as the child does himself. Consequently they do not oppose the child's phobic or obsessional arrangements; they even help actively in various ways to reinforce them. They help the child avoid the danger situations in which anxiety arises; they adapt themselves to bedtime ceremonials and to eating, dressing, and washing obsessions, etc. Their object is to spare the child the suffering inherent in his anxiety, and simultaneously to avoid the violent outbreaks that ensue whenever an obsessional act or phobic precaution is opposed or prevented. There are thus many infantile phobias and obsessional neuroses that exist under the surface and that are not felt as acutely painful by the child, although they cause endless trouble for the mother.

During the time of mass evacuations in England, 1940, many children became neurotic sufferers after separation from their parents. It would be erroneous to conclude that they had all acquired a neurosis due to their traumatic experiences. In many cases, their neuroses had merely not been in evidence while they lived with their mothers; acute anxiety and suffering appeared when they had to live with people who were less willing or able to show consideration for their phobic and obsessional arrangements.

To sum up: the presence or absence of suffering cannot be considered a decisive factor when making up one's mind about the treatment of a child. There are many serious neurotic disorders that the child bears with equanimity; there are less serious ones that cause pain. Since the decision to seek advice for the child normally lies with the parents, an infantile neurosis is more likely to be brought for treatment when its symptoms are disturbing to the environment. The parents will be guided in their assessment of the seriousness of the situation by the impact of the child's neurosis on themselves. They show more concern, for instance, about aggressive and destructive states than about inhibitions; obsessional acts are taken more lightly than anxiety attacks, though in reality they represent a more advanced stage of the same disorder; bed wetters are taken to clinics more regularly than any other group of cases; the beginning stages of passive femininity in young boys, though often decisive for their whole future abnormality, are almost invariably overlooked.

The Factor of Disturbance of Normal Capacities

An adult neurosis is assessed not only subjectively according to suffering, but objectively according to the extent to which it damages the two main capacities of the individual: the capacity to lead a normal love and sex life and the capacity to work. Patients usually decide to come into treatment when one or both of these functions are severely threatened.

The question arises whether there are any functions in the child's life, the disturbance of which is an equally significant indicator of the seriousness of the infantile neurosis.

The child's love and sex life, as revealed by psychoanalytic studies, is not less extensive and certainly not less intensive than that of the adult. But, after the first severe repressions of early childhood have occurred, it is inhibited in its aims. Though centered according to objects (oedipus complex), it is diffuse in its manifestations (component instincts), not organized under the primacy of any single one of them. Furthermore, it lacks a climax in its expressions, the disturbance of which could be taken as indicative of disturbance of function. The intactness of the child's sexuality is therefore more difficult to gauge than that of the adult. To measure the child's capacity for object love, we can only measure his libidinal urges directed toward the outer world as against his narcissistic tendencies. Normally, after the first year of life, object love should outweigh narcissism; satisfaction derived from objects should become increasingly greater than autoerotic gratification. An infantile neurosis can seriously interfere with these proportions. But the assessment of these factors in the diagnosis is too subtle and too complicated to be of immediate help as an indication for treatment.

It is equally difficult to find in the child's life a parallel for the disturbance of work capacity. It has been suggested by many authors that play is as important for the child as work is for the adult, and that consequently a test of the child's ability to play is indicative of the extent of his disturbance. This view seems to be borne out by the fact that neurotic children are invariably disturbed in their play activity. In certain types of neurosis, imaginative play is excessive, at the expense of constructive play. In its initial stages, this is sometimes construed as an asset by the parents, as the sign of a particularly vivid imagination and of artistic gifts. But when such play becomes repetitive, monotonous, and interferes with all other kinds of activity, the neurotic element is unmistakable: it is a sign that the child is fixated at a certain point of his libidinal development.

Although the child's capacity for constructive play is the nearest substitute for the adult capacity to work, the two functions remain so far removed from each other that it is hardly justifiable to give them an equal place in the diagnosis. Since play is governed by the pleasure principle, the disturbance of each of the two functions has a different clinical significance.

The Factor of Disturbance of Normal Development

It is thus impractical in the evaluation of an infantile neurosis to use the same criteria that we apply in the case of an adult. Childhood is a process *sui generis*, a series of developmental stages in which each manifestation has its importance as a transition, not as a final result. Its tasks and accomplishments cannot therefore be compared with those of the more static stage of adulthood. In childhood there is only one factor of such central importance that its impairment through a neurosis calls for immediate action; namely, the child's ability to develop, not to remain fixated at some stage of development before the maturation process has been concluded. The suggestion is therefore to assess the seriousness of an infantile neurosis, not according to its damage to the activities or attitudes of the child in any special way or at any given moment, but according to the degree to which it prevents the child from developing further.

Libidinal Development

The Sequence of Libidinal Development

On the basis of our present knowledge it is possible, even in a cursory examination, to establish whether a child's libidinal development corresponds to his age level. We roughly know the age limits for the pregenital organizations of the libido, and for some of the subdivisions. Gross disturbance in the order of events, or a child's failure to progress from any of these transitory stages when he is neither organically nor mentally deficient, points to serious neurotic interference.

But wide individual variation and the scantiness of our knowledge prevent us from making anything beyond rough estimates on this basis. Normally, we have to take into account the extensive overlapping of the various organizations. The oral phase, for instance, persists for months after the anal-sadistic organization has come into being; anal-sadistic manifestations do not disappear with the beginning of the phallic phase. The latency period is usually in existence for one or two years before the tendencies of the first infantile period fade into the background. It would, for instance, be erroneous to conclude, from a persistence of oral or anal forms of autoerotic gratification into the fourth or fifth year, that the child has failed to reach the phallic level. It never happens that the libido expresses itself wholly in the manifestations of the latest phase of development; some part of it invariably remains attached to earlier modes of expression. To insure normality it is sufficient if the major proportion of the libido reaches the organization appropriate to the age of the child. The manifestations of this level then predominate over the earlier ones, though never as fully as the genital tendencies of adult sex life predominate over the pregenital tendencies.

There are more reliable data on which an opinion about the libidinal development of a child could, theoretically, be based: namely, the fantasies that accompany the child's masturbatory activities. But practically this is of little help for the diagnosis. Such fantasies are always hidden, very frequently unconscious, and laid bare only in the course of an analysis, not in a consultation.

The Intactness of Libidinal Development

The libidinal normality of a child is also judged according to the fate of the individual component instincts. We would not expect any of the component instincts to be completely absent from the clinical picture (if the child is neither organically nor mentally deficient) except as a sign of severe neurotic disturbance.

But again, individual variation is sufficiently great for us to be cautious in our conclusions. The component instincts (including tendencies like exhibitionism and scoptophilia), or rather their manifestations, are not visible to the same degree in all children; nor does any individual child present us with equally clear pictures of all the different libidinal tendencies. Usually some of the component instincts are clearly in evidence, others remain faint and shadowy. In some children, cruelty, exhibitionism, or greed may appear to have played no appreciable part in their lives; in others, these urges may be unmistakable, while other component instincts are seen only on closer observation. Individual differences of this nature are based on constitutional factors, and are not due to neurotic interference; but they create points of special libidinal interests in the child's life, so-called fixation points, which play an important role in later neurotic development.

Neurotic Interference with Libidinal Development; The Factor of Spontaneous Recovery

Neurosis in an adult damages the intactness of the sexual organization; an infantile neurosis also interferes directly with the forward movement of the libido.

In the beginning stage of a neurotic conflict the libido flows backward (regression), and attaches itself once more to earlier libidinal wishes (fixation point), in order to avoid anxiety that has arisen on a higher level of sexual organization. The ego of the child thus finds itself confronted with primitive desires (oral, aggressive, anal), which it is not prepared to tolerate. It defends itself against the instinctual danger with the help of various mechanisms (repression, reaction formation, displacements, etc.), but if such defense is unsuccessful, neurotic symptoms arise which represent the gratification of the wish, distorted in its form by the action of the repressive forces. While these symptoms persist, they are the central expression of the child's libidinal life.

From the developmental point of view it is immaterial whether such symptoms are a little more or a little less painful. What counts is that with the onset of the neurotic disturbance the libido has been arrested in its course. Instead of moving on toward more adult levels, it has been forced backward, and important gains have thereby been relinquished. Qualities and achievements that depend directly on the stage of libido development are lost. The child who regresses to the oral level, for instance, simultaneously reverts to the emotional attitudes connected with it: he becomes once more insatiable, exacting, impatient for wish fulfillment, 'like a baby.' Regression from the phallic to the anal-sadistic level destroys the so recently acquired attributes of generosity, manliness, and protectiveness, and substitutes for them the domineering possessiveness that belongs to the earlier libidinal level. But progress is made at the same time in other spheres that are not influenced directly by the neurosis. The child grows bigger and more intelligent, and his development becomes inharmonious since this growing body and mind are tied to an instinctual and emotional life that cannot keep pace with it. The need for treatment seems urgent at this stage, not because the neurosis itself is so severe, but because the presence of the neurosis hinders libido development.

On the other hand, this impression of a serious interruption is frequently misleading. After a shorter or a longer duration, symptoms may suddenly lose importance; the fixation may dissolve and the libido, freed from restrictions, may resume its normal progressive flow. The child has, as the popular saying goes, 'outgrown' his neurosis, and therapeutic help has become unnecessary.

As analysts, who collect their evidence from adult cases, we do not readily believe in the spontaneous cure of a neurosis, and we view such appearances with distrust when they are brought to our notice. We know that neuroses can, at best, change their manifestations. Neurotic anxiety, for instance, can disappear, but only to reappear later, centered around a different object or topic. Changes in life circumstances can alleviate a neurotic condition in various ways. Neurotic suffering can be exchanged for ordinary suffering; for instance, the real loss of an object through death can take the place of the imagined loss of love from that object, and thus make a particular symptom unnecessary. A masochistic desire which at one time manifests itself in neurotic symptoms can at another time find satisfaction in organic illness. Inhibitions or obessional restrictions that cripple a patient's activity may be given up when he is, for instance, in prison or in a concentration camp, that is, when he lives under crippling and inhibiting circumstances. A neurosis can further be relieved through separation from the love object onto which it has transferred its central issues; but such relief will be temporary, and the neurosis will soon re-establish itself completely when a new transference has taken place. Happenings of this kind, though often described as spontaneous cures, are merely slight fluctuations within the neurotic arrangement itself.

On the basis of our theoretical knowledge, there is little reason to expect the neuroses of adults to clear up spontaneously. The neurotic symptom, as a compromise between two opposing forces, can alter only when decisive changes take place, either in the instinctual tendencies or in the ego and superego of the individual. Neither kind of change is likely to happen in the adult. The infantile wish, to which the patient has regressed, will remain potent. The ego will retain its repressive energy (unless a serious deteriorating process sets in). Furthermore, the whole process is anchored in the unconscious, and therefore is not accessible to influence from conscious levels.

In this respect the conditions of an infantile neurosis are completely different. The child's libido organization is, as described before, in a fluid state, the libido moving on continuously toward new positions. A component instinct that is charged with libido in one phase may be devoid of interest at another. The child need not remain hopelessly tied to any fixation point to which it has been led back through regression. If the fixation is not excessively strong, the libido has a good chance of freeing itself again, carried forward by the next wave of development. This possibility is greatest at times when the biological urges are of special strength, as they are at the onset of the phallic phase (four to five years) and of puberty.

It is a common error to believe that as a result of the strengthening of the ego children become more neurotic in the latency period. On the contrary, the latency period marks a definite decrease in infantile neurosis. At that time the strength of the infantile sexual wishes dies down, partly for biological reasons, partly owing to the frustration of the child's oedipal wishes. This lessens the need for defense against the instincts and alters the compromise formations between ego and id which lie at the root of symptom formation. Many infantile neuroses therefore disappear at approximately that date, their spontaneous cure being due to these quantitative changes.

Puberty is rightly regarded as a time when numerous neurotic disturbances may be expected to appear. It is less well known that puberty also removes certain neurotic symptoms that are typical for the years preceding it. This refers especially to the neurotic behavior of boys who all through early childhood and latency fight against repressed wishes of a passive feminine kind. Their behavior is characterized by anxiety, due to their repressed castration wishes, and by a superficial and noisy aggressiveness which is a reaction against the underlying passivity. Puberty brings a biological increase in genital masculinity which, while it lasts, puts the anal, passive, and feminine tendencies out of action. This is a spontaneous cure in the real sense of the word: the neurosis not merely changes its form, but the underlying unconscious forces themselves undergo alterations. It depends on future developments whether the former constellation of instincts will come to the fore again in adult life; in this case the neurotic defense against it will be reinstated.

There are other typical examples of infantile neuroses which almost invariably disappear before adolescence: bed wetting, and some of the common eating disturbances. They also are swept away by the libidinal changes before or in puberty. Certain disorders affecting sexual potency, and certain nervous disorders of the stomach may, much later, appear in their stead, if the adult genital sex organization is not strong enough to maintain itself.

To sum up: the decision whether a child needs therapeutic help or not can be based on the state of the libido development. An infantile neurosis can be treated as a transitory disorder as long as the libido organization of the child remains fluid and shows progressive tendencies. Infantile neuroses disappear whenever the normal forward movement of the libido is strong enough to undo neurotic regression and fixation. When the libido constellations become rigid, stabilized, and monotonous in their expressions, the neurosis threatens to remain permanently. This means that treatment is indicated.

This view, that child analysis should be used only in cases where there is slight or no hope for a spontaneous recovery, is opposed to that of many analysts who hold that child analysis should be used prophylactically to remove the pathogenic fixation points.

Neurotic Interference with Ego Development

The threat which the occurrence of an infantile neurosis constitutes for the libido development is so apparent that it has not escaped notice. The same danger is less obvious in relation to the development of the ego. On the contrary, it is generally believed that neurotic development in children is associated with an especially good, frequently an especially early, blossoming of this side of the child's personality. It is left an open question whether it is the infantile neurosis that, as one of its results, overemphasizes the side of the ego forces, or whether it is an early ripening of the ego that predisposes the child to a severe infantile neurosis.

The following is an attempt to examine the questions whether a childhood neurosis helps or harms the development of the ego; what the interactions are between the two processes; and whether the degree of harm done to the ego can serve as a further indication for the therapeutic use of child analysis.

The Quantitative Factor in Ego Development

A neurosis can affect the ego quantitatively, that is, in its strength.

The term 'ego strength' is not meant to denote an absolute quantity of ego forces, which are in themselves not measurable. It refers to the relative efficiency of the ego with regard to the contents of the id (instinctual drives) and to the forces of the environment with which the ego has to deal. This ego strength varies repeatedly in the course of normal development.

In the beginning of life the instinctual drives are of overwhelming strength and the first crystallizations of the ego are completely under their domination and at their service. The child's growing awareness of the outside world, the beginnings of his ability to retain and connect memory traces, to foresee events, to draw conclusions from them, etc., are used exclusively for the purpose of instinct gratification. The better the ego development of an infant, the better are his chances to gratify his desires and to use the outside world for the fulfillment of his wishes.

This undisputed reign of the instincts does not outlast early infancy. As a result of his strong emotional ties to the parents, the child soon begins to consider their wishes, which are frequently in opposition to his own. To the degree in which he is able to identify with his parents, his ego develops hostile attitudes toward his instinctual demands and attempts to oppose and manage them. Simultaneously the ego begins to correlate conflicting emotions and tendencies instead of giving alternate expression to them. This means suppressing one or the other side of them (love or hate, active or passive desires, etc.), and creates new conflicts between ego and id. Although all these efforts are made by the ego to assert itself against the instincts, no real ego superiority is established in the first period of childhood. The pull of wish fulfillment is still too strong, and the principle that governs the child's life remains to a large extent the pleasure principle. It is only the final frustration of the oedipal wishes, with the consequent fading out of the early libido organizations, that changes the situation decisively in favor of ego strength.

While the sexual drives remain latent (latency period), the ego assumes superiority, directs the actions of the child, establishes the reality principle, and effects the first real adaptation to the exigencies of the outside world. Ego and id have now reversed their positions.

But the new order is by no means permanent. Ego superiority is overthrown again as soon as the first signs of adolescence appear. Because of the biological increase in pregenital tendencies during prepuberty, and genital tendencies during puberty, the libidinal forces rise in strength. Throughout adolescence, ego forces and id forces struggle with each other for the upper hand, a combat that is responsible for many of the conflicting and abnormal manifestations of that period.

It is impossible to predict before the end of adolescence whether the individual will emerge from this struggle with a strong or a weak ego, but this uncertainty is normal and necessary. It is essential for the development of a rich and vivid personality that this part of character formation (the establishment of a definite proportion between id strength and ego strength) should not be terminated too early. The changing flow of libidinal development should, while it lasts, find scope for at least transitory expression without being too crippled by the dictates of a strong ego. On the other hand, every new gain in the ego achievements should contribute something toward altering the balance between ego and id and mark a further step in perfecting a sensible management of the instincts.[2] The personality of the child will develop as long as the relationship between ego and id remains fluid and changeable.

The existence of an infantile neurosis acts like a calcification in the middle of a living organism. Every neurotic symptom represents an attempt to establish an artificial balance between an instinctual wish and the repressive forces of the ego, a balance that is rigid and, once established, not open to correction. If symptoms multiply and the neurosis organizes itself into a coherent structure, the whole relationship between ego and id becomes hopelessly paralyzed.

Another and more direct manner in which infantile neuroses reduce ego strength is due to the regression that occurs invariably at the beginning of symptom formation. Libidinal regression is always accompanied by a certain amount of ego regression; ego strength is to a degree dependent on the phase of libido development. The oral organization of the libido, for instance, always goes together with a special urgency of wishes and impatience for wish fulfillment. This means, practically speaking, that a child who regresses from the genital to the oral level simultaneously regresses from ego strength to ego weakness. Or, to put it differently, regression from the genital to the oral level implies regression from the reality principle to the pleasure principle.

The neurotic child may thus, at first glance, appear to possess a strong ego. But this appearance is misleading. The child's ego is committed to definite and irreversible attitudes toward instinctual drives, in order to maintain the delicate balance necessary for symptom formation. However, his ego is in reality weaker than that of a normal child since the id forces have gained a more or less lasting victory in the disguise of symptom formation.

The Qualitative Factor in Ego Development

From the first months of life onward the ego develops from a mere receiving station for dimly perceived stimuli into an organized center where impressions are received, sorted out, recorded, interpreted, and where appropriate action is undertaken. A separate part of the ego fulfills the task of supervising thoughts and actions from a moral point of view (superego). The essential ego functions in this respect are:

testing of inner and outer reality; building up of memory; the synthetic function of the ego; and ego control of motility. All through childhood a maturation process is at work which, in the service of an increasing knowledge of and adaptation to reality, aims at perfecting these functions, at rendering them more and more objective and independent of the emotions, until they can become as accurate and reliable as a mechanical apparatus. In the last resort, an individual's efficiency in life (under less civilized conditions, his chance of survival) is determined by the perfection or imperfection of these ego functions.

Simultaneously with this maturation process, however, another even more powerful tendency is at work in the child. These ego achievements are wholly acceptable to him as far as they serve instinct gratification and provide some mastery over the environment. But it soon becomes evident that this new way of functioning brings at least an equal, if not an overwhelmingly greater, amount of pain, discomfort, and anxiety. Each one of the new functions has its disagreeable consequences. The faithful testing and the recording of outer reality reveal to the ego the existence of countless alarming possibilities; the outer world is shown to be full of frustrations, disappointments, threats. The testing of the child's own inner reality reveals the existence of forbidden and dangerous tendencies which offend the child's conception of himself and therefore cause anxiety. The sorting and interpretation of stimuli as they arrive lead to a sharp distinction between the child's own self and the objects outside; before this faculty is developed, the infant has been able to feel himself at one with the world around, to ascribe anything pleasurable to himself, and anything disturbing to the 'outsider.' The development of the function of memory is equally disturbing, since it aims at retaining memory traces irrespective of their quality; the infant gives preference to pleasant memories and rejects painful ones. The synthetic function of the ego, which aims at unifying and centralizing all mental processes, is opposed to the free and easy manner in which the infant lives out his most divergent emotions and instinctual urges either simultaneously or alternately; as, for instance, loving his parents, and hating them; being a passive baby in need of comfort from his mother at one moment, only to confront her as an active lover and protector the next moment; destroying possessions, and then immediately afterward desiring and treasuring them passionately. Lastly, a strict ego control of motility permanently deprives the instinctual forces in the id of their former free expression.

Strictly objective functioning of this nature heightens the feeling of tension and anxiety for the ego. On the one side, the libidinal forces in the id, represented by the component instincts of infantile sexuality, are felt to clamor for satisfaction. On the other side, the child is aware of the threat of punishment from the adults in the outside world, or of the loss of their love, should he indulge in forbidden sexual or aggressive wishes and actions. From the side of the superego, i.e., from within, the ego is flooded with feelings of guilt and self-criticism whenever it fails to live up to its own standards.

The weak and immature ego of the child fails to stand up to the impact of these dangers. It consequently attempts to undo its own achievements as fast as they are made. It tries *not* to see outside reality as it is (denial); not to record and make conscious the representatives of the inner urges as they are sent up from the id (repression); it overlays unwelcome urges with their opposites (reaction formation); it substitutes for painful facts pleasurable fantasies (escape into fantasy life); it attributes to others the qualities it does not like to see in itself (projection); and it appropriates from others what seems welcome (introjection).

Normally these methods are used to a moderate degree in every childhood to defend the ego against anxiety. A certain retrograde movement in the development of the ego achievements is therefore the rule. It does no more than to create a certain amount of subjective and faulty functioning, which is usually overcome with the beginning of the latency period when the position of the ego is strengthened and anxiety lessens.

But events shape themselves differently if acute neurotic conflicts intervene either in the preoedipal phases or during the oedipal phase. In the face of excessive anxiety the ego makes excessive and more lasting use of the defense mechanisms at its disposal. Therefore, the harm done to the ego functions becomes considerably greater and is of more permanent importance.

Examples of the excessive use of the method of denial of outer reality can be found when the child is confronted with the facts of the difference between the sexes, which give rise to penis envy and castration anxiety.

Under the pressure of these painful emotions the ego waives reality testing, pretends to see what is not there (for instance, a penis on the mother), or ignores what is in plain view. (A little girl, on watching her newborn brother's penis, said, with satisfaction, to her sister: 'He has a belly button just like us,' thus remarking on their similarity instead of admitting the obvious difference between them.) Denial makes still greater inroads on reality testing where the central subject of observation of parental intercourse is concerned. Under the influence of their oedipal jealousy children will refuse to realize that their parents have a sex life with each other, and will uphold this denial in spite of all other advances in knowledge of biological facts, of propagation among animals, and even of the facts of life when they concern strangers. Evidence of such denial can be found in countless fairy tales, myths, religious beliefs, etc. Under neurotic conditions denial frequently out-lives the latency period and adolescence and continues into adult life. But even normally, as long as children avoid admitting reality in this all-important respect, they are not free to use their full intelligence for becoming acquainted with the outer reality. (An adult neurotic, by profession a medical man, began his analytic treatment with the follow-ing words: 'My parents never had anything to do with each other.' Since he was one of a long line of brothers and sisters, there was obviously no truth in his statement. But it contained the key to his neurotic and bizarre behavior which made his dealings with the real world somewhat unpredictable and unreliable.)

Examples of excessive use of the method of repression are by now common knowledge. Repression occurs invariably when a young child finds himself faced with the intolerable frustration of the component instincts of his early instinctual life. It is easier for the child to stand the clamoring for satisfaction that comes from the id when the representa-tives of the instincts are refused admittance into consciousness, i.e., are repressed. Since all instinctual manifestations are interrelated, such repression extends in ever-widening circles until ego and id become entirely estranged from each other. What the neurotic child knows about his own inner life is frequently negligible; at best it is scanty and faulty. Awareness of inner reality cannot be maintained under these conditions.

The most instructive instance of neurotic defense doing harm to an

223

ego function is the complete obliteration of childhood memories due to repression. To uphold belief in the asexuality of the parents, or to blot out coitus observations, or scenes of seduction, etc., the memory traces of whole periods of life are removed from consciousness, thus damaging the objectivity of the function of memory, and disrupting and disconnecting the individual's relationship to his own past. Normally, all children remove the memory traces of their earliest years in this manner, to spare themselves the memory of their primitively aggressive and crudely sexual infantile reactions; but this infantile amnesia should not cover more than the first years of life. (A young neurotic girl was able to remember most of her past childhood, with the exception of two years during the latency period, the memory traces of which were completely absent. Her analysis revealed that during this period her widowed mother had been unfaithful to her dead father, a fact the child had tried to ignore.)

Excessive use of projection is usually made by neurotic children when dealing with their hostile feelings against father or mother. They either ascribe these tendencies to the parents themselves or to another child, or to an animal. When used in a normal degree, this defense method is an important transitory help in the development of the personality. Used excessively, it once more blurs the newly made distinction between the child himself and the world outside. (A child of two and a half years was subject to violent temper tantrums against her mother substitute; she would shout and throw things at her. When she began to make attempts to overcome these tantrums, she suddenly got hold of the rocking horse of the nursery, rushed it against the nurse, shouting: 'Naughty Jane, Jiji bit you now.' When the nurse said: 'Oh no, the horse will not bite me, it is not cross with me, but you are,' the child laughed and said: 'No, me not cross, only Jiji.') Similarly, children ascribe their bad feelings to the 'big bad wolf,' or some other outside agency, with the result that they themselves can feel all 'good' and loving.

Another defense method for dealing with the negative side of the child's ambivalence against the parents is the splitting of the personality, with the resulting damage to the synthetic function of the ego. For certain periods many children go so far as to invent special names for their 'good' and their 'bad' selves, though normally they retain the knowledge that both the good and the bad child are themselves, with a vague feeling of responsibility remaining for both. In an outstanding case of this kind, a girl of six referred to her bad side consistently as 'the devil' and had ceased to feel any conscious responsibility for the devil's thoughts or actions.

One of the most important advances in ego development during early childhood is the control of actions by the ego itself. This is withdrawn when too many actions become invested with symbolic sexual or aggressive significance. The ego then tries first to inhibit them and, if unsuccessful, withdraws from certain forms of activity altogether, leaving the control of motility in these respects to the forces of the id. The child then presents a picture, partly of inhibitions, partly of unreliable, unpredictable functioning, that is not adapted to reality. (A little girl of three was hardly able to use her hands for any practical occupation. She would stretch them out in front of her, uplifted as if to ward off actions, her fingers spread wide apart. In this manner she kept herself from committing the aggressions against her little companions with which her mind was constantly occupied in fantasy.) Many boys are greatly disturbed in their urinary function by guilt feelings that arise when they have to touch the genital. They withdraw from action because, for them, it implies the wish to masturbate. A boy of eight was unable to use a knife at the table because he had the fantasy of cutting his mother with it; but withdrawing from this action was of little help since his aggressive wishes dominated other acts as well; for instance, holding a stick; accordingly, many activities suddenly took on the meaning of passionate attacks on his mother.

The common escape into fantasy, which is of the greatest help to every child, is used excessively under the pressure of neurotic conflicts, and can then become the basis for a complete withdrawal and estrangement from the real world and its demands.

This interference with the ego functions is of greater importance in childhood than under otherwise similar conditions in the adult neurosis. It occurs while the maturation of the ego is still in process. The function that is most directly attacked by infantile neurosis is kept back from further development, at least temporarily, while the other ego achievements continue to mature. Accordingly, ego development becomes one-sided and inharmonious.

The particular defense mechanism employed and the consequent ego damage depend on the type of infantile neurosis. In the various forms of hysterical neurosis, anxiety is warded off predominately with the help of repression. This may account for the fact that children of the hysterical type frequently possess a faulty and unreliable memory, with consequent difficulties in studying: damage to the function of memory has spread further than the emotionally dangerous memories with which the ego tried to interfere. Obsessional children usually have an excellent and undisturbed memory; but, owing to the excessive ego interference with the free expression of their anal-sadistic tendencies, they are estranged from their own emotions, and are considered cold and unresponsive, even when other than these primitive aggressive-sexual manifestations are concerned. Phobic children deal with their anxieties by withdrawal from their danger points. They tend to withdraw from many forms of activity altogether and give up motility, far beyond the original range of neurotic danger. As a consequence they frequently become altogether retiring and clumsy in their actions, with passionate and unpredictable outbreaks whenever the motility is governed by the id forces instead of the ego.

With this point of view in mind, it may be possible to assess the seriousness of an infantile neurosis, and with it the need for treatment, in an indirect way, through the harm done to the ego functions by the extensive use of one or several of the neurotic defense mechanisms. There is no reason for alarm or interference when one or another of the ego achievements is reduced or retarded in their development or temporarily put out of action. This is a normal and inevitable occurrence. But such retardations may become lasting; or several, or all, of the important ego functions may be severely attacked at the same time. If a child shows a faulty knowledge of the outer world, far below the level of his intelligence; if he is seriously estranged from his own emotions, with blank spaces in the remembrance of his own past beyond the usual range of infantile amnesia, with a split in his personality, and with motility out of ego control; then there can be little doubt that the neurosis is severe and that it is high time to take therapeutic action.

Conclusion

In the foregoing pages an attempt has been made to find indications for the therapeutic use of child analysis not so much in the neurotic manifestations themselves as in the bearing of these manifestations on the maturation processes, within the individual child. Emphasis is shifted thereby from the purely clinical aspects of a case to the developmental aspect.

When diagnosing cases from this point of view, the child analyst or child psychiatrist has to be as intimately familiar with the normal sequence of child development as he is with the neurotic or psychotic disturbances of it. He is actually faced with the task of judging the normality of the developmental process itself.

It is an open question how much help diagnosis of this kind can receive from academic psychology. The various mental tests so far devised assess circumscribed aspects of ego development; they are nearly indispensable in cases where a differential diagnosis has to be made between mental deficiency and defective awareness of reality through excessive denial. The Rorschach test goes furthest in inquiring into the state of libido development and its disturbances. Other tests try to disclose the fantasy life of the individual. It is to be expected that in time further testing methods will be devised to cover an increasingly wider range of factors on which a satisfactory diagnosis of infantile neuroses can be based.

At present our analytic knowledge about the developmental processes on the libido as well as on the ego side is still very incomplete. Besides, too little is known about the interactions between them, beyond the fact that a precocious ego is especially intolerant when coupled with the primitive pregenital component instincts. We are only slowly learning to distinguish the various characteristics that mark a neurotic disturbance as either transitory or permanent, although this distinction is of extreme importance for our diagnoses. Not enough is known about the relation between the development of the purely intellectual factors and the other important functions of the ego.

Until these gaps are filled by more clinical data from the psychoanalytic investigation of individual children, it will be necessary not to confine examinations to shortcuts of any kind, helpful as they may be in furnishing additional data, but to adhere to the former lengthy, laborious, and groping methods of individual approach.[3]

Notes

1. Detailed accounts of two different types of child analysis are contained in Melanie Klein's *Psycho-Analysis of Children* (1932) and in Anna Freud's *Introduction to the Technique of Child Analysis* (1926–1927).
2. A little girl of four and a half, when asked to behave and control herself nicely on a certain occasion in the absence of her nurse, answered sensibly: 'I think I can manage.'
3. [Some of the points made here are taken further in *Normality and Pathology in Childhood* (A. Freud, 1965).]

16

The Widening Scope of Indications for Psychoanalysis: Discussion (1954)

This paper was written at a time when the psychoanalytic treatment method was being applied to mental disorders different in nature to the neuroses. Before the Second World War, analysts in the United States and Switzerland were working with patients suffering from schizophrenic and manic depressive psychoses, with drug addicts and with people with severe personality disorders. This mostly took place in the United States. It is not surprising therefore that this paper was originally presented to the New York Psychoanalytic Society.

Much of the paper is devoted to the problems of transference which occur in the treatment of severely ill patients. To illustrate this, Anna Freud presents numerous clinical examples. She attributes the absence of transferences which can be used for therapeutic ends in these difficult cases not simply to 'narcissistic withdrawal' but to lifelong deficiencies in the capacity to relate to others. She backs up this hypothesis with the observations she had made of children who had been rescued from concentration camps. These children were no longer able to sustain relationships other than those of a needs-satisfying type.

While acknowledging the importance of attempts to widen the therapeutic range of psychoanalysis, Anna Freud is uncertain of the gains which can be obtained from this work when compared with what can be achieved with the neuroses. She writes: 'If all the skill, knowledge, and pioneering effort which was spent on widening the scope of application of psychoanalysis had been employed instead of intensifying and improving our technique in the original field, I cannot help but feel that by now we would find the treatment of common neuroses child's play, instead of struggling with their technical problems as we have continued to do.'

Finally, she turns to the issue of the real relationship between patient and analyst versus true transference reactions. A real relationship exists and this never disappears in the course of an analysis. Insensitivity on the analyst's part to the patient's recognition of him as a real person can, as Kohut (1971) was later to point out, cause severe resistance to the treatment.

> 'The Widening Scope of Indications for Psychoanalysis: Discussion' was a contribution to the Symposium on the Widening Scope of Indications for Psychoanalysis. The symposium was sponsored by the New York Psychoanalytic Society and held at Arden House, Harrison, New York in May 1954. The prepared papers were read by Leo Stone and Edith Jacobson. It was first published in the *Journal of the American Psychoanalytic Association*, 2: 607–20, 1954.

To open the discussion on the two prepared papers of this Symposium is an honor which I accept without hesitation. Mary O'Neil Hawkins has remarked very kindly that I am myself responsible for one well-known extension of psychoanalytic therapy; she has not mentioned the fact that I have had no hand in many others. This omission is due to certain principles which govern the selection of cases in the practice of a lay analyst, even in a country like Great Britain where authorities and public are extremely generous in their attitude to lay analysis. It is true that my clinical experience extends beyond the run of the common neuroses to character problems of all kinds, including those with severe ego deformities; to perversions, alcoholism, manifest homosexuality, etc.; but it stops short of the severe depressions, as described by Edith Jacobson (1954) or the prepsychotics and schizophrenics, mentioned by Leo Stone (1954), except where cases of this kind arrive with their disturbances well hidden under a neurotic aspect. You may find that this lack of firsthand experience in important directions detracts from the value of any remarks which I may have to offer.

On the other hand, the subject of analytic technique and its legitimate variations has been a fascinating one to me since the times when I, as a beginner, attempted to treat children; when I had occasion to watch Aichhorn adapt the orthodox technique to the treatment of delinquents; when I listened to Federn's descriptions of his variations of technique for psychotic cases, and to Rank's and Ferenczi's explanations of 'active therapy;' and when I witnessed Wilhelm Reich's exciting and promising beginnings of so-called strict defense analysis, etc. Later, when I was teaching, my interest was quickened by the attitude of some of our candidates who seemed to regard our classical technique as little more than the 'habits' or 'conventions' governing analysis, oblivious in many instances of their firm theoretical foundations. Since then I have nourished the secret ambition to write a really exhaustive, theoretically well-founded paper on the practical, technical aspects of psychoanalysis. Naturally, I feel envious that, in my place, Stone has made the attempt and has succeeded brilliantly in its execution.

In a recent lecture on psychoanalytic technique (1950b), I set myself the task of classifying the variations of analytic procedure according to their causes, dividing these into four groups. Stone says that 'any number and degree of parameters [i.e., variations of procedure] can be introduced where they are genuinely necessary to meet special conditions, so long as they are all directed to bringing about the ultimate purposes and processes of the analytic end requirements.' I agree fully with Stone. On the other hand, by no means all the variations of technique which we find in the analytic field today owe their origin to special conditions in the cases under treatment. An equal, if not larger, number of them are occasioned, not by a change in the type of disorder treated, but by a change in the analyst's outlook and theoretical evaluation of familiar phenomena. The intimate interrelation between theory and practice in psychoanalysis is responsible for the fact that every development in theory results inevitably in a change of technique. To the extent that classical psychoanalysis splits up into different schools of thought, the orthodox technique undergoes variations the value of which cannot be assessed except on the basis of the value of the theoretical innovations that have caused them. It seems important to me to separate off these innovations from the parameters (to use Eissler's term [1953]) which owe their origin to 'the widening scope of the application of psychoanalysis.'

There are, further, individual variations in dealing with material, which Stone acknowledges in passing. Years ago, in Vienna, we instituted an experimental technical seminar among colleagues of equal seniority, and equal theoretical background, treating cases with similar diagnoses and therefore supposedly similar structure. We compared techniques and found in discussion – not only as Stone put it today – 'that no two analysts would ever give precisely the same interpretations throughout an analysis,' but more surprisingly still, that such uniformity of procedure was never kept up for more than a few days in the beginning of an analysis. After that, the handling of the material would cease to run parallel, each analyst giving precedence for interpretation to another piece or even layer. These differences in timing would influence the emergence of the next material, and this in turn influenced the trends of interpretation. Even though the final results might be the same, the roads leading there were widely divergent. So far as I know, no one has yet succeeded in investigating and finding the causes of these particular variations. They are determined, of course, not by the material, but by the trends of interest, intentions, shades of evaluation, which are peculiar to every individual analyst. I do not suggest that they should be looked for among the phenomena of countertransference.

It is different with the fourth and last variation of technique, which is determined by the patients' personalities and transferences and the analyst's individual counterreactions to them. Just as 'no two analysts would ever give precisely the same interpretations,' we find on closer examination that no two of a given analyst's patients are ever handled by him in precisely the same manner. With some patients we remain deadly serious. With others, humor, or even jokes, may play a part. With some the terms in which interpretations are couched have to be literal ones; others find it easier to accept the same content when given in the form of similes and analogies. There are differences in the ways in which we receive and send off patients, and in the degree to which we permit a real relationship to the patient to coexist with the transferred, fantasied one. There is, even within the strictness of the analytic setting, a varying amount of ease felt by analyst and patient.

These wholly unintended and unplanned variations in our responses are imposed on us, I believe, not so much by the patients' neuroses but by the individual nuances of their personalities which may otherwise escape unobserved. If we become aware of these often minute variations in our own behavior and reactions, and cease to treat them as unimportant chance occurrences, their observation and scrutiny lead us directly to important findings. In the personal pressure which the patient exerts on us in this manner, he betrays the subtleties of his healthy personality, the degree of maturity reached by his ego, his capacity to sublimate, his intellectual gifts, and his ability to view his conflicts at least momentarily in an objective manner. In the variations of the analyst's 'acting out' in technical behavior, we may, therefore, find new clues for the systematic study of character structures and personalities. Efforts of this type serve to deepen and intensify our work rather than to extend its scope.

This brings me to the one and only point where I find myself in disagreement with Stone. In concluding his paper, Stone calls psychoanalysis 'the most powerful of all psychotherapeutic instruments' and expresses the opinion that 'it is basically a greater error to use it for mild or incipient or reactive illnesses than for serious illnesses.' Although I appreciate the weight of his arguments, I do not share the conclusions drawn from them. For years now, our most experienced and finest analysts have concentrated their efforts on opening up new fields for the application of analysis by making the psychotic disorders, the severe depressions, the borderline cases, addictions, perversions, delinquency, etc., amenable to treatment. I have no wish to underestimate either the resulting benefits to patients or the resulting considerable gains to analysis as a therapy and science.

But I sometimes regret that so much interest and effort has been withdrawn from the hysteric, phobic, and compulsive disorders, leaving their treatment to the beginners or the less knowledgeable and adventurous analytic practitioners. If all the skill, knowledge, and pioneering effort which was spent on widening the scope of application of psychoanalysis had been employed instead of intensifying and improving our technique in the original field, I cannot help but feel that by now we would find the treatment of the common neuroses child's play, instead of struggling with their technical problems as we have continued to do.

How do analysts decide, if they are given the choice, between returning to health half a dozen young people with good prospects in life but disturbed in their enjoyment and efficiency by comparatively mild neuroses, or to devote the same time, trouble, and effort to one single borderline patient who may or may not be saved from spending the rest of his life in an institution? Personally, I feel the pull in both directions, perhaps with a bias toward the former task; as a body, the Psychoanalytic Association has in recent years inclined toward the latter.

Let us hope that the future analysts, who now occupy our training institutes as candidates, will be numerous enough to spread their energies over both fields.

I turn next to the problems of transference, discussed by both speakers. Stone has enumerated many types of transference which raise special problems for the analyst, such as the primitive overwhelming transferences of the narcissistic disturbances; the insatiable demands of the oral types; the need to control and tyrannize the analyst, etc. He also mentioned the dreaded confusion in the patient's mind between the images of analyst and patient, as I have described it elsewhere in individuals who ward off *Hörigkeit*,[1] i. e., complete emotional surrender, to the analyst. Jacobson's lucid descriptions of variations of transference in severe depressions I found especially helpful and instructive.

That Stone expresses doubts regarding the so-called 'narcissistic incapacity for transference' leads me to mention another type of case where the difficulty of establishing full transference relations originates not from narcissistic withdrawal caused by regression, but from certain basic defects in emotional development which date back to the patients' earliest years. I refer here to individuals whose relationship to their mothers was interrupted traumatically during their first year of life, or soon thereafter, either by the death or removal of the mother, or by the disruption of the whole family, the child being cared for afterward by repeatedly changing mother substitutes or in institutions.

In London, we had the opportunity to analyze emotional deviations of this kind in children and adolescents who had been rescued from concentration camps. The degree of their abnormality depends, naturally, on the specific age when they lost their object ties. When this happened before they had reached the stage of object constancy, adults were for them only need-satisfying objects. They are important as protectors, as the suppliers of food and clothing, at best as sources of pleasure; but they are not love objects in the proper (object-libidinal) sense of the word. Relations with the environment are usually shallow, subject to quick changes and promiscuousness. In the analyses of such patients, we find that there is no hidden fund of archaic object love or hate on which the transference can draw. Relations to the analyst remain superficial and insecure, built on the only available pattern of relationships; since libido has never been concentrated fully on any one object, the concentration of material in a transference neurosis does not seem to come about.

The technical problems which face the analyst here are obvious ones. We all agree with Stone's statement that 'the mobilization of the transference neurosis holds a central place' in analysis and, equally important, that 'an adequate positive transference is necessary even to the *acceptance* of . . . interpretations.' Transference to the analyst as a need-satisfying object does not lend itself to either of these purposes; cathexis is withdrawn from the therapist and placed elsewhere whenever interpretations are painful and resistances increase, thus continually interrupting the formation of a transference neurosis. On the other hand, the intimacy of the analytic setting is well suited to reproduce – or, where necessary, to produce for the first time – the intimacy of the mother–child relationship. The technical question which arises here approximates the one concerning the psychotic patient who has been helped toward object cathexis by his analyst. Has the analyst automatically disqualified himself from continuing the treatment by using deviations in technique while ministering to the patient's object needs? This is a question raised by Eissler (1953). Or, obversely, to quote Stone, 'Is more lost by a change of therapist than is gained by an uncontaminated transference?' If the patient succeeds in establishing a more mature relationship to the analyst, will the change of therapist not repeat the traumatic separation from the mother, with renewed disastrous results for the newly won capacity for object love?

When we were reading and discussing Eissler's paper on technique in London, one of the cases in our Hampstead Clinic supplied us with a striking illustration of his views on the close connection between variations of technique and variations in the patient's ego structure. In this instance, it was the young patient herself who suggested the parameter to her analyst in the context of her free associations. The patient in question was an adolescent girl, a victim of the Nazi regime, who had been smuggled out of a Polish ghetto as an infant and, from then onward, had been handed on from person to person in an endless series of 'rescues,' from one station in life to another, always cutting all her ties, including those to her possessions. There was no single figure, or even toy or other material object, in her life which dated back to her past. There were, before the treatment, also no memories or cover memories. (Incidentally, this raises the question how far our childhood memories are usually structured and kept alive by their intimate connection with the image of cathected and stable love objects.)

After several months of struggles in the treatment during which relations to the analyst went up and down, wavered, threatened to dissolve, to peter out, to extend to other figures in the environment in turn, the girl said to the therapist: 'You analyze me all wrong. I know what you should do: you should be with me the whole day because I am a completely different person when I am here with you, when I am in school, and when I am at home with my foster family. How can you know me if you do not see me in all these places? There is not one me, there are three.'

It struck me that here, disguised as a piece of 'technical advice,' we were offered some insight into the basic deficiencies of her ego structure. There had been, in her past, no opportunity to introject any one object sufficiently to build up inner harmony and synthesis under the guidance of a higher agency, acting as a unifying superego. Her personality shifted, following the promiscuity of her relationships. She was well able to adapt herself to the varying environments in which her life was spent, but in none of these relationships could she build up a real feeling of self, or correlate the self experience in one setting with that experienced in another setting. What she asked the therapist to do was, as it were, to offer herself in the flesh as the image of a steady, ever-present object, suitable for internalization, so that the patient's personality could be regrouped and unified around this image. Then, and only then, the girl felt, would there be a stable and truly individual center to her personality which she could transfer and offer for analysis. To carry out a plan of this kind resembles the initial periods of psychotherapy which Knight (1946) proposes as necessary for psychotic cases. Again, we are faced with the technical question whether such preparatory assistance, if undertaken in all earnest, would be compatible with later analytic work.

It seems possible to me that our concept of incapacity for transference on narcissistic grounds has detracted our attention from further instances where, for other reasons, no or an insufficient object love is available for the purposes of analysis. I have in mind here patients of an altogether different type and background from the one described last. In these cases, the relationship to an existing mother failed early in life, with a severe ego distortion taking its place soon after. I had occasion to observe and analyze these phenomena in two young girls in their twenties who came to me with a diagnosis of severe ego deformities which had led to complete failure in their love life and their studies.

The first patient came from a highly irregular, intellectual family, her father being known as an eccentric and pervert, her mother as hopelessly promiscuous and addicted to alcohol. The parents were divorced, and both had remarried several times. The child was made a ward of the court, but remained in contact with both parents, who made no secret to her of their sexual and other abnormalities. The young girl herself was attractive and intellectually brilliant, but completely unstable. She was promiscuous to the degree of not remembering either the names or the number of her lovers, and she lived in a whirlwind of changing plans, attempts at either intellectual or artistic careers, in constant uncertainty of the future, with debts, emotional upheavals with her friends, etc. Her human relationships were governed by passionate desire for any partner who refused her, with this attitude changing to contempt and utter rejection of him as soon as she could feel accepted. This was the one and only pattern of object relationship available for transference onto the analyst, and it had brought several attempts at treatment to an abrupt end.

Here, too, she desired the analysis passionately while no vacancy was available with the analyst of her choice, to reject it completely after she had been taken into treatment. She spent a short year with me during which I gained the impression that her acting out inside and outside of the analysis represented an identification less with the abnormal behavior of her parents than that of their respective partners, whom she considered worthless for objective as well as for subjective reasons. Her erratic behavior seemed addressed to the mother especially and to express, as it were, the plea: 'I am as bad and worthless as the drunkards, the homosexuals, the good-for-nothings with whom you associate. If you want to love such people, you might as well love me.' True to her usual pattern, during treatment she seemed to reject not only my person but also all the interpretations given by me. It was all the more surprising that, soon after leaving me and England, she married, became pregnant, had a baby, and told me the news on the very day of the birth over a long-distance telephone. Evidently, more had happened in the transference than I had been able to discern.

I began to see a little more light after treating a second, not dissimilar case. This patient's parents were also divorced. Her abnormalities centered around a deeply dissatisfying mother relationship. Her mother, whom she feared, was gifted, masculine, dissatisfied in her marriage, successful in an artistic profession, and had spent much time away from her children, fostering the careers of young artists. After a series of unsuccessful attempts to keep the family together, the child developed hostile reactions, unsatisfactory character traits, and a severe work inhibition. There was only one condition under which she continued to react positively. She needed only to enter a studio to be transformed in her feelings from a lonely, unloved person to one who glowed with the secret satisfaction of being a member in the warm and sympathetic atmosphere of a close-knit community. Since she had no artistic gifts herself, this led nowhere so far as accomplishments and sublimations were concerned; on the contrary, her craving for this particular atmosphere rendered her unfit for other forms of life. What emerged in the analysis was that her passionate desire to join the 'artists' had taken the place of her object relationship to the mother as well as to other people. In fact, she did not love artists. She loved being with the objects of her mother's concern; the atmosphere of the studio replaced that of a nursery, where she could feel loved, cherished, appreciated. The development of her ego had been placed wholly in the service of wooing the mother in the disguise of one of her imagined objects.

What troubled me in both patients was their inability to produce a transference neurosis, at least during the first year of treatment. The first patient seemed to transfer merely her instability, promiscuity, and rejection of objects. The second patient went one step further; although she was apparently not attached to me, she developed a heightened attention for every detail of the analytic setting. Unreliable and forgetful as she was in other matters, she had an excessive memory for every one of my words and sentences, for every arrangement concerning the sessions, the analytic rules, the other patients, etc. She seemed to replace at least some of her passion for the artistic atmosphere by a similar passion for the analytic one. But this devotion did not extend to my person; it avoided it; what should have been an object tie had been turned into an ego interest. Obviously, there are important differences between such a transferred ego distortion and a transference neurosis.

On the other hand, such identifications not with the mother herself but with her supposed or real love objects are familiar enough occurrences. We often find that the children of doctors, dentists, analysts, will act ill, or in pain, or sad, to draw their parents' interest and care away from the legitimate patients; the children of policemen and of workers with dissocial individuals will often develop dissocial behavior for the same reasons. The most striking, pathological instance of this kind has been reported recently by Dr. Alice Weiss-Stadthagen from Israel in the case history of a severe borderline patient of latency age, a study which we hope will be published soon.

This patient, a little girl, has grown up in the Children's House in one of the *Kvutzahs* (modern agricultural communities) in Israel where her parents were members. The mother worked in the stable, tending the cows, and the child developed very early an excessive identification with the animals under her mother's care. This went so far that she actually gave up her human interests, abilities, and behavior, and acted, walked, and lived like a cow. Her relationship to the mother deteriorated and she showed little or no interest in other people; the tie to the mother remained fixed in the wholly pathological form of her imitation of and identification with the animals.

Here, as in the cases mentioned before, the analytic task obviously consists in the undoing of the ego distortion and its retransformation into the object relationship from which it is derived.

I turn next to what Jacobson describes as the 'highly illusory, magic quality' of the patients' transference feelings of what Stone calls the patients' 'magical expectations and demands,' their need for the therapist to be 'omnipotent, omniscient, Godlike.' Such transference attitudes are known to be dangerous to the analysis when they remain unrecognized and uninterpreted. What interests me especially is the fact that they do remain so quite often and for considerable periods of time, at any rate more often than most other, more turbulent and less well-hidden transference reactions. For example, for the highly obsessional patient, the analyst's omnipotence is a fact which is so obvious that it need not be commented on; it is simply accepted and taken for granted without further question. Since for the patient this omnipotence 'goes without saying,' it may sometimes escape the analyst's attention until something happens in the environment to overthrow the established safety of the analytic setting and causes the analyst to 'lose face.'

Those colleagues who come from Nazi countries, as I do, will remember how this 'magical' transference relationship of certain patients dropped to zero when Hitler seized power. Being ourselves victims of the regime rendered us unfit for the role of powerful, Godlike beings in which these patients had cast us. Outbreaks of severe and intolerable anxiety on the patients' part under such conditions testified to their urgent need to retain this particular transference defense.

I experienced two further amusing as well as instructive instances of this kind during the war years. In the first year of the war I began the analysis of a highly intelligent, severe neurotic who, although himself not British-born, was in public service. Since this was the period when suspicion of spy activities was at its height, and since I myself was classed among the 'enemy aliens,' I wondered why his free associations never alluded to the possible adverse consequences which might arise for him under the Secrecy Act if it was discovered that he was in analysis with me. Finally, I myself referred to the omission. He replied airily: 'Oh, yes, I have thought of that quite often. But if it is found out, you can always set it right with the Government!' Another obsessional patient of mine reacted similarly in the London Blitz. He continued his attendance, undisturbed by the bombing, and resisted all temptations to leave London until one night when a bomb was dropped at the entrance to my street. This shattered not only the house on which it fell but also his belief in my omnipotence. After an outbreak of uncontrollable anxiety with hostile reactions against me for having disappointed him, he interrupted his analysis for the duration of the war.

Examples of this type are revealing, although hurtful to the analyst's professional pride. I cannot help feeling that, without this technical interference from outside, I might have analyzed both patients for a long time without realizing that, in their eyes, I controlled the British Government as well as Hitler's war machine. It makes me wonder just how often, without such help, patients' magical beliefs in us remain unrevealed.

Further, I refer briefly to Stone's remarks concerning the 'real person relationship' between analyst and patient versus the 'true transference reactions.' To make such a distinction coincides with ideas which I have always held on this subject. Many analysts express the opinion that the patient's transference, i.e., his fantasied relationship to the analyst, is strongest when he enters the treatment, and has to be worked through gradually by means of interpretation until, at the very end of treatment, a real relationship can come to the surface. This may be true for psychotic and borderline cases; for the common neurotic case, the reverse order seems to me to be the rule. We see the patient enter into analysis with a reality attitude to the analyst; then the transference gains momentum until it reaches its peak in the full-blown transference neurosis, which has to be worked off analytically until the figure of the analyst emerges again, reduced to its true status. But – and this seems important to me – to the extent to which the patient has a healthy part of his personality, his real relationship to the analyst is never wholly submerged. With due respect for the necessary strictest handling and interpretation of the transference, I still feel that somewhere we should leave room for the realization that analyst and patient are also two real people, of equal adult status, in a real personal relationship to each other. I wonder whether our – at times complete – neglect of this side of the matter is not responsible for some of the hostile reactions which we get from our patients and which we are apt to ascribe only to 'true transference.' But these are technically subversive thoughts and ought to be 'handled with care.'

I turn next to Stone's point that 'the decisive factor is the [analyst's] ability to stand the emotional strains of the powerful tormented and tormenting transference,' a remark which I illustrate from my experience with a particular patient whose transference I, as well as his former analysts, found almost intolerable. This patient had a 'good' and a 'bad' side to his life, representing his anal and phallic strivings which alternately claimed his attention. The phallic tendencies had been projected onto other men who became his official, treasured, homosexual partners, while the anal tendencies were projected onto secret, despised objects, contact with whom he avoided phobically and with the help of a complicated obsessional system.

His greatest wish was to merge with the phallic object; his greatest fear was to be forced into unwilling union with the anal object. In the first instance he felt raised to the status of a glamorous male; in the second instance he felt dragged down to the depth of anal passivity, dirt, depression, loss of personality. This complicated state of affairs was revealed in the transference, where the analyst had to play both the phallic as well as the anal role. So far as the analyst stood for the anal partners, the patient had to defend himself against contact with him by refusing to cooperate; so far as the analyst symbolized the phallic partners, i.e., in the last resort the penis, the patient had to cling to the analysis to avoid self-castration. Under these circumstances to carry out the analysis became as frightening for the patient as the idea to give it up.

In this particular instance it could be demonstrated clearly that the specific torment which the patient experienced in the transference was identical with the most tormenting element of his neurosis, namely, his inability to decide between two equally desired and equally dreaded instinctual urges. I believe that the specifically tormenting element for the analysts of this patient lay in the quick succession in which they had to fulfill the role of the desired glamorous and the dreaded dirty partner with whom contact was sought and avoided almost simultaneously.

And now, briefly, a last addition to these discussion remarks. There is, I believe, a similarity between the 'good' and the 'bad' side of the last-named obsessional patient's transference and the 'good' and 'bad' side of the book produced by Jacobson's depressive patient. Jacobson describes how this book, which had become a 'devouring, obsessional interest' of her patient, 'on the one hand the one great goal of his life; on the other hand, a monster which tortures him day and night with depression and anxieties.' Within the framework of Jacobson's interpretation this means to me also that the book, during the act of writing, symbolizes a phallic erection; once produced it is no more than a piece of anal dirt.

By describing what she calls her 'deliberate supporting counter-attitude,' Jacobson offers a further instructive example of a parameter for the treatment of severe depressives. To 'share' in the transference the patient's belief in the 'goodness' of his book here serves to reinforce his hopeful phallic strivings against the impact of his depressive archaic attitudes. But the same measure, if applied, for example, to my severe obsessional, would prove useless, or even dangerous. No doubt, he would revolt with hostility against the analyst's singling out for 'sharing' (i.e., for approval) one side of his strivings only. His ambivalence would force him to react to the implied condemnation of the other side by throwing his own weight wholeheartedly in that direction.

I have reached my point, having already taken up more time than should be allowed to any single contributor to a symposium. To return to my beginning: when the organizers of this Symposium suggested 'The Widening Scope of the Application of Psychoanalysis' as the topic of discussion, I doubted the wisdom of their choice. While listening to the opening speakers, and while collecting my own thoughts, I realized that no other subject would have offered better opportunities for fulfilling the long-standing need of approaching the practical problems of psychoanalysis from the side of psychoanalytic theory.

Notes

1. See A. Freud, 1952a [1949–1951]–(Part II).

17

Problems of Technique in Adult Analysis (1954)

There are really two parts to this paper – one essentially practical, the other theoretical. The theoretical part comes first and sets the scene for the other. Here Anna Freud answers in detail questions asked by analysts at the symposium. In many ways the paper adds to the one on 'The Widening Scope of Indications for Psychoanalysis' (chapter 16). In the second half of the paper she highlights the problems of technique which arise in the treatment of severe mental disorders. That these difficulties occur is no surprise because the psychical conditions existing in these states are entirely different from those present in the neuroses. In the former, the stability provided by repression directed against unacceptable wish phantasies is absent in the psychoses and in borderline states. The tie to the analyst is tenuous compared with that which develops in the course of the treatment of the neuroses.

Symptoms by themselves, even in the case of the neuroses, cannot be used as the sole means of assessing whether or not an analytic treatment is possible and will continue satisfactorily. This depends on the integrity of the ego and this can only be gauged with any certainty once the analysis has started. An important criterion is the patient's capacity to form a therapeutic alliance. The alliance must be sufficiently strong to withstand the buffetings of affects which arise from painful memories and transference repetitions. When there is an alliance, no essential modification of the basic technique is necessary. It is only in the psychoses and severe personality disorders, where the patient cannot distance herself from her immediate experiences and so cannot respond positively to the analyst's interventions, that major modifications of technique are necessary.

'Problems of Technique in Adult Analysis' was a contribution to a symposium held by the Philadelphia Association for Psychoanalysis, Philadelphia, Pennsylvania, on 10 May 1954. The meeting was chaired by Robert Waelder. The participants were Douglas

D. Bond, Nathan H. Colton, K. R. Eissler, Anna Freud, Dora Hartmann, Mary O'Neil Hawkins, Maurits Katan, Marianne Kris, Edward Kronold, Rudolph M. Loewenstein, Margaret S. Mahler, Eli Marcovitz, Annie Reich, Daniel Silverman, Paul Sloane, Jenny Waelder-Hall and Sidney U. Wenger. The paper was first published in the *Bulletin of the Philadelphia Association for Psychoanalysis,* 4: 44–69, 1954. Section I was sent in as an outline for distribution before the meeting.

Every discussion of therapeutic procedure in psychoanalysis derives added interest from the fact that it can never remain for long on purely practical grounds. In the history of psychoanalysis every advance in insight has been followed closely by an advance in technique; conversely, every technical rule has been considered valid only when rooted in a specific piece of analytic theory. Any doubt concerning the justification of a particular technique, therefore, had to be dealt with by inquiry into the theoretical assumptions which had given rise to it.

Analysts always had to defend their technique against opposition from outside on the grounds of complexity and cost; against the patients' resistance on the grounds of pain and frustration; and, moreover, against their own sense of dissatisfaction with the inevitable slowness and, often, incompleteness of results. In recent years, two more challenges have been added to these familiar ones. One is due to the widening of the field of application of the analytic therapy to patients with character structures different from those for which the analytic technique was devised originally. In this field, Eissler (1953) has shown in a stimulating paper which deviations from our standard technique become necessary to meet deviations in the patient's ego structure and – more than that – how technical experimentation in this respect may lead to new insight into abnormalities of structure. In this particular instance, theory profits from advances in technique.

The second challenge to our technique originates from the theoretical disagreements between the various analytic schools of thought, every innovation, advance, discussion or regression in theory being inevitably expressed by concomitant forward or backward technical moves or by side-stepping of well-established technical procedures. This has led to difficult and conflicting practical situations with which the psychoanalytic teaching institutes have not always coped successfully. To disentangle disagreement in psychoanalysis is, as mentioned before, not possible without disentangling theoretical clashes of opinion.

According to an old 'classical' definition, a therapeutic procedure has the right to be called psychoanalytic if it recognizes and works with two processes in the patient's mind: *transference* and *resistance* – a pronouncement which is neither as loose nor as permissive as it sounds. It means, translated into other words, that our 'orthodox' or 'classical' technique is based on an idea which is at the same time dynamically, genetically, qualitatively, and structurally determined. We assume that the patient suffers from a conflict, not with the environment but within the structure of his own personality; that this conflict has arisen in his remote past and is not accessible to his consciousness; further, that the instinctual strivings, lodged in the id, though unconscious, are possessed of a permanent urge to rise upward and manifest themselves in the present, making use for that purpose of any available object in the outer world. Here the analytic technique comes to the patient's help by offering him such an object in the person of the analyst, on whom the past unconscious experience is made conscious and relived. On the other hand, the analytic technique deals with the resisting counterforce lodged in the patient's ego, which is intent on keeping down the id strivings and on preventing them from becoming manifest. Here the technique is directed at making the patient aware of his defensive devices, thereby depriving them of much of their efficiency. Therefore, to deal with both transference and resistance inevitably brings about the revival of all those moments in infancy and childhood when id and ego forces clashed with each other; it implies reactivating these conflicts and finding new solutions for them.

With this overall definition of analytic technique in mind, it becomes easier to place what is commonly known as our analytic rules, and to discuss the current objections to, and digression from, them. There is the basic rule of *free association*, rooted in the theoretical conviction of a spontaneous upsurge of the id contents. There is the *use of the couch*, based on the idea that associations can be allowed to flow freely and safely only under the condition that motility is inhibited. There are the *reality arrangements* with the patient concerning his behavior under analysis with regard to time, money, length, and form of treatment, which bear witness to our belief in a healthy part of his ego with which we can make a pact. There is *dream interpretation* as the model procedure for disentangling id contents from superimposed ego distortions. There are the rules and regulations meant to safeguard the purity and, with it, the analytic usefulness of the *transference manifestations* by restricting all extra-analytic contact with the patient to the barest minimum. There are the strict rules on the noninterference with the spontaneous flow of material in the patient's mind, except in certain specific instances when the upsurge from the unconscious is blocked completely by successful defense, as, for instance, in the phobic disorders.

Logical as these regulations appear in the light of the definition of analytic technique given above, not one of them has remained unchallenged. I name as examples – probably well-known ones – a few only: the denouncing of the rule of free association in a recent Congress paper by Burke (1949); the break with regular hourly work advocated by Lacan (1953–1955); the distrust of the unlimited development of transference by members of the Chicago Institute (Alexander and French, 1946); the sole use of transference interpretations by part of the English school of analysts, etc. Discussion of technical digressions of this nature is fruitful and interesting when it includes their theoretical background. Digressions which are not based on theory but on practical, or financial, or other personal motives of their originators are of a different nature altogether and cannot be discussed with profit.

Certain technical questions which have recently agitated analysts are answered by implication in the above-mentioned definition of analytic technique. There is – at least so far as I understand it – no such thing as either an 'id analysis' or a 'defense analysis;' there is only one analytic procedure which embodies both. Working on the basis of both transference and resistance, it is the analyst's task to undo the interlocking of the id and ego forces, i.e., to direct his efforts from one side to the other, following the movement of the material in the patient's mind. No other form of work would do justice to our conception of conflict within the structure of the mind.

There are many other technical problems which remain unanswered and fill the analyst's mind with a constant string of worries. Does our standard technique equip us for the undertaking of character analyses as adequately as it has equipped us for the analysis of the various forms of hysteria and the obsessional neurosis? Do the various forms of perversion, fetishism, homosexuality, etc., which we now consider accessible to treatment, justify deviations of technique, or do they fall within the range of application of our present rules? Knowing that complete absence of anxiety dries up the flow of material and arrests the progress of therapy, do we ask – or even urge – the patient to tolerate anxiety for analytic reasons, and how much of it? What are the legitimate technical means for keeping anxiety on a level optimal for the treatment? Do analysts in such cases still use an 'active' technique in Ferenczi's sense of the word? Is the old rule still valid which advises that, on the whole, analysis should be carried out in an atmosphere of frustrated wish fulfillment? And there are many similar questions.

II

When Robert Waelder invited me to send a written introduction for this discussion, I was hesitant to do so, feeling that I did not know enough about this Association's needs and wishes. After I had complied with his request, I began to wonder whether you would not object to the simplicity of the points which I had raised and think it inappropriate to discuss with experienced analysts such well-known matters as the analytic rules themselves. Actually, when making my points, my intention was merely to lay before you the arguments which I employ for my own use whenever I meet in myself doubts and misgivings concerning the technique of analytic treatment. Like all analysts, I feel at times dissatisfied with the nature of my work, its rigidity, the restrictions placed upon analyst and patient, the length of time needed for a cure, etc. In such moods I wish I could drop all rules of procedure and act impulsively and on my own. These, I find, are the occasions when an analyst should take a firm stand, distrust his own emotions, look at the situation from a strictly theoretical perspective, and treat such technical rule for what it is, namely, the result of theoretical thinking of long standing.

There are two ways in which young analysts tend to react toward analytic technique. One is reminiscent of the manner in which small girls behave when they first learn to sew. They would find sewing quite easy if only they were not expected to wear a thimble. How can anybody, they complain, accomplish anything with such a heavy obstruction on their fingers? That, precisely, is the attitude of many of our analytic candidates: how can anybody be expected to maintain his human feeling and understanding while complying with a whole host of complicated rules? Here arises the dangerous wish to throw off regulations which are felt to be too restrictive. The other attitude consists of a wish to hide behind the rules, to meet the patient not squarely, but protected by a barrier which, at least in the ordinary run of cases, eliminates the need for independent action. It takes a long time to convince some students in training that the analytic technique was not devised for their protection.

The most profitable view to adopt toward analytic technique seems to consider the use of the couch, free association, the handling of the transference, the handling of the transitional forms of acting out, etc., as mere tools of treatment. Tools of any trade are periodically inspected, revised, sharpened, perfected, and, if necessary, altered. The technical tools of analysis are no exception to this rule. As in all other cases, alterations should not be carried out arbitrarily and without sufficient cause.

In a recent Symposium held by the New York Society on 'The Widening Scope of Psychoanalysis' (1954), Bertram Lewin pointed out that whenever an unusual situation occurs during the course of an analysis, it is impossible for the analyst to keep to the usual analytic procedure. He remarked that when faced with the suicide attempt of a patient, for example, the analyst quickly drops what he considers appropriate analytic behavior and concentrates on saving the patient's life, behavior in an emergency of this kind being a matter of necessity and practical consideration only.

Convincing as this argument may sound, I feel that it may lead us into danger. The question remains *when* a situation deserves to be considered an emergency. We notice, in ourselves and others, a tendency to declare emergency situations where, in fact, none exists. What we call an emergency may sometimes merely be the result of a delay in understanding and interpretation on our part which has created a so-called 'chaotic' upheaval in the material. So long as we define an emergency only in practical terms, we run the risk of interfering blindly with the correctness of our own technique. I suggest, therefore, that it is wise to substitute for the terms 'emergency' or 'necessity' other concepts of a more theoretical nature.

A situation in treatment which justifies a change of analytic technique would be one where something has happened to overthrow the basic conditions for analytic therapy which I have set out in my introduction. There is general agreement that we base the analysis of our patients on two main processes: transference and resistance. Of the two, the transference phenomena are caused by the spontaneous upsurge of repressed material and reveal the exigencies of the id; the resistance phenomena oppose this upsurge and thereby reveal the intricate activities of the ego side of the personality. In the so-called emergency situation, either the upsurge from the unconscious or the resisting, defensive forces are quantitatively or qualitatively different from what we expect them to be; therefore, our rules of procedure cease to apply, wholly or in part.

At this point I remind you of the fact that the particular relationship between id and ego (uprising and defensive forces, transference and resistance) on which our analytic technique rests are valid only for the neurotic disorders. In all other instances, whether psychosis, delinquency, addiction, childhood disturbances, etc., there are deviations in quantity or quality from the neurotic pattern to be found in the id or ego, or in their relations to each other. This point of view, I believe, also underlies Eissler's paper (1953) on the introduction of parameters into the technique of psychoanalysis.

This particular outlook on the variations of psychoanalytic technique seems to me so basic that I venture to dwell on it longer, at the risk of repeating myself. Whenever the field of application of psychoanalysis is widened to include mental disturbances other than the neuroses, the position may be examined from the sides of id and ego (transference and resistance) variations. With schizophrenic patients the question always arises whether their narcissistic withdrawal is deep enough to make access to them impossible; with paranoid patients, whether their transference will remain within the limits which are controllable in analysis. With delinquents and near-criminals, the destructive quality of the transferred id urges poses serious problems. With the atypical character disturbances where libidinal relationships were interrupted or otherwise disturbed in the first years of life, not enough object relationship may be available to supply the necessary positive tie to the analyst; or the libidinal urges may be split up and disconnected to a degree which makes it nearly impossible to reassemble them for reconstruction.

On the resistance side, on the other hand, we usually ask ourselves two main questions. The most important one concerns the healthiness of the resisting forces, i.e., in the last resort of the ego and the superego. Even though in the analytic technique we fight against the resistances, we expect that the resisting agency itself will not collapse under our onslaught but will persist. A sudden, complete, and unopposed breakthrough from the unconscious is not intended in analysis and comes as an unwelcome surprise to both analyst and patient. Such breakthroughs happen in prepsychotic cases, and such events have led to repeated warnings from the side of experienced analysts; I name as their representatives Paul Federn who wrote and spoke on these matters for many years (1952), and Robert Knight who emphasizes this point in many of his writings (1949, 1952, 1953a, 1953b). The modifications of analytic technique introduced by August Aichhorn (1925, 1936a, 1936b, 1937) for the treatment of delinquent adolescents are based on the same considerations.

There are, further, cases where it represents a serious risk to increase the resistance of the patient. These patients employ self-destructive urges as their defense and use this most powerful weapon to, as it were, blackmail the analyst until he has to lay his tools and, in fact, 'concentrate on saving the patient's life.' The most striking examples of this type are the cases of anorexia nervosa where the patient refuses to take nourishment in periods of resistance, as well as all patients with strong suicidal tendencies. There are probably other cases where this particular mechanism of defense against the analysis is present although less obvious. Similar to the question which we have asked with regard to uncontrollable transference, we have to put the query here: can we, by means of our usual technical devices, meet all the forces of resistance which the analytic situation calls forth in the patient?

In the light of these considerations we may say that variations in analytic technique become necessary whenever the aspect of a case leads us to expect manifestations of transference or resistance which exceed in force or in malignancy the amounts with which we are able to cope. In our estimation of the position we have to be guided not by a descriptive diagnosis of the case but by insight into its *structure*.

At the beginning of analysis, before we have insight into the structure of a neurosis, it is impossible to predict how the patient will respond to treatment. There is no guarantee that two individuals with the same *symptomatology* will react similarly to the same technical procedure. Well-established analytic rules which prove helpful and necessary when applied to one case may be disturbing and unnecessary in another. To illustrate quandaries of this kind, I quote an example from my own experience with the analysis of addictions and perversions.

In the classical technique of analysis we learn that there is little chance for the successful therapy of any disturbance which approximates an addiction while the addiction has free scope, i.e., while the patient indulges in, and derives pleasure from, practicing it, be it some perverse activity, alcoholism, or drug taking. In our times, analysts no longer interfere with their patients' behavior in the strict meaning of Ferenczi's 'active therapy,' i.e., by using prohibitions [Ferenczi, 1921 – eds.]. Instead, still in Ferenczi's sense, patients are asked to postpone the pathological form of satisfaction for periods of increasing lengths while tolerating as much as possible of the ensuing anxiety to intensify the treatment. Thoroughly familiar with this rule and convinced of its usefulness as I was, I proceeded at one time to apply it in the customary manner to two manifestly homosexual patients who were under treatment with me simultaneously [A. Freud, 1952a].

I had heard of the first patient years before while he was under analysis with a close colleague of mine, not his first analyst by any means. She found him completely inaccessible, resistant, and hostile whenever the question of restraining his homosexual practices was touched on. In discussion with her, I attributed his lack of progress toward normal sexual behavior to her apparent inability to apply the above-named rule. As luck would have it, this patient – still homosexual – came to continue his analysis with me in later years when I looked forward to trying out my own technique on him and winning him over to cooperation. I was wholly surprised when I failed miserably in this endeavor; even the slightest attempt to move the patient toward restraint of his homosexuality was met by outbreaks of hostility and anxiety which threatened the continuation of the analysis. My colleague had been one hundred percent right; to insist would have been not only impossible but a grave technical error. But, to my still greater surprise, the application of this particular technical device (restraint of the perverse satisfaction) did not prove as important here as I had assumed. After long endeavors in other directions, the analysis took a beneficial course in spite of the patient's manifest homosexuality being indulged in freely, and the patient eventually became heterosexual, a successful husband and father. I was left with the problem why an otherwise well-established analytic rule had proved neither applicable nor essential in this case.

The second patient, on the other hand, whose manifest homosexuality was complicated by severe alcoholism, behaved according to pattern. Difficult as it was for him to bear the anxiety, he cooperated for the sake of treatment, his perverse outbursts decreased in frequency, lengthening the periods when the analysis could penetrate into greater depth. Eventually he, too, became heterosexual, free of his alcoholism, married and had children. There was no doubt that in his case cutting down on his perverse practices had played a most beneficial part in the technique.

Happenings of this kind are instructive and thought-provoking for the analyst. I asked myself: if our rules are correct and well founded, why do they not apply with equal success to cases which appear to be so similar? The answer is, of course, a simple one. It is not the rule which is at fault here but the analyst's reasoning. Similar or even identical symptomatology may be based on very different psychopathology, and it is the latter, not the former, which determines how a case should be dealt with from the technical angle.

In the two cases mentioned, I came to the following explanation for their divergent behavior under analysis. For the second patient his outbursts of alcoholism coupled with passive homosexual practices served to reduce the anxiety which was aroused by his active, aggressive, masculine urges which he regarded as destructive to the female partner as well as to himself. Drink as well as passive advances to male partners served as reassurance and lowered his anxiety. In his own words, he felt 'held down' and protected. The lower he sank in his alcoholic stupors and escapades, which sometimes literally landed him in the gutter, the safer he felt. During the treatment it became possible for him to reduce the addiction to alcohol because in the transference a new addiction, that to the analyst, took its place. He gave me the role of protecting him against his dangerous, masculine, destructive impulses, in short, of 'holding him down.' While I filled this role in his imagination, he could do without alcohol or male partner. This implied, of course, that I had to be at his disposal without fail, and that interruptions of the analysis could not be tolerated. He would find me at the other end of the telephone even in the middle of the night, which is, of course, the usual striking deviation from the orthodox technique whenever it is applied to an addiction.

It is worthwhile to pause here and put the question to ourselves whether this particular rearrangement of forces in the transference is, perhaps, the condition for this particular technical interference with the patient's behavior. Where the relationship to the analyst takes the place of the satisfaction or reassurance gained from the system, the analysis turns into a battle between the two addictions, the addiction to the analyst holding the fort temporarily until the unconscious material appears and is analyzed. This may well prove to be the classical situation for which this technical rule was originally set up.

The same reasoning did not apply to the first patient, whose perverse activities served a completely different purpose. I have described his case in another context (A. Freud, 1950a, 1952a) as one of those instances where men become homosexual due to having invested other men with the attributes of their own phallic masculinity. They cannot then bear to be without these other male figures – ideal either in the bodily or mental sense – and proceed to pursue them everywhere. This is the type of man who will roam the streets like a true fetishist for a glimpse of the male organ which represents his own. By urging a patient of this type to restrict his homosexual practices you urge him to commit self-castration – and who will stand for that? The immense resistance and hostility which this patient displayed toward his analysts whenever they adopted a restrictive attitude was therefore the measure of his castration anxiety. This type of handling was not relevant and not applicable to his case. Interpretation of the origins of his projection of masculinity had to come first and enable him to reassume his phallic properties. Then, of course, male partners lost their importance and he became able to do without them.

So much for this particular point, from which we can draw the inference that blind obedience to technical rules can be as misplaced as blind divergence from them. Since the rules have to fit the cases to which they are applied, there has to be constant confrontation between task (case) and tool (technical device).

III

May I add here an example from my own practice which centers on the question of denial raised by Douglas Bond.[1]

Some time ago a patient was sent to me who presented a problem which I have so far been unable to solve in my own mind. He was a man of approximately forty years, independent, rich, in a most favorable social position. He suffered from a serious affliction of the eyes (detachment of the retina) and, in spite of repeated attempts at surgery, was threatened with complete blindness in the near future. He knew of the medical verdict, but he denied the knowledge. In his preliminary interview with me, I found him in a state of extreme anxiety and excessive restless agitation; he wished to enter analysis at once, since he found his state of mind intolerable. Talking to me, he repeatedly referred to the eye-surgeon's diagnosis and to the threat hanging over him, always with the proviso that he did not believe for a moment that it would really happen, that one operation had already done some good, that he was fully confident that the next operation would finish the job, etc.

It was quite impossible for me to put in a word or question edgeways. It was evident that he had to keep talking so as to prevent me from saying anything which might heighten his anxiety. I foresaw how, in the analysis, his free associations would proceed wholly on the basis of denial. What would happen if the analyst intervened here in the direction described by Bond in his case, by telling the patient that I did believe the doctor's diagnosis and that he would have to face the prospect of blindness? This particular man, in his fortunate outward circumstances, had every possibility of making a tolerable and even useful life for himself, even after the loss of his eyesight. Thus, if analysis helped him to face the threat and master his anxiety, he still had a worthwhile life ahead of him. The question was: could it be done? What would the consequences be if the remains of his inner equilibrium, precariously held together with the help of excessive denials, were thrown out of balance and the underlying immense amount of castration anxiety released? I was spared making up my mind about it by the simple fact that I had no immediate vacancy and the patient, in his urgency, was not prepared to wait. Moreover, he was not a case to be undertaken without ample time at one's disposal to see him whenever needed. He entered analysis elsewhere, but committed suicide after a few days, incidentally, *before* the analyst had had time to confront him with his violent denials.

We are left here with the question whether this man would have been analyzable and, if so, what would have been the best technical approach to his particular problem.

[After a discussion by K. R. Eissler:] To return once more to the blind patient. If I had had the analytic courage in my interview with him to say: 'You know that there is the possibility that you will become blind,' this might have changed his intolerable castration anxiety into a tolerable reality fear. But the unanswered question remains: would it really have had that desired effect? And if not – if his ego had been unable to stand the strain – would I not have been responsible for his suicide? K. R. Eissler has said that the outcome depends on the structure of the patient and the situation; I would say that in the last resort the success or failure of our intervention depends on the intactness of the ego. It is sometimes possible to re-establish the reality aspect which the patient has lost. This is probably what Bond succeeded in doing. The patient then responds on the basis of reality instead of on the basis of his neurosis. But can we really determine *when* this will happen? I doubt it.

IV

[In response to Dora Hartmann, who stated that in certain emergency situations (e.g., when a young unmarried girl is in danger of becoming pregnant as a consequence of acting out), the analyst should interfere to prevent lasting damage to the patient's future life.] Here it is not a question of changing the methods of analysis, but a question of interrupting the analysis for the sake of a reality situation. We should not confuse the two instances with each other.

[And in response to Jenny Waelder-Hall, who described problems similar to those mentioned by Dora Hartmann.] I feel that our discussion changed its direction to a certain degree. We do not mean to enumerate those instances when we are forced by circumstances to act nonanalytically. We attempt to widen the concept of 'analytic' behavior by perfecting our technique. To meet new or unusual challenges we need, probably, new or modified technical prescriptions. Whenever we overthrow established procedure, we feel, quite rightly, that we may be approaching a state of anarchy. That is the reason why analysts discuss these technical matters so infrequently. Our analytic technique is hardwon and should not be abandoned easily. Whenever rules are altered, we have the right to expect a theoretical justification for the step taken which remains on purely analytic ground.

V

Maurits Katan's example[2] is useful as an illustration for our purposes. There is no analytic rule which the patient's neurosis cannot pervert and use for its own purposes. Analysts should collect and pool instances from their own cases which show how a technical rule of procedure can be converted to serve neurotic purposes. May I begin with a striking example from my own practice: I have an obsessional patient in whose neurosis the fear of contact with his fellow beings plays an important part. His fellow beings, as is only natural, will sometimes address him unaware; this is felt by him as a terrible happening since it interrupts the compulsive flow of his inner thoughts which have to reach a satisfactory end before he can detach himself from them and pay attention. He suffers from the fact that he cannot control the people in his environment and keep them quiet. Some people even want to shake his hand. This is worse; who knows what germs they may pass on to him? People move about unaccountably and, in the interest of his neurosis, he has to try and keep them strictly confined to their places, etc.

Now mark what ideal circumstances this man meets in the analytic situation. The analyst does not touch him, does not shake his hand, does not interrupt his speech or thought, does not move about the room during the analytic hour. Everything is strictly under control, nothing unexpected happens, and our man is perfectly happy so long as the analyst remains strictly within his analytic reserve. It was only when − not intentionally but by chance − I stepped out of my role once or twice and addressed a harmless remark to the patient on arrival that I noticed how deeply shocked he was by my breaking through the protective barrier behind which he was sheltered.

We may ask ourselves here whether we are always sufficiently aware of the meaning which our own behavior, although correct in the analytic sense, assumes for the patient.

A similar example was discussed in the recent Symposium of the New York Society (1954a). It was shown how obsessional patients with magical ideas use the image of the analyst as the 'unknown' figure and build up his image exclusively on the basis of their transference fantasies, uncorrected by any reality factors. This constellation fits their needs for a mysterious being, invested with magical powers, who can control the world for the patient. In most cases these transferred fantasies become obvious in the material and are open to interpretation in the ordinary manner. Occasionally they are so well hidden and fitted to the reality of the analytic setting that the analyst may overlook them.

As a further example, take the use of the couch. Ordinarily, the patient uses the couch for the purpose for which it is intended (relaxation plus inhibition of motility). But there are some passive male patients for whom the use of the couch becomes an addiction since it provides the perfect opportunity for acting out their passive strivings. I have a patient, for instance, who cannot wait until he reaches the couch. He rings the doorbell, somebody has to run to answer it, he rushes to the lift, arrives upstairs, pulls open my door and throws himself on the couch, with all the springs creaking under him; then, at last, he can begin to be passive. I always tell him that his is the most active passivity which I have met! What should be a help to the analyst becomes an expression of the neurosis. And we have to be grateful if it is done so openly. What threatens to defeat us are all the occasions when this tendency remains subtly hidden under perfectly correct analytic behavior from both sides.

There are, of course, the familiar instances when patients use free association for the purpose of exhibitionism, or, as in one of my cases, for the purpose of dramatization. With my patient this perverted use of free association was revealed in one small feature. She talked like other patients, with the exception that she used to report whatever other people had said in the form of direct speech. Thus, instead of merely associating, she acted, in fact, a continuous drama on the couch.

Perhaps our technical rules should be given to us with an addendum, setting out their most common misuse for the purpose of the neurosis. We might also invite colleagues to note all those instances in their practice where such misuse of the technique had remained undiscovered for a length of time until the analyst became aware of the occurrence and interpreted it.

VI

Paul Sloane has presented a very helpful and interesting piece of material indicating that there are two possibilities; the analytic rule may be misused for defensive purposes – that is what I stressed first – or it may be misused, as Sloane emphasized, for purposes of satisfaction. In the one case it is the resistance side of the patient which exploits and distorts the analytic technique; in the other case it is the id side which does the same. It is useful to differentiate between the two possibilities.

VII

I want to make two brief points to prevent misunderstandings. I did not mean to say that a patient's misuse of a technical rule justifies in any way the alteration or abandonment of this rule; on the contrary, it provides the opportunity of safeguarding the rule by interpreting its misuse. The patient has to keep up free association, has to continue to lie on the couch, etc.; through interpretation these actions should recover their character as technical helps for the analysis and cease to be methods employed for defensive or symptomatic purposes.

Further, I want to stress that I did not intend to introduce the concept of intactness of the ego as a last resort of explanation. I mentioned the capacity of the ego for healthy reaction in connection with the defense by denial. How much denial an analysis can undo may, I believe, depend on the capacity of the individual ego to tolerate anxiety without breaking down into states of panic.

VIII

I feel that, by now, our discussion has begun to serve the purpose for which we undertook it. The intention was to make our rules of analytic procedure come alive. So that we could scrutinize them individually, see what meaning each one has for us, as well as what meaning they may have for the patient. When we interfere with them in any way, we shall then feel that we interfere with something that is real, living, and meaningful to us, more than a mere tradition or convention.

In answering the various speakers, may I begin with Sidney Wenger's question concerning the treatment of agoraphobic patients who are unable to leave their house. Although I have no special experience with severe cases of this kind myself, I cannot conceive of any procedure here except the classical one: to direct the whole analytic effort toward enabling the patient to meet the anxiety on the very spot and in the very situation where it is most severe. While the patient is defended against his anxiety by staying home, he may never produce the material which we need to analyze. In the analysis of an agoraphobic, or of any phobic patient, and even in the phobic situations which arise in a transitory manner during a treatment, we should always work, I believe, toward the patient's tolerating increasing amounts of the anxiety against which the phobia has been built up, until he can expose himself to the full amount of it and analyze it fully. I am interested to know whether members here agree with this point of view. Personally, I cannot imagine completing the analysis of a phobia while the phobic restrictions are kept up. Other analysts may have different experiences to tell.

Marianne Kris[3] made a most interesting contribution here which coincides with a point raised earlier by Robert Waelder. In working with her patient, she succeeded in reviving a conflict which had been dead and buried. For a time, before the patient's neurosis was fully established, this woman must have been torn between wanting to go out into the street and fearing to do so. This conflict was solved when the phobia appeared and the wish to go out disappeared. She became unable to leave the house and was not conscious any more of any desire to do so. To make the patient first *want* to try, and then to try going out actually, leads in the direction of analyzing the conflict. Cases of this type offer excellent opportunities for learning to use the classical technique with the minimum of demands made on the patient.

I was especially interested in Annie Reich's remark about the analysis of a paranoid patient, since one of my earliest patients was a paranoid woman (not selected as such) who placed me in a very similar quandary. The paranoid traits were displayed very soon in the transference and – very naturally for a beginner – I became uncertain and upset. I acted as Annie Reich did. I abandoned the analytic procedure in situations where the paranoid transference occurred. Or rather, for short periods, I permitted myself to become the receiver of her projections and her persecutor and then, periodically, proceeded to point out to her just enough of the reality factors to enable the patient to withdraw the projection again. Miraculously, the patient was cured. I know that this happened because I had not permitted the transference to develop to the full strength of its original force. It was this experience, probably, which provoked my interest in technique and its variations from the start. Since then I have heard of many cases of paranoia treated where analysts have given full scope to the transference and have reported good success. I still believe that I could not have handled this particular patient otherwise and that, with her paranoid suspicions fully transferred onto me, she would have broken off the treatment in despair.

By now we have elicited some useful illustrations for variations of technique in analytic treatment. The classical rule, for instance, prescribes: the analyst shall not interfere with the transference phenomena except by interpretation; but in the case of the two paranoid patients, neither Annie Reich nor I have complied with this rule. We have reduced the transference phenomena by other than interpretive action, which is a definite qualitative variation of technique. In the severe cases of denial discussed here, the deviation from the classical rule was of a quantitative rather than a qualitative nature. Instead of interpreting fully and on the spot it has been suggested that interpretations should be given in small doses and gradually, so as not to upset the precarious inner balance of the patient in too drastic a manner. As Marianne Kris suggested, this may apply especially in borderline cases, or with patients under a severe threat to their life or bodily health. I believe that in all instances of this kind we have to weigh the various dangers against each other. The danger of panic, suicide, self-destruction, etc., has to be very serious indeed to warrant a reduction in our interpretive activity. If we are too careful, or too frightened in the face of the patient's negative reactions, we run the opposite risk of unnecessarily delaying the progress of the analysis, and of permitting the patient to keep up defenses which we could have interpreted and thereby removed with benefit to the patient.

I welcome Edward Kronold's suggestion that we should distinguish between modification of rules as such and the adjustment of (unmodified) rules to the clinical features of the individual patient. Actually, I made a similar distinction in the recent Symposium (1954a) held by the New York Society and Institute. I suggested that we should recognize four different causes for the modification of techniques which are current today: (1) modifications made necessary by the application of psychoanalysis to new fields (psychosis, delinquency, borderline states, etc.); (2) modifications following on changes in theoretical outlook; (3) personal variations due to the individual bias of the analyst; (4) modifications forced on the analyst by the individual features of the patient's personality and transference [see chapter 16 in this volume – eds].

Nathan Colton spoke of the analyst's personal analysis which should clear up all these doubtful points for him. I believe that this is true merely within limits. It is in our own analysis that we acquire the conviction that analysis works (provided our own analysis has worked!). Without that conviction we should find ourselves unable, probably, to apply any analytic techniques to our patients. On the other hand, our personal analytic experience covers a certain area only. With the varied types of disturbance with which we have to deal, there will always be many which do not correspond to our personal experience. Thus, although we acquire the basic convictions in our own analysis, we do not acquire the experience necessary to prepare us for what we are going to meet in terms of type of disturbance, variation in structure, in ego strength, etc. After our own analysis, we need several years of practice until we have approached the many constellations which may arise, and even after that period we are still in for many surprises.

Daniel Silverman, when quoting his patient who had to be restrained with regard to drinking before being analyzable, emphasized the alterations of technique characteristic of the treatment of addicts. Where the transference temporarily substitutes for the addiction, the analyst can succeed only by being more accessible for the patient than is the rule otherwise. Where the analyst fails to do so, he cannot replace the drug; a drug has to be at hand to play its role. In many treatments of addicts we find it confirmed that the original addiction returns during the temporary absence of the analyst, whether for weekends, during holidays, or for reasons of illness. There is, doubtless, a direct correspondence between the drug and the presence of the analyst, knowing which we have to increase the time and attention usually given to an analytic patient. It is true that thereby we transgress ordinary analytic procedure, but only to the limits to which the structure of an addiction differs from the structure of an obsessional neurosis or hysteria. When such cases respond well to analysis, the weaning from the transference corresponds in striking ways to the usual weaning from a drug. We are familiar with people who can stop drinking or smoking only under the condition of taking not even one drop of alcohol or of smoking not even a single cigarette. Some cured addicts behave similarly. Once weaned from the transference, they neither need nor want further contact with the analyst.

Eli Marcovitz extended what used to be said concerning free association to the patient's behavior toward all analytic rules, namely, that
they can be followed wholly only at the end of the treatment. With
free association this is certainly as it should be, since the inner interference
with the basic analytic rule (free association) provides us with our best
clues for the understanding of the patient's ego defenses. It is not always
the same with the other technical prescriptions. Sometimes, in the
beginning of the treatment, when we make our pact with the conscious
and healthy part of the patient's personality, it is not too difficult for
the patient to cooperate. As the transference neurosis develops, the
disturbances of cooperation appear and open up a wide field of possibilities for the interpretation of the unconscious forces which are working
behind them.

There are, further, specific analytic rules and procedures which are
directly opposed to specific neurotic disturbances. In such instances,
the patient is unable to comply, not really for reasons of transference
or resistance in the strict sense of the terms, but because this particular
piece of behavior is impossible for him according to the symptomatology
of the case. An obsessional patient of mine, for instance, follows as his
main maxim of life the prescription to 'let sleeping dogs lie.' He tries
to avoid dangers by not thinking of them; he avoids contact of all kinds;
he does not mention death, illness, cancer, etc. What he can think or
speak of is actually restricted to a very small area. Far from this having
begun as a resistance in analysis, this tendency is an integral part of his
neurosis and has persisted throughout his life. Imagine what would
happen if you confronted this patient with the basic analytic rule, free
association, which is diametrically opposed to his own, neurotic manner
of functioning. Much as he might want to cooperate, he could not do
so. What could happen is that his attempts to comply with the rule,
futile as they are, would make him realize the extent of the restrictions
which are governing his life.

All analysts are familiar with patients who enter analysis with an
inhibition of speech. Structurally, this particular symptom does not
differ from other neurotic inhibitions. But the patient has entered a
treatment where speech is the main vehicle and he therefore finds
himself in a most precarious position. He ought to speak to be cured,
but he cannot do so before he is cured. The patient may reproach the

analyst, as one of mine did, by saying, 'Do not put the cart before the horse. You cure me, and I shall cooperate fully,' to which the analyst feels like answering, 'You speak, and I shall cure you in due course.' Or you may have a patient for whom the analysis presents a forbidden situation for other reasons. One of my patients suffers from the fear of finding himself alone with a woman; when this happens to him, he will either fall asleep on the spot or make a desperate bid for company. This is transferred into the analytic situation by avoidance of the analyst through being late, or by talking endlessly and for hours about the troubles of others, maneuvering these figures from the environment skillfully until they, as it were, take his place in the analytic situation. When this defense fails, he falls into a deep sleep on the couch. It is true that this behavior is no more than the literal repetition of his actions toward his wife; he invites endless company to his house to avoid being alone with her, although he loves her. He delays joining her in bed at night. And when he has finally succeeded in being with her, he immediately falls into a deep and trancelike sleep. You may say that his behavior in the transference reflects and reveals in an admirable manner what is wrong with his marriage. But it is also true that the precise nature of the inhibition, opposed as it is to the very intimacy of the analytic setting, places him at a disadvantage in the treatment. Compared with patients whose symptomatology is of a different kind, his main avoidance has to be overcome somehow before he can even approach the material sufficiently to have it analyzed.

Notes

1. [Douglas Bond described his treatment of a case of anorexia in a young girl. He emphasized her fantastic denial in the face of evidence of destruction – a denial he countered by telling her that she would die.]
2. [M. Katan described a patient who attempted to induce the analyst to forbid intercourse with his wife, an apparently normal activity which had the hidden purpose of defending against homosexual transference feelings.]
3. [Marianne Kris related how she initiated treatment with one agoraphobic patient by first going several times to the patient's home, and with another one by allowing the patient to be accompanied to the office by a relative, who was in fact the object of the patient's phobia.]

18

Difficulties in the Path of Psychoanalysis: A Confrontation of Past with Present Viewpoints (1969 [1968])

The purpose of this paper – of which parts of two sections are reproduced in this chapter – is to draw attention to some major changes which have, in recent years, characterized psychoanalytic theorizing and technique. In Anna Freud's opinion, these trends are one-sided in that they emphasize single aspects of normal and abnormal mental life while neglecting others. This is illustrated by the contemporary concentration on the vicissitudes of the infant–mother relationship. The fate of later relationships, for example the oedipus complex, will be wholly determined by those early psychical experiences. This one-sidedness is also reflected in techniques which are designed to reach the adult patient's (infantile) pre-verbal period. This can be achieved, if sufficient attention is given to the transference. It is here that enactments of the pre-verbal relationships with the mother are to be observed and analyzed. The result is technique in which analysis of the transference takes precedence over memories, free associations and dreams. Even if it is possible to connect with a psychopathology created in the pre-verbal period, there is, as yet, no evidence to indicate that what has been acquired at such an early time is necessarily reversible.

Anna Freud enters a plea for a return to theorizing which retains the closest connections with the observable phenomena. Freud's metapsychology (theory of mind), she believes, accommodates the dynamic (conflictual), the topographic (relationship of mental contents to consciousness), the economic (the quantitative factor) and the genetic aspects of mental life. This conceptualization offers the best opportunity for avoiding the tendency to overemphasize one of these factors to the neglect of the others.

'Difficulties in the Path of Psychoanalysis: A Confrontation of Past with Present Viewpoints' was delivered as the 18th Freud Anniversary Lecture of the New York Psychoanalytic Institute, New York, on 16 April 1968. It was first published in the *Freud Anniversary Lecture Series*, The New York Psychoanalytic Institute, by International Universities Press, New York, 1969.

The Patients

... When Freud wrote of *earliest* defensive struggles or of analyzing the prehistory of the oedipus complex, what he had in mind, probably, were events of the anal and oral phases, the period immediately after ego and id had separated off from each other. There is little or no evidence that he thought it possible to deal therapeutically with preverbal experience, in spite of his knowledge and conviction that this is an all-important period in the individual's life when essential lines for development are laid down, when reaction patterns are preformed, and when basic deprivations and frustrations exert an influence which threatens to be lasting.[1]

Departing from this position, a considerable cross-section of the psychoanalytic community today pins their faith on the analysis of the first year of life, with the purpose of therapeutically modifying the impact of the earliest happenings. Freud's discovery that every neurosis of the adult is preceded by an infantile neurosis and that the latter has to be analyzed before the former can be reached, is paraphrased by them as follows: every infantile neurosis in the oedipal period is preceded by fateful interactions between infant and mother in the very first days and months of life, and it is this archaic, preverbal phase which has to be revived in the transference and analyzed before the later infantile neurosis can be approached effectively.

This view is held today by many analysts of otherwise widely divergent opinions.[2] Interestingly enough, it has been described systematically, not by a member of one of the more independent and revolutionary analytic sections, but by Jeanne Lampl-de Groot. In a recent paper 'On Obstacles Standing in the Way of Psychoanalytic Cure' (1967), she goes through the list of difficulties cited by Freud, referring each back to some happening during the earliest mother–infant interaction: the (masochistic) *negative therapeutic reaction* of some patients who have a need for self-punishment, to 'the primitive fear of their own aggressive drives and the destruction of their omnipotence fantasies' directed against the mother; the *incapacity to tame the instinctual drives*, to the modes of drive discharge initiated when the ego is helpless *vis-à-vis* the drives and 'strongly dependent on the mother's support';

irregular and distorted ego development, to failures in the original dyad between infant and mother; the *bisexual problems*, to the infant's fear of merging with a dominating mother, a fear of passivity which later, in the phallic phase, acquires sexual meaning.

Any attempt to carry analysis from the verbal to the preverbal period of development brings with it practical and technical innovations as well as theoretical implications, many of which are controversial.

What strikes the observer first is a change in the type of *psychic material* with which the analysis is dealing. Instead of exploring the disharmonies between the various agencies within a structured personality, the analyst is concerned with the events which lead from chaotic, undifferentiated state toward the initial building up of a psychic structure. This means going beyond the area of intrapsychic conflict, which had always been the legitimate target for psychoanalysis, and into the darker area of interaction between innate endowment and environmental influence. The implied aim is to undo or to counteract the impact of the very forces on which the rudiments of personality development are based.

Analysts who work for this aim assure us that this can be achieved. They feel enthusiastic about the new therapeutic prospects which they see opening out before them. Jeanne Lampl-de Groot, in her paper, confesses to being 'far from optimistic' in cases in which the damage done during the initial mother–infant interaction has been massive. I myself cannot help feeling doubtful about trying to advance into the area of primary repression, i.e., to deal with processes which, by nature, are totally different from the results of the ego's defensive maneuvers with which we feel familiar.

As regards *technique*, it is obvious that different methods are needed for the approach to the earliest rather than to the later phases. Lampl-de Groot mentions 'nonverbal modes of communication' which become unavoidable. Others speak of 'silent communion' between analyst and patient, or use other terms to stress the need for the analyst's intuitive understanding of the patient's signs and signals, his empathy, etc. However that may be, there is no doubt that neither memory nor verbal recall reach into the depth of postnatal, preverbal experience. Therefore, remembering yields its place to repetition, verbal communication to re-enactment. This explains the heightened significance of communication via the transference in many present-day analyses, where transference interpretations are considered the only therapeutically effective ones and where the transference phenomena are perforce given preference over memory, free association, and dreams, as the only real road to the unconscious.

It is, in fact, this central and unique role given to the transference in the psychoanalytic process, to the exclusion of all other avenues of communication, which is, to date, one of the points of controversy in the analytic world. There is, further, the question whether the transference really has the power to transport the patient back as far as the beginning of life. Many are convinced that this is the case. Others, I among them, raise the point that it is one thing for preformed, object-related fantasies to return from repression and be redirected from the inner to the outer world (i.e., to the person of the analyst); but that it is an entirely different, almost magical expectation to have the patient in analysis change back into the prepsychological, undifferentiated, and unstructured state, in which no divisions exist between body and mind or self and object.

The argument that it is the quality of the analytic setting itself which promotes such deep regressions also does not necessarily command belief. In many respects, the mother–infant and the analyst–patient relationship are dissimilar rather than similar. What is characteristic for the former is the infant's need for an ever-present, exclusive, timelessly devoted, giving, and comforting partner, while the latter is characterized by the existence of rivals, restriction in time, demands for punctuality and cooperation, release of anxiety, withholding of reassurance, frustration of wishes, at best token gratifications. Taken altogether, the question is left open whether, in fact, the re-enactment of life after birth does, or does not, take place in the patient's mind.

Another controversial point concerns the role of the ego within the analytic process. In the classical procedure, as described above, this role is considered decisive in various respects: for the initial pact with the analyst; for the patient's willingness to reduce or suspend defenses and thereby promote upsurges from the id; for accepting insight; for incorporating the result of interpretations within its own organization, etc. Furthermore, the aim itself of analysis is geared to the concept of a mediating ego that is helped to abandon defensive structures built up in infantile life on faulty premises and to replace them by more adequate and rational solutions.

Perhaps it has never been spelled out explicitly that such considerations cease to apply where analysis aims to penetrate into pre-ego strata, where the power of a quasi-delusional transference is meant to carry the patient far beyond the confines of ego functioning into the reliving of primary emotional experience. What is expected of the ego under these altered circumstances is not only the undoing of its own faulty moves but also the undoing of the impact of the very processes which have led to its formation.

More important than these mainly technical considerations seem to me *two theoretical assumptions* which are implied in them.

The first of these is a revision of the distinction between inherited and acquired characteristics. According to Freud (1937), 'We have no reason to dispute the existence and importance of original, innate distinguishing characteristics of the ego' (p. 240), which, is, after all, initially, one with the id. Nevertheless, the extent of an individual's innate endowment has been under dispute in recent years, based partly on psychoanalytic reconstructions, partly on the direct observation of mother–child couples. Both types of data have produced in us the conviction that much that used to be considered innate can now be shown to have been acquired during the first year of life and to have been added to the inherited constitution.[3]

But if there is unanimous agreement on this point, there is, in contrast, vivid disagreement concerning a theoretical inference drawn from it. The new technical proposals aimed at the beginning of life imply the assumption that whatever is acquired is reversible. This is by no means proved. It may well be that the very basis on which personality formation rests is, in fact, bedrock.

The Analyst

. . . The analyst's task is not to create, i.e., to invent anything, but to observe, to explore, to understand, and to explain. It is in respect to these latter activities that an important quality appears to me in danger of getting lost.

Psychoanalytic thinking, in classical terms, implied the specific demand that every clinical fact should be approached from four aspects: *genetically*, as to its origin; *dynamically*, as to the interplay of forces of which it is the result; *economically*, with regard to its energy charge; *topographically* (later *structurally*), concerning its localization within the mental apparatus.[4] It was the psychology based on this view of mental functioning which was singled out by the name of *metapsychology*.

Nevertheless, in our times, the term metapsychology has assumed a very different meaning. What it denotes now is largely theory building, distant from the area of clinical material, an activity which demands and is reserved for a specific, speculative quality of mind. As such it has become the bugbear of the clinically oriented analyst who feels wholly divorced from it. This brings about a division which, in the long run, threatens both areas with sterility: the theoretical field, due to the absence of clinical data; the clinical field, due to a diminution in their theoretical evaluation and exploration. What is lost, finally, is what used to be considered as a *sine qua non* in psychoanalysis: the essential *unity* between clinical and theoretical thinking.

A look at the history of the four metapsychological aspects may take us a step further. Although they were meant to exist and be developed simultaneously, this did not happen according to intention. There were always periods when one or the other of them gained ascendancy to the comparative detriment of the remaining ones.

The first to be given widespread approval was, no doubt, the *dynamic* aspect. In fact, to approach mental functioning and mental illness in terms of conflict between opposing forces seemed so obvious and acceptable, not only to the analysts themselves, that for a while it dominated the scene and became the hallmark of enlightened thinking, especially in psychiatry. On this basis, psychoanalysis used to be alluded to as a 'dynamic psychology.' This, of course, disregarded the fact that in metapsychological thinking an interplay of internal forces as such remains inconclusive unless information is added where in the mental apparatus these forces are localized; whether they possess the same or different psychical qualities (unconscious, preconscious, conscious); whether they are able to meet each other on the same level and within the same mental area; to reduce each other; to enter into compromises with each other, etc.; or whether they are walled off from each other by defensive activity. In short, the dynamic point of view is not profitable for the analyst, except in combination with the *topographical* one. But acceptance of the latter was more hesitant and less wholehearted and did not become prominent in the analytic literature until 1926 when *Inhibitions, Symptoms and Anxiety* put it into the foreground in its revised form as the '*structural* aspect.'

There was never any doubt about psychoanalysis as a *genetic* psychology. The genetic point of view had a recognized existence from the moment when psychoanalytic exploration turned from the neurotic problems of adult life to their forerunners in childhood and demonstrated the impact of early on later happenings and patterns.

In contrast, the *economic* aspect had a chequered career and not only because 'the term "mental energy" may give rise to criticism on the part of psychologists, psychiatrists, and psychoanalysts' (Lampl-de Groot, 1967, p. 24). Freud himself was always convinced of the highly important part quantity plays in the defensive struggles against unpleasure which go on in the mental apparatus early in life and play havoc with the normality of the ego. He was equally convinced of the fact that the outcome of every analytic treatment depends essentially on quantitative factors, i.e., on the strength of the patient's resistances and negative reactions measured against the amounts of energy upon which analysis can draw. Nevertheless, he admitted with regret that 'our theoretical concepts have neglected to attach the same importance to the *economic* line of approach as they have to the *dynamic* and *topographical* ones' (1937, p. 226f.).

To return from here to the analysts of today and the problems of present and future development of analytic thinking:

What may give rise to concern is a comparative neglect of the fact that the relations of the four metapsychological aspects to the notion of a psychoanalytic cure are not on an equal level. While alterations of the economics, dynamics, and structure of the patient's personality are the essence of analytic therapy, exploration of the genetic roots is not the aim in itself, but is the means to the end of understanding and interpretation. Heinz Hartmann, who in psychoanalysis is the genetic explorer par excellence, expressed this very succinctly when in 1939 he wrote concerning his own efforts to disentangle the roots of ego development: 'Many of these lengthy . . . considerations are not psychoanalytic in the narrow sense, and some of them seem to have taken us quite far from the core of psychoanalysis' (p. 108).

However that may be, one look at the analytic scene of today can convince us that the desire to unearth ever earlier and deeper antecedents, not only of the ego but of human emotions, anxieties, and struggles in general, has taken hold of the analysts' imagination. For the moment it outstrips most other interests, and it may take some time until the other metapsychological aspects catch up again with the genetic one, which has strayed ahead.

But this, exactly, is what we should be waiting for. The newly discovered facts about early and earliest life need to fall into place within the dynamics, the economy, and the structure of the personalities for which they prepare the ground. Only in this way can metapsychology regain its former status. It is also only in this way that we shall approach once more what the Ad Hoc Committee for Scientific Activities calls hopefully

'a creative era in psychoanalysis.'

Notes

1. See also M. Balint (1958) on 'basic faults.'
2. See, for example, René Spitz, D. W. Winnicott, Melanie Klein, Herbert Rosenfeld, and others.
3. On this point see also Martin James (1960) and others.
4. A fifth aspect, the *adaptive* one to be added later; see Hartmann (1939) and Rapaport and Gill (1959).

Bibliography

Adatto, C. (1958) 'Ego Reintegration Observed in Analysis of Late Adolescents',
    Int. J. Psycho-Anal., 39: 172–7.

Aichhorn, A. (1925) *Wayward Youth*, New York: Viking Press, 1935.

Aichhorn, A. (1936a) 'On the Technique of Child Guidance: The Process of
    Transference', in *Delinquency and Child Guidance*, New York: International
    Universities Press, 1964, pp. 101–92.

Aichhorn, A. (1936b) 'The Narcissistic Transference of the "Juvenile Impos-
    tor" ', in *Delinquency and Child Guidance*, New York: International Universi-
    ties Press, 1964, pp. 174–91.

Aichhorn, A. (1937) *Einführung in die Erziehungsberatung: Kurse für Pädagogen*,
    Vienna: Internationaler Psychoanalytischer Verlag.

Alexander, F., French, T., *et al.* (1946) *Psychoanalytic Therapy*, New York:
    Ronald Press.

Arlow, J. (1981) 'Theories of Pathogenesis', *Psychoanal. Q.*, 50: 488–514.

Balint, M. (1958) 'The Three Areas of the Mind', *Int. J. Psycho-Anal.*, 39: 328–40.

Bergmann, T. (1945) 'Observations of Children's Reactions to Motor
    Restraint', *Nerv. Child*, 4: 318–28.

Bergmann, T., and Freud, A. (1965) *Children in the Hospital*, New York:
    International Universities Press.

Bernfeld, S. (1923) 'Über eine typische Form der männlichen Pubertät', *Imago*,
    9: 169–88.

Bibring, G. (1959) 'Some Considerations of the Psychological Processes in
    Pregnancy', *The Psychoanalytic Study of the Child*, 14: 113–21.

Blos, P. (1962) *On Adolescence: A Psychoanalytic Interpretation*, Glencoe, Ill: Free
    Press.

Bonnard, A. (1949) 'School Phobia – Is It a Syndome?' Read at the International
    Congress of Psychiatry, Paris, *Archives*, Paris.

Bowlby, J. (1951) *Maternal Care and Mental Health*, Geneva: World Health
    Organization.

Bowlby, J., Robertson, J., and Rosenbluth, S. (1952) 'A Two-year-old Goes
    to Hospital', *The Psychoanalytic Study of the Child*, 7: 82–94.

Burke, M. (1949) 'The Fundamental Rule of Psycho-Analysis'. Abstract in *Int.
    J. Psycho-Anal.*, 30: 200.

Burlingham, D. (1951a) *Twins: A Study of Three Pairs of Identical Twins*, New York: International Universities Press.

Burlingham, D. (1951b) 'Present Trends in Handling the Mother–Child Relationship During the Therapeutic Process', *The Psychoanalytic Study of the Child*, 6: 31–7.

Burlingham, D. (1972) *Psychoanalytic Studies of the Sighted and the Blind*, New York: International Universities Press.

Burlingham, D. (1979) 'To Be Blind in a Sighted World', *The Psychoanalytic Study of the Child*, 34: 5–30.

Burlingham, D., and Freud, A. (1942) *Young Children in War-time*, London: George Allen and Unwin.

Coleman, R., Kris, E., and Provence, S. (1953) 'The Study of Variations of Early Parental Attitudes: A Preliminary Report', *The Psychoanalytic Study of the Child*, 8: 20–47.

Couch, A. (1995) 'Anna Freud's Adult Psychoanalytic Technique: A Defence of Classical Analysis', *Int. J. Psycho-Anal.*, 76: 153–71.

Couch, A. (1997) 'Extra-Transference Interpretation: A Defence of Classical Technique', paper presented to the Northern Ireland Association for the Study of Psycho-Analysis; a revised version of 'Extra-Transference Interpretation: The Debate Continues' given to a Scientific Meeting of the British Psycho-Analytical Society on 1 November 1989.

Deutsch, H. (1967) *Selected Problems of Adolescence*, New York: International Universities Press.

Dubo, S. (1950) 'Psychiatric Study of Children with Pulmonary Tuberculosis', *Amer. J. Orthopsychiat.*, 20: 520–8.

Dyer, R. (1983) *Her Father's Daughter: The Work of Anna Freud*, New York: Jason Aronson. [Includes Appendix: 'Chronological List of the Publications of Anna Freud, 1922–1982', pp. 269–83.]

Eissler, K. (1950) 'Ego-Psychological Implications of the Psychoanalytic Treatment of Delinquents', *The Psychoanalytic Study of the Child*, 5: 97–121.

Eissler, K. (1953) 'The Effect of the Structure of the Ego on Psychoanalytic Technique', *J. Amer. Psychoanal. Assn*, 1: 104–43.

Eissler, K. (1958) 'Notes on Problems of Technique in the Psychoanalytic Treatment of Adolescents', *The Psychoanalytic Study of the Child*, 13: 223–54.

Erikson, E. (1959) *Identity and the Life Cycle* [Psychological Issues, Monogr. 1], New York: International Universities Press.

Federn, P. (1936) 'On the Distinction between Healthy and Pathological Narcissism', in *Ego Psychology and the Psychoses*, London: Hogarth Press, 1952, pp. 323–64.

Federn, P. (1952) *Ego Psychology and the Psychoses*, London: Hogarth Press, 1952.

Fenichel, O. (1941) *Problems of Psychoanalytic Technique*, New York: The Psychoanalytic Quarterly.

Ferenczi, S. (1921) 'The Further Development of an Active Therapy in Psycho-

Analysis', in J. Rickman, ed., *Further Contributions to the Theory and Technique of Psycho-Analysis*, London: Karnac Books, 1980, pp. 198–217.

Fraiberg, S. (1955) 'Some Considerations to the Introduction of Therapy in Puberty', *The Psychoanalytic Study of the Child*, 10: 264–86.

Frankl, L. (1963) 'Self-Preservation and the Development of Accident Proneness in Children and Adolescents', *The Psychoanalytic Study of the Child*, 18: 464–83.

Freeman, T., Cameron, J., and McGhie, A. (1958) *Chronic Schizophrenia*, London: Tavistock Publications; New York: International Universities Press.

Freud, A. (1922) 'Beating Fantasies and Daydreams', in *The Writings of Anna Freud*, Vol. 1, pp. 137–57. New York: International Universities Press. [Hereafter referred to as *Writings*, with volume number from this series.]

Freud, A. (1927 [1926]) *Four Lectures on Child Analysis*. Revised translation, *Writings*, 1, pp. 3–69. First published as *Introduction to the Technique of Child Analysis*.

Freud, A. (1928 [1927]) 'The Theory of Child Analysis'. *Writings*, 1, pp. 162–75.

Freud, A. (1930) *Four Lectures on Psychoanalysis for Teachers and Parents*. Revised translation, *Writings*, 1, pp. 73–133. First published as *Introduction to Psycho-Analysis for Teachers: Four Lectures*.

Freud, A. (1936) *The Ego and the Mechanisms of Defence*. Revised edition, 1966. *Writings*, 2.

Freud, A. (1939–1945) *Reports on the Hampstead Nurseries, 1939–1945. Writings*, 3, pp. 3–540.

Freud, A. (1942) *Young Children in War-time: A Year's Work in a Residential War Nursery. Writings*, 3, pp. 142–211, as chapter 12, 'Annual Report January 1942 – Summary of First Year's Work'. In collaboration with Dorothy Burlingham.

Freud, A. (1945) 'Indications for Child Analysis'. *Writings*, 4, pp. 3–38.

Freud, A. (1946) 'The Psychoanalytic Study of Infant Feeding Disturbances'. *Writings*, 4, pp. 39–59.

Freud, A. (1947) 'The Establishment of Feeding Habits'. *Writings*, 4, pp. 442–57.

Freud, A. (1949a[1948]) 'Notes on Aggression'. *Writings*, 4, pp. 60–74.

Freud, A. (1949b) 'On Certain Difficulties in the Preadolescent's Relation to His Parents'. *Writings*, 4, pp. 95–106.

Freud, A. (1950a) 'Some Clinical Remarks Concerning the Treatment of Cases of Male Homosexuality'. Abstract in *Bull. Amer. Psychoanal. Assn*, 7: 117–18, 1951.

Freud, A. (1950b) 'Variations of Psychoanalytic Technique'. Abstract in *Bull. Amer. Psychoanal. Assn*, 7: 129–30, 1951.

Freud, A. (1951a [1950]) 'Observations on Child Development'. *Writings*, 4, pp. 143–62.

Freud, A. (1951b) 'An Experiment in Group Upbringing'. *Writings*, 4, pp. 163–229.

Freud, A. (1952a [1949–1951]) 'Studies in Passivity'. *Writings*, 4, pp. 245–59.

Freud, A. (1952b) 'The Role of Bodily Illness in the Mental Life of Children'. *Writings*, 4, pp. 260–79.

Freud, A. (1953) 'James Robertson's *A Two-Year-Old Goes to Hospital*, Film Review'. *Writings*, 4, pp. 280–92.

Freud, A. (1954a) 'The Widening Scope of Indications for Psychoanalysis: Discussion'. *Writings*, 4, pp. 356–76.

Freud, A. (1954b) 'Problems of Technique in Adult Analysis'. *Writings*, 4, pp. 377–406.

Freud, A. (1955) 'The Concept of the Rejecting Mother'. *Writings*, 4, pp. 586–602.

Freud, A. (1956) 'Comments on Joyce Robertson's "A Mother's Observations on the Tonsillectomy of her Four-Year-Old Daughter"'. *Writings*, 4, pp. 293–301.

Freud, A. (1958a [1957]) 'Child Observation and Prediction of Development: A Memorial Lecture in Honor of Ernst Kris'. *Writings* , 5, pp. 102–35.

Freud, A. (1958b [1957]) 'Adolescence'. *Writings*, 5, pp. 136–66.

Freud, A. (1961 [1959]) 'Answering Pediatricians' Questions'. *Writings*, 5, pp. 379–406.

Freud, A. (1962) 'Assessment of Pathology in Childhood – Part I'. *Writings*, 5, pp. 26–37.

Freud, A. (1965) *Normality and Pathology in Childhood: Assessments of Development*. *Writings*, 6.

Freud, A. (1966a) 'The Effects of Bodily Illness on the Child'. Lecture at Guy's Hospital Medical School.

Freud, A. (1966b) 'The Interaction between Body and Mind in the Child's Physical Illness'. Lecture at the University of Amsterdam.

Freud, A. (1967 [1953]) 'About Losing and Being Lost'. *Writings*, 4, pp. 302–16.

Freud, A. (1969 [1968]) 'Difficulties in the Path of Psychoanalysis: A Confrontation of Past with Present Viewpoints'. *Writings*, 7, pp. 124–56.

Freud, A. (1970) 'The Symptomatology of Childhood: A Preliminary Attempt at Classification'. *Writings*, 7, pp. 157–88.

Freud, A. (1974a [1973]) 'A Psychoanalytic View of Developmental Psychopathology'. *Writings*, 8, pp. 57–74.

Freud, A. (1974b) 'Beyond the Infantile Neurosis'. *Writings*, 8, pp. 75–81.

Freud, A. (1976 [1975]) 'Psychopathology Seen Against the Background of Normal Development'. *Writings*, 8, pp. 82–95.

Freud, A. (1981) *Psychoanalytic Psychology of Normal Development*, *Writings*, 8.

Freud, A. (1983 [1981]) 'Problems of Pathogenesis: Introduction to the Discussion', *The Psychoanalytic Study of the Child*, 38: 383–8.

Freud, A. (1992 [1952]) *The Harvard Lectures*, J. Sandler, ed., London: The Institute of Psycho-Analysis and Karnac Books.

Freud, A. and Burlingham, D. (1942) *War and Children,* New York: International Universities Press.

Freud, A., and Burlingham, D. (1944) *Infants Without Families: The Case For and Against Residential Nurseries. Writings, 3,* pp. 541–664.

Freud, S. (1894) 'The Neuro-Psychoses of Defence' in *The Standard Edition of the Complete Psychological Works of Sigmund Freud* (translated by James Strachey and Anna Freud, assisted by Alix Strachey and Alan Tyson), Vol. 3, pp. 45–61. London: Hogarth. [Hereafter referred to as *S.E.* with volume number from this series.]

Freud, S. (1896a) 'Further Remarks on the Neuro-Psychoses of Defence'. *S.E., 3,* pp. 162–85.

Freud, S. (1896b) 'Heredity and the Aetiology of the Neuroses'. *S.E., 3,* pp. 143–56.

Freud, S. (1896c) 'The Aetiology of Hysteria'. *S.E., 3 ,* pp. 191–221.

Freud, S. (1900) *The Interpretation of Dreams. S.E., 4–5.*

Freud, S. (1901) *The Psychopathology of Everyday Life. S.E., 6.*

Freud, S. (1905) *Three Essays on the Theory of Sexuality. S.E., 7,* pp. 125–245.

Freud, S. (1909) 'Analysis of a Phobia in a Five-Year-Old Boy'. *S.E., 10,* pp. 5–149.

Freud, S. (1911 [1910]) 'Psycho-analytic Notes on an Autobiographical Account of a Case of Paranoia'. *S.E., 12,* pp. 9–82.

Freud, S. (1913) *Totem and Taboo. S.E., 13,* pp. 1–161.

Freud, S. (1915) 'Instincts and Their Vicissitudes'. *S.E., 14 ,* pp. 117–40.

Freud, S. (1916–1917 [1915–1917]) *Introductory Lectures on Psychoanalysis. S.E., 15 and 16.*

Freud, S. (1919) 'A Child is Being Beaten: A Contribution to the Study of the Origin of Sexual Perversions'. *S.E., 17,* pp. 179–204.

Freud, S. (1920) *Beyond the Pleasure Principle. S.E., 18,* pp. 3–64.

Freud, S. (1922) 'Some Neurotic Mechanisms in Jealousy, Paranoia and Homosexuality'. *S.E., 18,* pp. 221–32.

Freud, S. (1923) *The Ego and the Id. S.E., 19,* pp. 12–59.

Freud, S. (1925) 'Preface to Aichhorn's *Wayward Youth'. S.E., 19,* pp. 273–5.

Freud, S. (1926) *Inhibitions, Symptoms and Anxiety. S.E., 20,* pp. 87–172.

Freud, S. (1937) 'Analysis Terminable and Interminable', *S.E., 23,* pp. 209–53.

Freud, S. (1940) *An Outline of Psycho-Analysis, S.E., 23 ,* pp. 144–207.

Fries, M. (1946) 'The Child's Ego Development and the Training of Adults in His Environment', *The Psychoanalytic Study of the Child,* 2: 85–112.

Geleerd, E. (1958) 'Borderline States in Childhood and Adolescence', *The Psychoanalytic Study of the Child,* 13: 279–95.

Goldstein, J., Freud, A., and Solnit, A. (1973) *Beyond the Best Interests of the Child,* New York: Free Press.

Goldstein, J., Freud, A., and Solnit, A. (1979) *Before the Best Interests of the Child,* New York: Free Press.

Goldstein, J. Freud, A., and Solnit, A. (1986) *In the Best Interests of the Child*, New York: Free Press.

Greenacre, P. (1944) 'Infant Reactions to Restraint: Problems in the Fate of Infantile Aggression' in *Trauma, Growth, and Personality*, New York: Norton, pp. 83–105.

Greenson, R. (1967) *The Technique and Practice of Psychoanalysis*, New York: International Universities Press.

Hall, J. Waelder (1946) 'The Analysis of a Case of Night Terror', *The Psychoanalytic Study of the Child*, 2: 189–228.

Hartmann, H. (1939) *Ego Psychology and the Problem of Adaptation*, New York: International Universities Press.

Hartmann, H. (1950) 'Psychoanalysis and Developmental Psychology', in *Essays on Ego Psychology*, New York: International Universities Press, 1964, pp. 99–112.

Hellman, I. (1958) 'Research on Adolescents in Treatment', *Proc. Roy. Soc. Med.*, 51: 942–3.

Hoffer, W. (1950) 'Oral Aggressiveness and Ego Development', *Int. J. Psycho-Anal.*, 31: 156–60.

Hoffer, W. (1952) 'The Mutual Influences in the Development of Ego and Id: Earliest Stages', *The Psychoanalytic Study of the Child*, 7: 31–41.

Holder, A. (1995) 'Anna Freud's Contribution to the Psychoanalytic Theory of Development', *Journal of Child Psychotherapy*, 21: 326–46.

Jackson, E. (1942) 'Treatment of the Young Child in the Hospital', *Amer. J. Orthopsychiat.*, 12: 56–63.

Jacobson, E. (1954) 'Transference Problems in the Psychoanalytic Treatment of Severely Depressed Patients', *J. Amer. Psychoanal. Assn*, 2: 595–606.

Jacobson, E. (1961) 'Adolescent Moods and the Remodeling of Psychic Structures in Adolescence', *The Psychoanalytic Study of the Child*, 16: 164–83.

Jacobson, E. (1964) *The Self and the Object World*, New York: International Universities Press.

James, M. (1960) 'Premature Ego Development: Some Observations upon Disturbances in the First Three Years of Life', *Int. J. Psycho-Anal.*, 41: 288–94.

Jessner, L., Blom, G., and Waldfogel, S. (1952) 'Emotional Implications of Tonsillectomy and Adenoidectomy in Children', *The Psychoanalytic Study of the Child*, 7: 126–69.

Jessner, L., and Kaplan, S. (1949) 'Emotional Reactions to Tonsillectomy and Adenoidectomy', in *Problems of Infancy and Childhood*, M. Senn, ed. New York: Josiah Macy, Jr Foundation, pp. 97–118.

Jones, E. (1922) 'Some Problems of Adolescence', in *Papers on Psycho-Analysis*, London: Baillière, Tindall & Cox, 5th ed., 1948, pp. 389–406.

Katan, A. (1937) 'The Role of Displacement in Agoraphobia', *Int. J. Psycho-Anal.*, 32: 41–50, 1951.

Katan, M. (1950) 'Structural Aspects of a Case of Schizophrenia', *The Psychoanalytic Study of the Child*, 5: 175–211.

Kennedy, H. (1950) 'Cover Memories in Formation', *The Psychoanalytic Study of the Child*, 5: 275–84.

Kestenberg, J. (1967–1968) 'Phases of Adolescence: Parts I, II, and III', *J. Amer. Acad. Child Psychiat.*, 6: 426–63; 6: 577–614; 7: 108–51.

Klein, M. (1932) *The Psycho-Analysis of Children*, London: Hogarth Press.

Knight, R. (1946) 'Psychotherapy of an Adolescent Catatonic Schizophrenic with Mutism: A Study in Empathy and Establishing Contact, *Psychiatry*, 9: 323–39.

Knight, R. (1949) 'A Critique of the Present Status of the Psychotherapies', in *Psychoanalytic Psychiatry and Psychology*, R. Knight and C. Friedman, ed., New York: International Universities Press, 1954, pp. 52–64.

Knight, R. (1952) 'An Evaluation of Psychotherapeutic Techniques', in *Psychoanalytic Psychiatry and Psychology*, R. Knight and C. Friedman, ed., New York: International Universities Press, 1954, pp. 65–76.

Knight, R. (1953a) 'Borderline States', in *Psychoanalytic Psychiatry and Psychology*, R. Knight and C. Friedman, ed., New York: International Universities Press, 1954, pp. 97–109.

Knight, R. (1953b) 'Management and Psychotherapy of the Borderline Schizophrenic Patient', in *Psychoanalytic Psychiatry and Psychology*, R. Knight and C. Friedman, eds., New York: International Universities Press, 1954, pp. 110–22.

Kohut, H. (1971) *The Analysis of the Self*, New York: International Universities Press.

Kris, E. (1938) 'Review of Anna Freud', *Int. J. Psycho-Anal.*, 19: 136–46.

Kris, E. (1950) 'Notes on the Development and on Some Current Problems of Psychoanalytic Child Psychology', *The Psychoanalytic Study of the Child*, 5: 24–46.

Kris, E. (1951) 'Opening Remarks on Psychoanalytic Child Psychology', *The Psychoanalytic Study of the Child*, 6: 9–17.

Lacan, J. (1953–1955) 'Commentaires sur des textes de Freud', *Psychanalyse*, 1: 17–28.

Lampl-de Groot, J. (1960) 'On Adolescence', *The Psychoanalytic Study of the Child*, 15: 95–103.

Lampl-de Groot, J. (1967) 'On Obstacles Standing in the Way of Psychoanalytic Cure', *The Psychoanalytic Study of the Child*, 22: 20–35.

Laufer, M. (1964) 'Ego Ideal and Pseudo Ego Ideal in Adolescence', *The Psychoanalytic Study of the Child*, 19: 196–221.

Laufer, M. (1965) 'Assessment of Adolescent Disturbances: The Application of Anna Freud's Diagnostic Profile', *The Psychoanalytic Study of the Child*, 20: 99–123.

Laufer, M. (1966) 'Object Loss and Mourning during Adolescence', *The Psychoanalytic Study of the Child*, 21: 269–93.

Laufer, M. (1968) 'The Body Image, the Function of Masturbation, and

Adolescence: Problems of Ownership of the Body', *The Psychoanalytic Study of the Child*, 23: 114–37.

Leupold-Löwenthal, H. (1992), 'Austria: The Viennese Psychoanalytical Society from 1918 to 1945', in *Psychoanalysis International: A Guide to Psychoanalysis throughout the World, Vol. 1 – Europe* ed., Stuttgart-Bad Cannstat, 1992, pp. 1–15.

Levy, D. (1928) 'Finger Sucking and Accessory Movements in Early Infancy', *Amer. J. Psychiat.*, 7: 881–918.

Levy, D. (1944) 'On the Problems of Movement Restraint: Tics, Stereotyped Movements, Hyperactivity', *Amer. J. Orthopsychiat.*, 14: 644–71.

Levy, D. (1945) 'Psychic Trauma of Operations in Children', *Amer. J. Dis. Child*, 69: 7–25.

Lipton, S. (1962) 'On the Psychology of Childhood Tonsillectomy', *The Psychoanalytic Study of the Child*, 17: 363–417.

Lorand, S. and Schneer, H., eds. (1962) *Adolescents: Psychoanalytic Approach to Problems and Therapy*, New York: Hoeber.

Mahler, M. (1952) 'On Child Psychosis and Schizophrenia: Autistic and Symbiotic Infantile Psychoses', *The Psychoanalytic Study of the Child*, 7: 286–305.

Mahler, M. (1968) *On Human Symbiosis and the Vicissitudes of Individuation*, New York: International Universities Press.

Mahler, M., Luke, J., and Daltroff, W. (1945) 'Clinical and Follow-up Study of the Tic Syndrome in Children', *Amer. J. Orthopsychiat.*, 15: 631–47.

Masson, J., ed. (1985) *The Complete Letters of Sigmund Freud to Wilhelm Fleiss, 1887–1904*, Cambridge, Massachusetts: Harvard University Press.

Mayes, L. and Cohen, D. (1996) 'Anna Freud and Developmental Psychoanalytic Psychology', *The Psychoanalytic Study of the Child*, 51: 117–41.

Meng, H. (1934) *Strafen und Erziehen*, Bern: Huber.

Meng, H. (1943) *Praxis der seelischen Hygiene*, Basel: Schwabe.

Michaels, J. (1955) *Disorders of Character*, Springfield, Illinois: Charles C. Thomas.

Miller, J. (1996) 'Anna Freud: A Historical Look at Her Theory and Technique of Child Psychoanalysis', *The Psychoanalytic Study of the Child*, 51: 142–71.

Murray, J. (1994) 'Anna Freud: A Beacon at the Centre of Psychoanalysis', in *Centres and Peripheries of Psychoanalysis: An Introduction to Psychoanalytic Studies*, R. Ekins and R. Freeman, eds., London: Karnac Books.

Nagera, H. (1966) *Early Childhood Distrbances, the Infantile Neurosis, and the Adult Disturbances*, New York: International Universities Press.

Noshpitz, J. (1957) 'Opening Phase in the Psychotherapy of Adolescents with Character Disorders', *Bull. Menninger Clin.*, 21: 153–64.

Pearson, G. (1941) 'Effect of Operative Procedures on the Emotional Life of the Child', *Amer. J. Dis. Child*, 62: 716–29.

Pfister, O. (1920) *Some Applications of Psycho-Analysis*, New York: Dodd, Mead, 1923.

Pfister, O. (1922) *Psycho-Analysis in the Service of Education*, London: Kimpton.

Putnam, M., Rank, B., and Kaplan, S. (1951) 'Notes on John I.: A Case of Primal Depression in an Infant', *The Psychoanalytic Study of the Child*, 6: 38–58.

Rapaport, D., and Gill, M. (1959) 'The Points of View and Assumptions of Metapsychology', *Int. J. Psycho-Anal.*, 40: 153–62.

Rexford, E., ed., (1966) *A Developmental Approach to Problems of Acting Out*, New York: International Universities Press.

Robertson, J. (1952) *A Two-Year-Old Goes to Hospital* [Film], London: Tavistock Clinic.

Robertson, J. (1956) 'A Mother's Observations on the Tonsillectomy of Her Four-Year-Old Daughter', *The Psychoanalytic Study of the Child*, 11: 410–27.

Rosenblatt, B. (1963) 'A Severe Neurosis in an Adolescent Boy', *The Psychoanalytic Study of the Child*, 18: 561–602.

Sandler, J. with Anna Freud (1985) *The Analysis of Defense: The Ego and the Mechanisms of Defense Revisited*, New York: International Universities Press.

Sandler, J., Kennedy, H., and Tyson, R. (1990) *The Technique of Child Psychoanalysis: Discussions with Anna Freud*, London: Karnac Books and the Institute of Psychoanalysis.

Solnit, A. (1959) 'Panel Report: The Vicissitudes of Ego Development in Adolescence', *J. Amer. Psychoanal. Assn*, 7: 523–36.

Spiegel, L. (1951) 'A Review of Contributions to a Psychoanalytic Theory of Adolescence', *The Psychoanalytic Study of the Child*, 6: 375–93.

Spitz, R. (1947) *Grief: A Peril in Infancy* [Film], New York: New York University Film Library.

Spitz, R. (1965) *The First Year of Life*, New York: International Universities Press.

Sprince, M. (1962) 'The Development of a Preoedipal Partnership between an Adolescent Girl and Her Mother', *The Psychoanalytic Study of the Child*, 17: 418–50.

Sterba, R. (1982) *Reminiscences of a Viennese Psychoanalyst*, Detroit: Wayne University Press.

Stone, L. (1954) 'The Widening Scope of Indications for Psychoanalysis', *J. Amer. Psychoanal. Assn*, 2: 567–94.

Symposium (1954) 'The Widening Scope of Indications for Psychoanalysis', *J. Amer. Psychoanal. Assn*, 2: 567–620.

Symposium (1981) 'Problems of the Superego', *The Psychoanalytic Study of the Child*, 37: 219–81.

Trilling, L. (1947) *The Middle of the Journey*, New York: Viking Press.

Wallerstein, R. (1984) 'Anna Freud: Radical Innovator and Staunch Conservative', *The Psychoanalytic Study of the Child*, 39: 65–80.

Winnicott, D.W. (1949) *The Ordinary Devoted Mother and Her Baby*, London: Tavistock Publications.

Winnicott, D.W. (1953) 'Transitional Objects and Transitional Phenomena: A Study of the First Not-Me Possession', *Int. J. Psycho-Anal.*, 34: 89–97.

Yorke, C. (1996) 'Anna Freud's Contributions to Our Knowledge of Child Development: An Overview', *The Psychoanalytic Study of the Child*, 51: 7–24.

Young-Bruehl, E. (1988) *Anna Freud: A Biography*, New York: Summit Books.

Young-Bruehl, E. (1996) 'Anna Freud as Historian of Psychoanalysis', in *The Psychoanalytic Study of the Child*, 51: 56–68.

Zulliger, H. (1935) *Schwierige Schüler*, Bern: Huber.

Zulliger, H. (1950) *Über symbolische Diestähle von Kindern und Jugendlichen*, Biel: Verlag Institut für Psychohygiene.

Zulliger, H. (1951) 'Unconscious Motives for Theft', *Brit. J. Delinqu.*, 1: 198–204.

Index

and the ego *see under* Ego
Defences, xv, xviii, 3, 4, 271—2
  against affects, xviii, 3
  against aggression, 100
  altruistic surrender xx
  asceticism xix
  and child psychopathology, 139, 141
  defence against the impulses, 194—5
  defence against the infantile object
    ties, 189—94
  by displacement of libido, 189—91
  identification with the aggressor xx
  intellectualization xix
  meaning of term xx
  during puberty xix
  by regression, 193—4
  by reversal of affect, 191—2
  by withdrawal of libido to the self,
    192—3
Delinquency, xxix, 48, 51, 125, 127, 145,
  182, 183, 204, 230, 233, 250, 251,
  262
Delusions, 22, 114
Denial, 122, 222, 223, 255—6
  as a defence mechanism, 3
  in fantasy xix
  of positive feeling, 191
  replaced by repression, 157
  in word and act xix
Dependency, 115, 119
Depersonalization, 114
Depression, 47, 74, 90, 91, 114, 128, 167,
  182, 192, 206, 230, 233, 234, 242
  manic, 229
Depressive position, 44
Deprivation, 57, 61, 70, 99, 141, 267
Destructive impulses, xxiv, 38, 39, 43,
  45—8, 56, 97, 115, 209, 210
Deutsch, H., 179
Development
  aggressive, 51
  arrested, 123, 126—7, 128, 130, 138,
    150, 153
  atypical, 84
  defects, 130, 155, 160
  delay in milestones, 116, 121—2, 128
  delays and failures of, xxx, 106,
    121—3, 128, 139
  the depressive position, 44

drive, xxix, 122, 128
ego, xxiv, 45, 55, 63, 68—9, 83, 110,
  111, 116, 118, 128, 134, 135, 160,
  166, 171, 201, 218—27
erotic, 48
instinct, 71
irregularities in xxx
libidinal *see under* Libido
motor, 124
and projection, 25
psychotic, 84
retarded, 38
stages, interdependence of, 156—7
see also Abnormal development;
  Normal development
Developmental chart, 146, 149
Developmental deviations, 144, 151—3
Developmental lines, xxvii—xxviii, xxix,
  130, 134—42, 146, 151, 160, 267
Developmental point of view xiii—xiv,
  xvii, xix
Developmental Profile xxxi
Developmental reconstructions xv
Dewey, John xi
Diagnostic interviews, 132
Diagnostic Profile, 125—6, 133
Diagnostic recommendations xxvii
Dietary restrictions, 70—71
Differentiation, 141
Disappointment, 169, 171
Discharge, 136
Displacement, 25, 59, 99, 121, 205—6
  and aggression, 37, 46
  of cathexis, 55
  as a defence mechanism, 3, 9, 22
  and the ego, 214
  of feeling, 100
  hatred, 6
  of the libido, 189—91
  of wishes, 31
Dissociality, 38, 125, 167, 168, 188, 190,
  191, 204, 239
Distortion, 59, 205—6
Distractibility, 116
Disturbance of elimination, 109, 110
Doctors
  fear of, 120
  passive devotion to, 74—5
Doubting, 113

Drawings, 205
Dream work, 169
Dreams, xv, 205, 266, 269
  interpretation of, xi, 50, 204, 205, 247
  the lost object in, 102–4
  and the primary process, 55
  and the topographical point of view
    xviii
Drive derivatives, xviii, 3, 112, 114, 178,
    194
Drives
  aggressive, xxiv, 134, 267
  control of, 110, 119
  defences against, 3, 186
  development, xxix, 122, 128, 178
  drive activity, 115
  and the ego, 160, 267
  instinctual, xvii, 267
  regressions, 119
  sexual, xxiv, 219
Drug misuse, 229, 252, 263
Dubo, Sara, 70
Dyer, R. xxvi, xxvii
Dynamic point of view, xiii, xxix, 266,
    271–2, 273

Eating, xxiii, xxviii, 28, 52, 66, 135
  and destructive/erotic urges, 45
  disturbances, 88, 92
  obsessions, 210
  and penis envy, 9
  wrong feeding methods, 83
  see also Food
Ecker, Dr, 131
Economic point of view, xiii, xxix, 266,
    271, 272, 273
Eczema, 112
Education, xiv, xvii, 38, 51, 125, 126,
    168, 207
Ego, xv, xviii, 10, 144, 146
  achievements, 58, 59, 219–20, 221
  and adaptation to reality xix
  and the adolescent, 192–3, 193
  and affects, 4, 5, 11
  and aggression, 42, 203–4
  and analysis xviii, xxi
  and anxiety, 72, 117, 178, 222, 260
  arrest in the area of ego functioning,
    118

and arrested development, 123
control of motility, 221–2
defensive mechanisms, xx, xxi, 3–11,
    14, 20, 21, 45, 121, 150, 178, 214,
    222, 264, 268, 269–70
deformities, 230, 237, 239, 247
development of, xxiv, 45, 55, 63,
    68–9, 83, 110, 111, 116, 118, 128,
    134, 135, 155, 160, 166, 171, 201,
    218–27, 232, 238, 268
and the drives, 160, 267
and the environment, 153, 218
functions, 220–27
and guilt, 222
and the id, xxiii, 10, 106, 112–13,
    124, 127, 134, 135, 138, 139, 142,
    152, 156, 178, 179, 185, 188, 194,
    195, 218, 219, 220, 223, 225, 226,
    246, 247, 250, 267, 270
and identification with the aggressor,
    15, 21
immaturity and weakness of, 183
and instincts, 5, 14, 25
instincts, 42
integrity of, 244
interest, 148
and introjection, 10, 11, 20–21
and the libido, 134
maturation, 147, 160
modification, 9
and morality, 13
oversensitivity, 119
and phobia, 8
and preadolescence, 167, 169, 170
and projection, 10, 11, 20, 21, 25
psychology xviii
and regression, 49, 57, 115, 124, 128,
    153, 220
regression, 49
and repression, 8, 10, 153, 214, 216,
    220
resistance, 5, 251
restriction, 124, 128
restrictions, 113
retardation, 122
role within the analytic process,
    269–70
severity of, 203
and sexual impulses, 203–4